Reflective Writing

in Counselling
and Psychotherapy

SAGE has been part of the global academic community since 1965, supporting high quality research and learning that transforms society and our understanding of individuals, groups and cultures. SAGE is the independent, innovative, natural home for authors, editors and societies who share our commitment and passion for the social sciences.

Find out more at: **www.sagepublications.com**

Reflective Writing
in Counselling
and Psychotherapy

Jeannie Wright and Gillie Bolton

Los Angeles | London | New Delhi
Singapore | Washington DC

First published 2012

SAGE Publications Ltd
1 Oliver's Yard
55 City Road
London EC1Y 1SP

SAGE Publications Inc.
2455 Teller Road
Thousand Oaks, California 91320

SAGE Publications India Pvt Ltd
B 1/I 1 Mohan Cooperative Industrial Area
Mathura Road
New Delhi 110 044

SAGE Publications Asia-Pacific Pte Ltd
3 Church Street
#10-04 Samsung Hub
Singapore 049483

Library of Congress Control Number: 2011936865

British Library Cataloguing in Publication data

A catalogue record for this book is available from the British Library

ISBN 978-0-85702-327-8
ISBN 978-0-85702-328-5 (pbk)

Typeset by C&M Digitals (P) Ltd, Chennai, India
Printed by MPG Books Group, Bodmin, Cornwall
Printed on paper from sustainable resources

For Mum, Liam and Katie

Contents

List of Figures

About the Authors

Jeannie Wright PhD was Associate Professor at Massey University in Aotearoa New Zealand while writing this book. She is now Director of Counselling and Psychotherapy Programmes at Warwick University in the UK. Reflective writing has helped during the separation, transition and relocation periods, as ever.

For Gillie Bolton PhD, the self-educative healing power of creative writing has been inspirational: the focus of her research and practice for nearly 30 years. Author of *Reflective Practice: Writing and Professional Development*, Third Edition (2010; www.uk.sagepub.com/bolton), and author or editor of six other books on similar subjects (one co-edited with Jeannie Wright), Gillie writes poetry and fiction and keeps a daily personal journal. A freelance consultant, she lectures and facilitates workshops worldwide, as well as mentoring and supervising one-to-one (www.gilliebolton.com). *Reflective Journal Writing* has been a very happy collaboration in a busy life which also includes being a devoted grannie to three little ones. Gillie lives and works in the Hope Valley, Derbyshire, and Bloomsbury, London.

Foreword

It has always seemed to me that here are two essential elements to any form of counselling and psychotherapy that is genuinely helpful for people. First, there is the opportunity to enter into a relationship with someone who is consistently on your side, who represents a safe 'other' who can be trusted and relied on. Second, therapy offers the possibility to stand aside from the pressure and demands of everyday life, to reflect on what that life means and to make choices around the direction in which you want your life to go.

This second strand of therapeutic experience can be pursued in a variety of ways. Obviously, reflecting on one's life it can be accomplished in conversation with a therapist. However, it can also be pursued by other means, such as walking along a beach, meditation and prayer, or making music; there are many activities that can serve as vehicles for personal reflectiveness. Writing comprises one of the most widely-used and effective forms of reflection that exists. The process of committing thoughts and feelings to words operates on a number of levels. As ideas, phrases, feeling or images that may have been rattling around in and out of awareness become fixed on the page, they become externalised and open to scrutiny: 'Is that what I really mean?', 'Is that the totality of what I feel, or just a part of it?' Putting the words or feelings 'out there', on the page, allows the rational, sense-making part of the writer to be more involved.

In addition, there is a magical quality to the human capacity to use language that introduces the potential for new understanding. Much of language is based on metaphor. Without being consciously aware that we are doing it, the act of writing brings forth metaphors and other aspects of the intrinsic creativity of language, which invite further thought and which can take us forward in our understanding. For example, earlier in this paragraph I used the word 'strand'. Looking at that word now, what does it mean to me? I think that, among other things, it refers to my sense that therapy, or life as a whole, is like a cloth that consists of threads that go on and on and that come together to make patterns. No doubt other meanings are also implicit in my use of the word 'strand'. This is a small example of how reflecting on something that has been written can open up a wider appreciation of the meaning of some aspect of one's own position on a topic.

It is important to recognise that writing stops time. Words that are written out, or written down, are captured and are able to be revisited and reinterpreted at any point in the future. In this way, the meaning of 'now' – the moment at which a sentence is written, can be expanded and filled out at some point in the future. In face-to-face therapy, the meaning of what is said 'now' can be explored and filled out through the responsiveness of the therapist. By contrast, in therapeutic and reflective writing, the writer is creating the conditions for dialogue with himself or herself.

I believe that it is also important to recognise that the invention of writing, several thousand years ago, marked a fundamental transformation in human culture, for good and ill. Being able to know what writing does is therefore a means of opening up a personal awareness of some fundamental aspects of what it means to be a person in modern literate societies.

I hope that these brief remarks convey the significance with which I regard personal writing as an essential activity for therapists, both as a vehicle for the growth of self-awareness and as a method of working with clients. I always encourage my students and clients to write. Some of them take to it like a duck to water. For others it is harder, for a variety of reasons. What Jeannie Wright and Gillie Bolton have done in this book is provide a way in to the discipline of writing. The book offers a gentle and creative invitation to the use of reflective writing in counselling and psychotherapy. In supplying a clear account of different approaches to reflective writing, and a large number of stimulating writing tasks, *Reflective Writing in Counselling and Psychotherapy* makes a timely, welcome and necessary contribution to this area of therapeutic training and practice.

John McLeod
Professor of Counselling
University of Abertay Dundee

Preface

Reflective Writing in Counselling and Psychotherapy aims to enable practitioners and students of counselling and psychotherapy to develop their own ways of personal reflective journal writing. For humanistic practitioners, keeping a personal reflective journal or personal learning journal will be required from the very beginning stages of introductory training. Equally, this book supports experienced therapists and lecturers and teachers who facilitate personal and professional development in how to use writing creatively and reflectively.

THEORETICAL FRAMEWORKS: THE TERRAIN

Personal development in counselling and psychotherapy is at the heart of initial training and continuing professional development (CPD); it cannot exist in a theoretical vacuum. Yet, no one therapeutic theory has all the answers. In repeated research findings, it is the 'heroic client' and the personal qualities and presence a therapist brings to the relationship and working alliance that make the difference in therapeutic outcome, rather than any particular technique or therapeutic orientation preferred by the therapist. According to some outcome research, client factors contribute most powerfully to change and positive outcomes in counselling and psychotherapy; and next to what the client brings to therapy, the client's perception of the therapeutic relationship is responsible for most of the gains resulting from the therapy (Duncan, Miller & Sparks, 2004). Different modalities and techniques are less important than previously thought in terms of positive outcomes. This book points out agenda variations for personal and professional development for those committed to different approaches in counselling and psychotherapy education and practice, for example, person centred or cognitive behavioural therapy. Signposts for those practising or training in different modalities will indicate specific activities and writing exercises which work within the frame of those different theoretical approaches. We take a pluralistic view of the theoretical underpinnings of writing for personal development.

At last count there are well over 400 different approaches to counselling and psychotherapy. In this book you will be presented with a 'no one way is the right way' view.

Oversimplification is one danger in aligning certain writing activities with specific approaches to counselling and psychotherapy. Theories guide our every therapeutic intervention, however, and without theory, practice is blind. Some writing activities, such as thought monitoring, could clearly be associated with cognitive therapy, for example.

SELF-AWARENESS: MAPS, AND HOW TO USE THIS BOOK

Through the voices of three fictional UK-based students, Philip, Anita and Jo, we show how writing develops self-awareness. The very concept of self-awareness begs an awful lot of questions. In telling the story of keeping personal reflective journals through the characters of Philip, Anita and Jo, and through extracts from their journal entries, we provide maps of changing self-awareness and personal development landscapes.

Exploring personal experience is at the very heart of therapy, and essential to the practices in this book. You will notice that we use an archetypal journey metaphor to represent how you might navigate the territory of personal reflective journal writing. Starting out by going straight to the chapter that gives you detailed instructions about different kinds of writing (Chapter 4) is one way to go. Certainly if you have never kept a diary or reflective journal before, reading Chapters 1 and 2 will be useful in enabling you to see how others have explored writing for self-understanding, and how such writing fits with counselling and psychotherapy and reflective practice.

There is no one right way to use this book. You might want to start reading at the very beginning; we strongly recommend you read Section One before launching into any of the writing exercises. Your particular interests might lead you from chapter to chapter, trying out different activities. The 'Try this' activities are designed to relate closely to particular examples or sections in each chapter. In the end, you will find some of the suggested writing activities help you build self-knowledge and self-awareness, and some won't suit you. You will gain *much* more if you *do* the writing and not just think about the suggested activities.

Each chapter ends with a series of writing exercises and activities entitled *Write!,* in addition to those you've already encountered within the chapter. Please try these once you've read the advice in Chapter 4 on beginning writing.

ASSESSMENT CRITERIA

Criteria for assessing personal development are currently in embryonic form in terms of professional accreditation in the UK and some other countries, and very much established in others, such as in the USA. Some standards of competence and accreditation for counselling and psychotherapy are under discussion, and where appropriate we have referred to those criteria and referenced the relevant professional body. At the time of publication, for example, the British Association for Counselling and Psychotherapy (BACP) has produced lists of requirements for individual, organisational and training course accreditation, including the place for self-awareness in your way of working with clients and how issues of difference and equality impact upon the therapeutic relationship. The information on the BACP website is regularly updated (www.bacp.co.uk). It is well worth checking for the most up-to-date lists of requirements for professional accreditation with the particular professional organisation to which you belong.

FROM THE FAR SIDES OF THE WORLD

We have written together before and share a passion for the therapeutic and reflective potential of different kinds of writing. This book was written when Jeannie was living and working in Aotearoa New Zealand, and Gillie was living and working in the UK. Keeping a reflective journal seemed to be a taken-for-granted requirement for most therapists in practice and in training as part of personal and professional development, but nobody seemed to say why or how.

You will hear both our voices as you read. Jeannie and Gillie have discussed every element of this book. Jeannie is the major author of Chapters 1, 2 and 5–11, with small additions by Gillie. Gillie wrote Chapters 3 and 4. We wrote Chapters 12 and 13 together.

Examples from practice have been included with authors' written consent. Mostly real names have been used, but occasionally authors requested a pseudonym. Many examples from therapeutic practice are drawn from Aotearoa New Zealand. We would be wary of making comparisons between one culture and another, especially given the unique indigeneity of Aotearoa New Zealand; however there are broad, common features between therapeutic practice in Aotearoa New Zealand and the UK, including a requirement to demonstrate cultural and self-awareness, for example, in applying for membership of professional organisations. Those organisations have similarities too, such as a recent move towards voluntary registration for practitioners. It is possible to learn about the general from the particular. Becoming aware of the cultural soup that we swim in is a major part of the explorations of 'personal development' in this book.

It has sometimes been difficult to find a writing activity's original source; if we have inadvertently used an exercise or idea without proper acknowledgement, please let us know. We would like to acknowledge contributions appropriately in future editions.

Acknowledgements

Building a text like this workbook requires firm foundations. We would like to thank all those counsellors, colleagues, psychotherapists, students, clients and supervisees who have contributed their writing, providing us with solid rock for this book. Some contributors have used their own names, and some have not, preferring pseudonyms. Your voices and the details of your stories not only add depth but also bring this book to life.

We have loved working together. Jeannie says: 'Gillie Bolton has been a wonderfully creative companion throughout the architectural, construction and finishing stages of this project. Thank you Gillie.' Gillie says: '*Reflective Writing in Counselling and Psychotherapy* would never even have had footings dug without Jeannie's insight and dedication. She has been the driving and creative force; I've felt a bit like the grannie I am! I've found her fictional writing about Jo, Philip and Anita particularly wonderful. Most of all I've appreciated her humour: always a laugh and a light way through any difficulty, stuckness, or exhaustion. Thank you Jeannie.'

Thank you too to Liam Wright Higgins for illustrations that, in the words of one reviewer, 'help evoke reader awareness of the felt sense of the feelings or states of mind' and use a different, non-verbal kind of intelligence.

We would like particularly to thank Alice Oven for being a wonderful editor and Kate Wharton for valuable support, as well as Juhani Ihanus, Brendan Boyle, Linda Garbutt, Ilona Singer, Judy Clinton, Kate Billingham, Dan Rowland, Alice Rowland and particularly Stephen Rowland for his patience and endless cooking of meals at the right time.

PART ONE

MAPS

1

Preparing for the Journey

What this book is and how to use it

Unlike 'processing things in my head', writing in my reflective journal means that, potentially at least, thoughts and feelings are open to others to read.

(Counsellor)

Like jazz musicians, counsellors and psychotherapists improvise. This book does not provide navigation equipment with precise instructions, nor a musical score; but at the end of each chapter there are exercises to help improve your own sense of direction and ability to improvise. The exercises introduce the links between self-awareness and being able to tell your story in different ways in counselling and psychotherapy and expressive and reflective writing.

WHO IS THIS BOOK FOR? INTRODUCING PHILIP, ANITA AND JO

This book is for practitioners, supervisors, teachers and students in counselling and psychotherapy. You may be an experienced practitioner who is looking for new ways to continue personal and professional development using writing; you may be new to counselling, coaching or psychotherapy and have started initial training; you may be involved in some further study for continuing professional development (CPD). At some stage you may have been asked to keep a reflective journal and would like to know more about how to do that writing most successfully and enjoyably. To help illustrate this task, we follow three characters throughout the book; all are in various stages of therapeutic training in the UK.

Philip: I can understand why we have to keep a personal journal during this course, but I don't really know how. I've decided I'm going to join a person centred group for the personal therapy requirement. I went out and bought a new writing book for this reflective journal, small enough to fit into a pocket, with white paper and no lines.

Anita: Sitting there in the lecture theatre I thought to myself, 'No way,' keep a personal journal? Me? I don't think so! They are also encouraging us to go to the student counselling service. I know it's free, and I know it would give me an experience of sitting in the client's seat – but, what would I talk about?

Jo: Hmmm, keeping this journal is a bit like blogging, except I don't write it on the Internet. I asked if I could use online counselling for the personal therapy requirement on the course but they said no. I'll find out if there is a narrative therapist or somebody solution focused I could go and see locally. Writing this personal journal feels exposing – like a snail coming out of its shell, I feel too pale and vulnerable and want to protect my privacy.

Try this: Why do I work as a therapist – what do people say about me?

Listing personal qualities and values

Find somewhere you feel comfortable to write and allowing yourself no more than 10 minutes to write a list of those personal qualities or values that brought you into training and work in counselling and psychotherapy. If it helps, write what other people have said about you, for example:
   Peter is:

- warm and approachable
- creative
- helping others is important to him
- the peacemaker in family of origin.

By completing this exercise, you have already started preparing for your journey to reflective writing skills. Where did you decide to write? Did you use paper, pencils, the Internet, a digital platform? There is no wrong or right way to do this self-writing in practical terms, only the way that suits you best.

PROFESSIONAL AND PERSONAL DEVELOPMENT

Personal and professional awareness or development are terms that tend to go together, especially from a humanistic point of view (Wilkins, 1997). They are often linked in the counselling and psychotherapy literature, and it can sometimes be a pointless exercise to attempt to disentangle one from the other. It seems certain that personal and professional development continue throughout a career in counselling and psychotherapy. Over 10 years ago, Hazel Johns suggested that personal development never ends for therapists:

> Personal development is not an event but a process, life-long and career-long: it must and will happen incidentally before and after any training course, through all aspects of life and work. (1996: xii)

Since then, professional bodies in the psychological therapies have considered what might define personal development competence. For example, the British Association for Counselling and Psychotherapy (BACP) and other professional bodies have referred to self-awareness as one necessary criterion for professional accreditation, but have not yet provided more specific detail about what self-awareness is or how it might be measured. In the USA, the Council for the Accreditation of Counseling and Related Education Programmes (CACREP) states that the presence of self-awareness is a pre-requisite for counsellor fitness to practice, yet also leaves aside exactly what is meant by self-awareness and how it might be assessed. The need to demonstrate how you have developed personally and professionally and the role of writing in that process is considered in more depth in Chapter 12.

In this book, professional development and the kind of writing we provide practice for is hard to separate from personal development. We cover a terrain, akin to writing for reflective practice, where you might not be certain where the path you're taking will lead, and where your assumptions will be challenged (Bolton, 2010). Keeping a reflective journal is one way of noticing how your experience changes, how your values and the background you come from play a part in your ability to create and maintain therapeutic relationships:

> To be an effective therapist, it is necessary to develop a way of being with people that is genuinely grounded in one's own personal experience, values and cultural context. Over and over again, research studies have found that what makes the difference to clients are the personal qualities of the counsellor, and his or her capacity to form an accepting and facilitative relationship.
>
> (McLeod, 2010: 3)

Whether the terminology in your particular counsellor education or practice refers to self-awareness or personal development, the centrality of knowing yourself in order to develop effective therapeutic alliances makes sense. Personal development could include 'a unique pattern of moral, emotional, sexual, social and intellectual concerns' allowing the practitioner or trainee to 'identify her own strengths, limitations and oddities' (Johns, 1996: 59). You may be working in a personal development group as part of your practice or involved in personal therapy, so this self-writing may only be part of that journey of self-exploration. Although there is little conclusive evidence for the effectiveness of personal therapy and therapy groups for the personal development of trainees in counselling and psychotherapy, research continues (Norcross, 2005).

When asked for the advantages and disadvantages of writing compared to personal therapy or personal development groups, some counselling students on an integrative programme used words such as 'reflection, time/space, a means of clarifying thinking, expressing and identifying feelings, confidential, honest, freedom of expression' (Daniels & Feltham, 2004: 184).

In the same study, one student said 'Writing enables me to articulate in a non-vocal way material what I wouldn't dare express in any other way'.

There is increasing evidence for the professional and personal benefits of expressive and reflective writing (Bolton, 2010; Pennebaker & Chung, 2007). There is also a long tradition of self-therapy in various schools of the psychological therapies, such as Karen Horney's (1942) pioneering work in self-analysis or the increasing use of self-practice and self-reflection in cognitive behavioural therapy training (Bennett-Levy, Turner, Beaty, Smith, Paterson & Farmer, 2001).

CONFIDENTIALITY, AND SAFEGUARDING YOUR PERSONAL WRITING

It is your responsibility to ensure that your writing remains private until you choose to communicate about it with others. Whether you use encryption in a digital environment, or make sure that your writing is not left where others could read your thoughts and feelings, you must decide now how you are going to store this writing in a way that is comfortable for you.

You will write differently, and tend to censor your thinking/writing, if you write for an audience, or even suspect that someone else might read this raw material. In some initial counsellor and therapist education programmes, autobiographical writing is required. Who is to read that writing and, if it is to be assessed, by whom and according to whose criteria, are essential pieces of negotiation. These questions also bring up important ethical points:

> We were asked to write our life story and hand it in by the following week. It was my first experience of counsellor education. I knew why I wanted to retrain as a therapist and it had taken a huge amount of effort to get into this particular programme. Refusing to do the first 'homework' we were given seemed downright daring. I sat for hours and finally wrote a letter to the tutor, a man I had never met, explaining why I didn't want to write my autobiography and 'hand it in'. At different stages of my therapeutic development and training this same process has been repeated. I need to know who's going to read my writing and why. (Jeannie Wright)

I still have a copy of the letter I wrote to the tutor in my initial training. How did writing that letter contribute to my personal development? It is an example of reflective writing, and in re-reading I ask various questions: What did the refusal to write an autobiographical piece for a stranger say about me? The tutor on that first counsellor education programme would have learned that I am wary (still am), not always compliant, and liable to question instructions. I can't remember now if that was an insight I gained from that whole exercise, but reflecting on it now is useful and reminds me about some important personal characteristics that emerge from time to time. That's exactly why we are asking you to start writing straightaway. You then have a record you can look back over and learn from. Like birds peck for worms, if there is no soil, there is nothing to find. You need to create the soil and then see what inhabits it.

You are in charge of the 'self-writing' we encourage you to do in this book. You choose how to use the writing and who can read it. That means finding a safe way to store your writing.

This kind of autobiographical and reflective writing works best without a critic or judge looking over your shoulder, even if that critic is part of you.

THE WRITING

What to write about

If you are ready to start writing, you could choose from any of these suggested themes (Clarke, 2000). They are based on *The New Diary* (Rainer, 1978), a classic in the journal-writing literature. The journal is a place for many purposes:

- To communicate with and advise yourself – how have you overcome personal prejudices, for example?
- To clarify your beliefs or goals – in what ways has past history and family of origin experience impacted on your current thinking?
- To make and evaluate decisions.
- To indulge yourself.
- To reflect upon your dreams and disappointments.
- To work through difficult situations.
- To rehearse future behaviour.
- To focus on immediate events and experiences – how far are you able to give and receive personal feedback in an acceptable way, for example to clients, course members and staff?
- To work towards clarity and order.
- To exercise responsibility for yourself.

- To reflect upon and further enjoy various pleasures.
- To be simply free and creative.
- To examine things you find hard to raise with others.
- To respond to and apply psychological and counselling theory.

What kind of writing is this?

> It makes sense to me, to map a journey in expression through writing, when I was young I read somewhere about writing people a letter when (you) wanted to tell them something but were too afraid to say it, not necessarily to send, in fact they all ended up in the bin, but I always felt better after 'getting it out on paper', so to speak.
>
> ('Jenny' in Tan, 2008: 13)

Autobiographical and professional development or reflective writing clearly calls for a more personal style from the academic or formal kind expected for college and university assignments; for a start it uses the first person, 'I'. It is also possible to throw this writing away; you are in charge of what happens to it. When asked about the benefits of journal writing, even though some therapists are sceptical to start with, most find great value in it:

> Seeing them (my feelings) on paper also helps me to understand them.
> Looking back and seeing how I've grown.
> Insight and understanding.
>
> (Daniels & Feltham, 2004: 184)

or as a cognitive behavioural therapy (CBT) student commented about their journal:

> Mine was initially about the course content and about clients and my own feelings and anxieties. And more about inner beliefs and now it's become more philosophical but in a positive sense really.
>
> (Sutton, Townend & Wright, 2007: 395)

Re-reading is an important part of this kind of writing, to reflect further on what you have written about. Here's an example of 'raw' journal writing from Anita, which started out as a list, merely describing a day without exploration or more meaningful observations:

> When it's sunny I find it easier to get out of bed. I have a full day, with three counselling appointments before lunch, two after lunch and then I go to supervision. All of the morning clients showed up, but there was a gap in the afternoon, with no notification, so I caught up on notes. (Anita)

This writing tells us little about Anita's day that we couldn't have found out from reading her office diary. It is not reflective. There is little exploration of her emotional or evaluative sense of each of her counselling sessions or her agenda for supervision. When she re-read it, she went further:

> After 22 days without seeing the sun, finally this morning there it was. I notice how my mood changes immediately and I'm ready to go into work much earlier than usual. I decided to walk to the office – part of the self-care strategy I've discussed with my supervisor. I'm looking forward to seeing him today, particularly to work on my risk assessment and guiding formulation with B. I should see B. this afternoon if she turns up. I think the grey weather in the winter affects her depression too. I shall be disappointed if she doesn't attend today. (Anita)

This writing took about 5 minutes, even the second version where Anita is much more reflective.

Making time

Students on a CBT diploma training course reported various ideas about how often and how much to write:

> I try to do at least half an hour each week at work on the computer, now I'm a bit wary because I'm already up to 8000 words.

> I try to do it every week.

> I seem to do it either when I've had a really, really good session and I'm very, very happy and had a good supervision or I'm really, really cheesed off.

> (Sutton, Townend & Wright, 2007: 394)

In this kind of self-writing, it can be useful to create specific spaces, even rituals, so that the usual everyday 'busyness' isn't allowed to crowd out the writing. You might be a morning journal writer, preferring to stay in bed and write before starting the day. You might choose to add a writing space to supervision appointments, leaving time before and after each session to write in your journal. Like any other kind of activity which we've been told is 'good' for us, you need to know what will help motivate you (see Exercise 1.2 at the end of this chapter).

Time alone

Apart from writing enabling you to keep a record of self-discoveries and changes, it also makes time for solitude: time for yourself. For some, this may feel uncomfortable.

Being alone is different from feeling lonely. Solitary time is essential for creativity; we're not suggesting you have to work alone all the time. You are responsible for your own learning and know your own learning styles better than anybody else. What is likely to work for you? For some people, writing in the morning before they've got up and started the day is most helpful:

> Well, I'm sitting up in bed and I've probably done the first, the kind of opening routine I do which says, how are you? Then, how did you sleep? How was yesterday? – Possibly following up something like that, how did it go? Or how did you feel with that?
>
> (Wright, 2009a: 237)

For others, keeping a notebook always with them so to catch thoughts and feelings on paper at any time becomes habitual and essential (see Exercise 1.3 at the end of this chapter).

THEORETICAL FOUNDATIONS OF SELF-AWARENESS AND WRITING

Personal development in counselling and psychotherapy sits within theoretical frameworks. Some of the theoretical foundations we will draw from include the traditional 'forces' in psychology, counselling and psychotherapy: the psychodynamic, cognitive behavioural, humanistic and multi-cultural. Positive psychology and therapies based on the postmodern or 'narrative turn' will also form an important theoretical base for what we mean by 'self'.

Research into expressive, therapeutic writing using randomised controlled trials and other 'scientific' methods is largely associated with cognitive and behavioural approaches.

In addition to physiological and psychological benefits which emerged from such research into expressive writing, the very act of writing has been shown to improve communication and relationship with others:

> The cognitive changes themselves now allow the individuals to begin to think about and use their social world differently. They talk more; they connect with others differently. They are now better able to take advantage of social support. And with these cognitive and social changes, many of their unhealthy behaviors abate. As recent data suggest, expressive writing promotes sleep, enhanced immune function, reduced alcohol consumption, etc.
>
> (Pennebaker & Chung, 2007: 38)

Communicating with yourself, using expressive and reflective writing, can offer physiological as well as psychological benefits (Bolton & Wright, 2004). It may be that you are not particularly drawn to words and writing. You may be more visual and find yourself drawing, painting or using photography and other less verbal ways of expressing yourself. These could be included in your journal.

PREPARING FOR THE JOURNEY AND DEVELOPING YOUR MULTIPLE INTELLIGENCES

A further theoretical framework we draw from is multiple intelligences (Chen, Moran & Gardner, 2009; Gardner, 2006). The two intelligences that are valued most highly in most Western educational systems are skill in language, or linguistic intelligence and skill in logical-mathematical operations. Here's a student on a cognitive behavioural psychotherapy training programme talking about her experience of writing a journal (called a 'learning log' on her course) and dyslexia:

> [Y]ou know the difficulties I was having on the course and the intelligence and dyslexia and all those kinds of things which came to me. I was writing about them and some conversations I'd had with the tutor and it was almost (laughs) this is going to sound really sad, but knowing that the tutor was going to read it, I was almost winning my argument through my learning log.

> (Wright, 2005: 513)

This student's difficulties with reading and writing did not prevent her succeeding in therapy training. Grammar, spelling or school rules which have created such obstacles for those who struggle with writing are irrelevant in personal journal writing. The kind of activities we are suggesting you develop hinge less on linguistic intelligence and more on other ways of expressing yourself, such as photography, collage or music. We also agree with Gardner that all of us could fulfil our potential more depending on motivation and resources available. Whether or not you agree with Gardner's theories, which come from a particular view of psychology and human development, you can probably think of examples of how these intelligences can be developed through your work. Gardner's theories make two claims: first, that all human beings possess these intelligences; second, that no two human beings possess exactly the same profile of strengths and weaknesses (Chen, Moran & Gardner, 2009).

Activity: Writing and 'mindfulness'

Start by clearing a space where you can 'be' rather than following the driven or 'doing' mode as Jon Kabat-Zinn (2005: 6) and mindfulness practitioners call it: . You might need to turn off telephones and make sure you won't be interrupted. In later

(Continued)

(Continued)

chapters we will ask you to follow guided meditations, but the point of this short exercise is to slow your thoughts down using writing.

- Where are you right now?

  - Describe the place you are in.
  - Are you inside or outside?
  - Is it warm, cold, stuffy or airy?
  - What are some of the colours you can see?

- Now close your eyes and allow yourself to relax, letting go of any tension. Focus on the sounds where you are.
- When you're ready, open your eyes and write down what you can hear.

Many of the exercises we will ask you to take part in will benefit from this kind of mindful observation and reflection before writing.

CONCLUSION

There is no right or wrong way to write a reflective journal. The writing is for you and not to be read by others until you're ready. You must take responsibility for deciding where to keep this writing so that you can control who accesses it.

The practicalities of self-writing include: making time alone; choosing paper, screen or digital platform for writing – a way that suits you; ignoring critics, including all rules you learnt in school about spelling and grammar. As well as writing you could choose to draw, photograph, speak and then record those words in writing.

The words we use to describe ourselves may be slippery and elusive but we can observe changes in how we think, feel and behave by keeping a personal journal. The next chapter explores the rationale for writing a reflective journal – why should I write?

Write!

Each chapter in this book will end with ways to try out some writing. Don't just think it, ink it!

1.1 Choose your materials

- What are you going to write on? List the possibilities.
- What is your preferred medium for writing? This could range from recycled paper journals, the backs of envelopes, to digital platforms, to a voice-recognition option.

1.2 When to write: writing routines

Think of the time when you started a new, beneficial activity. Perhaps it was joining a gym, cycling to work or meditating.

- What helped you build this new activity into your daily routine?
- How were other people involved, if at all?
- How did you find it easier to make time and how were you derailed (if you were)?

1.3 How will you start writing?

It may be that you have been writing your autobiography or keeping a reflective journal for a long time. If that is the case, continue from where you left off. If you are still unsure about where to begin, you might want to go to Chapter 4 on how to start writing.

2

Why Take the Journey?

The rationale for personal and professional journal keeping

What a useful tool this writing is – quiet, costs very little, no need for electricity even.

(Counsellor)

Philip: Now comes the part of the course I won't find difficult. I've kept a journal since I was old enough to write and that teacher started us doing it, so this is normal for me. Maybe it's because I had older brothers and sisters who seem to talk more than me and were less shy? Writing is an obvious way for me to keep track of what's going on – in many ways easier than saying things. It's unpredictable – I never know what will come onto the paper – but it's OK because I'm the only one who reads it. The community group is so much harder. I blush, stammer, and can't meet other people's eyes. I get sweaty palms just thinking about it.

Anita: I really don't see the point of this. I don't want to do it. I want to learn about how to work with people therapeutically not how to become a writer. They seem to be asking us to be our own therapists – trying out techniques we'll be using with clients on ourselves. OK, but I do that in my head. It's been a chore so far, writing slows me down.

Jo: It's OK on the Internet – I use a pseudonym. But are they asking me to talk about parts of my life story in this journal? I'm saying things online that I've never disclosed to anyone before. […] the trouble was there was nobody to tell. Ask for help? Me? But I am supposed to be the one learning how to help other people. I could see in the online writing I was getting worse and worse – more depressed, more angry than any of my clients at that particular time. I had no idea when I started how far I would go in writing it down.

A counselling student admitted to me several months into the course that his first response to my session on how to keep a reflective journal was, 'You've got to be joking!' Several months later, he told me how his personal development writing had helped him to make his voice heard, with doctors in particular.

Others have claimed this space for themselves from an early age; Philip, one of the counsellors whose story runs throughout this book, is a keeper of journals. Anita is not.

This chapter will signpost the what, how and why – the rationale – for keeping a personal and professional reflective journal. We have chosen six or seven reasons for starting and developing the journal. The list keeps growing and changing and will develop as this chapter and the whole book unfolds.

WHY WRITE A JOURNAL?

There are many reasons to write a journal:

1 Writing slows you down, offers a time to pause and reflect and allows you to make time for yourself.
2 Writing allows you to express feelings and thoughts privately, to externalise them.
3 Writing organises your thinking.
4 Writing develops empathy and so benefits relationships with clients.
5 Writing leaves a record of your thinking and feeling – and changes.
6 Writing is a way to explore self-therapy and self-care.
7 Writing allows you to make time for yourself.
8 Writing identifies skills, strengths, gaps and growing edges.
9 Writing is a way to ensure ethical, reflective practice and identify prejudices.

We will now look at these reasons in detail. Always remember that *nobody has the right to read your personal journal* until you choose to share it.

1 Slowing down – pause and reflect

Have you ever had the experience of stopping so completely,
of being in your body so completely,

of being in your life so completely, that what you knew and what you didn't know,
that what had been and what was yet to come,
and the way things are right now
no longer held even the slightest hint of anxiety or discord?

(Kabat-Zinn, 2005: 243)

It may be that you are into meditation and are convinced of its benefits. If you have been keeping a journal or diary for some time, you will recognise the way in which this kind of writing slows you down, almost like a form of meditating. Pip Ranby, a New Zealand-based practitioner, talks and writes about 'composing herself' in her diaries:

> I began writing in a journal at ten years of age. My very first entries were small confessionals – 'I was mean today for no reason and I'm not sure why'; 'I'm having a wee cry tonight, I think it's because Dad is so unwell.' They were also the first markings of an instinct to represent my self, using my own words – an instinct that must have seen to its own increase because I've continued to write in journals ever since. For years now, I have been composing myself, double entendre intended. There's something in claiming time for myself to write that's important in and of itself too.

(Wright & Ranby, 2009: 58–59)

Making time, claiming time for reflection through personal development writing is one essential reason to write.

2 Expressing thoughts and feelings – privately

Expressive writing has therapeutic potential. If you have ever filled pages of your diary or banged words onto a screen while weeping or ranting, you will know what a relief it can be to express feelings in writing. These are heartfelt moments. A student on a CBT programme talks about expressing anger in journal writing:

> I mean when I wrote it, at the time if I was really angry about something I'd go to town with it, but that got it out of my system, it helped me.

(Sutton et al., 2007: 392)

The focus and pace of this writing is entirely in your control. Acting on strong feelings can be risky; being able to write them down first is like allowing yourself a cooling-off period.

3 Organising your thinking

For some people, the saying 'I don't know what I think until I've written it' holds true. Research supports the idea that structuring your random thoughts and feelings is beneficial:

FIGURE 2.1   Shaking with rage

© Liam Wright-Higgins. Reproduced with kind permission.

> Writing forces people to stop and to re-evaluate their life circumstance. The mere
> act of writing also demands a certain degree of structure as well as the basic labe-
> ling or acknowledging of their emotions. One particularly rich feature of the
> process is that these inchoate emotions and emotional experiences are translated
> into words. This analog-to-digital process demands a different representation of
> the events in the brain, in memory, and in the ways people think on a daily basis.
>
> (Pennebaker & Chung, 2007: 38)

One therapist who uses writing therapy for herself said, 'it allows me to articulate
fully without being distracted by physical surroundings or time pressure, or
another party's mood/mind set at that particular time' (Jane).

4 Benefits for clients of therapists who self-practice/self-reflect in writing

One essential finding from outcome research is that the relationship between
therapist and client is vital to positive change. The greater part of therapeutic
effectiveness can be accounted for independently of the counsellor's theoretical
orientation and technique, but the therapeutic relationship is key (Cooper, 2008;
Wampold, 2001). The quality of the relationship between therapist and client can

be improved through greater self-awareness on the part of the therapist. Personal therapy and group work in training have been questioned in terms of developing self-awareness. Research has also questioned how personal therapy affects therapy practice (Macran, Stiles & Smith, 1999). Self-practice followed by self-reflection is gaining ground in many training programmes because of the evidence that empathy is developed by such writing practices (Bennett-Levy, 2006). Keeping a reflective journal, not just in initial training but throughout a career in therapy, is part of this move towards more self-practice and self-reflection. Increased self-awareness then leads potentially to more effective relationships with clients.

For example, a student on a CBT training programme was asked to work with a negative automatic thoughts diary, practising this particular technique on herself. Negative automatic thought monitoring is a cognitive therapy technique; it involves noticing negative thoughts and writing them down as they come into your mind (Greenberger & Padesky, 1995). The student reflected on the experience:

> I did try a bit of that (negative automatic thought diary) when I had a down phase and it made me realise how hard it is when you give out homework to clients who are depressed or lead busy lives, how difficult it can be to complete it. So it can be really good to do some of those strategies yourself.
>
> (Sutton et al., 2007: 392)

The realisation that giving 'homework' to clients who already have full lives might cause some difficulties is crucial. Such insights increase the capacity for empathy with clients. This is one clear outcome of self-practice/self-reflection in writing.

5 Writing leaves a record of thinking, feeling – and what changes

Another student on a CBT training programme commented on the experience of keeping a reflective journal:

> I certainly look back on my first year's diary and sometimes it's hard to know when you are at a certain level, you don't tend to recognise where you have come from and how much you have developed and I think in that respect, having a learning journal to look back on, I suppose it is a bit like having a positive data journal to look back on in a sense, 'Wow, was I really thinking that? Was I really struggling with that?'
>
> (Sutton et al., 2007: 393)

The record of progress a reflective journal provides means that you have some evidence of your learning. You also gain a clear sense of your own achievements, and where some of the gaps might be in your knowledge and experience.

6 Self-therapy and self-care

Writing a reflective journal is a form of self-therapy. The kinds of writing exercises we suggest in this book draw from several therapeutic orientations. A student on a CBT training programme commented on the parallels between being asked to keep a reflective journal (called a 'learning log' on her course) as part of psychotherapy training and a client being asked to find their own insights: 'With CBT you are trying to get people to find the answers themselves and in essence that is what we are doing with the learning log' (Sutton et al., 2007: 392).

Shanee Barraclough, a New Zealand-based practitioner, writes:

Love Write Teach Learn Parent Create
Words to live by
for now
To live by or be inspired by?
To aspire to
and be guided by?

They grow, morph
I love them
I love that I have writing
For me, about me
A solace, a place to know me
Full of promise and possibility
Reminding me of who I am
Who I can be, might be
Strengthening my resolve
my value
To also love, parent, create
nourish, nurture, and grow
Yet they remain only words
Waiting to be translated into action
And they remind me of
the action I want to create
And move me closer to it
And to a sense of peace
in connecting so clearly, so strongly
To what sustains me ...

(SGB, personal correspondence)

There is now agreement that developing and maintaining resilience and self-care are part of the effective delivery of training and CPD across the spectrum of counselling and psychotherapy education and practice. In a study of therapists' responses to stress and trauma based in Aotearoa New Zealand, 'Beth' reflects on the aftermath of listening:

Sometimes I will be sitting working in this very room and listening to disclosures of awful stuff and then go out there [pointing to the tea room/kitchen area] for a cup of tea. I don't have a feeling of being in contact with something evil but I do have a feeling of almost like awe or disbelief that my mind is stretched about the human capacity for harm and about the unbelievability of the awful things that people will do to people. I won't be listening to any other conversation in the room. I'll be in a completely other place. It's about having gone on an unbelievable journey. So it's a kind of feeling of having to get my head around. It's about my mind stretched with human calamity.

(Pack, 2009: 52)

'I don't need to write,' some say, 'I've always processed things in my head.' There are many reasons why externalising is a good idea, including both the therapeutic benefits of 'getting it out' and the fact that you can re-read what you've written.

7 Identifying strengths, skills, gaps and growing prejudices

Remembering life as a first-year student, I can't stress how unsettling that first semester was. I don't know how my first semester compares with students from other years, but for instance, the two people I connected with the most both left before the end of the first semester. Some have struggled with lecturers, others with the course material … As a second year student – I feel that we are all at different stages of completion and this also brings anxieties within the group.

(Personal correspondence from a former student, now working as an integrative therapist.)

Your particular counselling and psychotherapy practice may involve small groups, personal therapy, experiential groups and other ways in which your peers and teachers provide feedback to you. However, when this is not possible or you find confusion and discomfort persists, writing down your thoughts and feelings about a particular experience may help make more sense of it. Here's a practitioner involved in group therapy who used writing to recognise transference:

And there was this person in the group, an older man, I just couldn't get on with. Others in the group noticed the tension, but it wasn't until I had described him in my journal that I realised how much like my father he was. (Jane)

Supervision will also be a part of your practice. You will be able to see clearly what you're good at, how your skills are developing and what you find more challenging by writing and re-reading this journal record before, during and after supervision. Meanwhile, some gaps and prejudices emerge in writing:

I always used to show my age by printing off the e-mails. So, although online therapy sounds so modern and high-tech, what I was doing was more like supported writing. With asynchronous e-mailing the 'sitting with' was the same, but instead of a person with hair or not, a body, clothing, colour, scent, a face with eyes and teeth, a voice – I would sit with their words on paper in my hands. At first I didn't enjoy it as much. I noticed my anxiety levels were higher. Sometimes there would be technical glitches, and one of the 'boys' would fix it. There seem to be more men working online – or is that my imagination? I know I'm biased. I certainly felt like an incompetent, technophobic woman at times. (Jeannie Wright)

You may be able to see patterns in your response to particular situations and begin to trace blind spots. Over time you will be able to step back and look at the taken for granted, the so-called 'normal' and see the cultural, socio-economic and gendered assumptions that are part of the frameworks of our lives and identities.

8 Keeping a record and re-reading

If you are still reluctant to start writing and prefer to process events and experiences in your head, it is possible to use other ways to record that processing. But the fact is that we forget. If you have ever kept a diary of a round-the-world trip or a particularly exceptional experience, such as childbirth, you will know that even six weeks after the train journey across Siberia or your child's arrival, not just details but major episodes will have been forgotten and will surprise you when you re-read them.

Keeping a reflective journal means that you have a record. This is crucially important, as illustrated below.

Philip: I've learned a lot about myself by re-reading my reflective journals. At the very beginning of the course I had read so much about genuineness. I knew it was important and I'd watch videos of Carl Rogers counselling people and I could see how authentic he was. It looks so simple. Well, Carl Rogers certainly makes it look easy. I still have moments where I think I'll never get there, but I can see examples in the writing about client work where I'm doing OK – that's what the client feedback says so I shouldn't ignore the positives. Old pattern: Only hear negative feedback.

Anita: I've not done much work with children. Last week I was asked to see a child, a 10-year-old who was refusing to go to school. The person who would usually have seen her was away and I had a cancellation. It was strange working in the room set aside, with smaller furniture and lots of crayons, trains, soft toys, big sheets of paper. We didn't talk much. She sat down straight away and started drawing. She drew a dandelion clock with all the seeds just about to be blown away. They were separate from the flower stem, but not way off in the air. When I was walking home, I picked a dandelion head and held the seeds, fluffy in my hand. I can see why it's important for work with children to use things you can touch, see, move around. Once I'd written up my notes in this journal thing I was clearer.

Jo: One of the things I like about e-mail counselling at the agency is that we collaborate on written responses to clients' messages. We don't promise an immediate reply and sometimes I can draft an e-mail to a client's message and come back in the next day to read it and confer with people in the team. Sometimes, I can see how what I've done is give advice. I know I do that sometimes face-to-face too, but when the words are there on the screen, it's so obvious! Even more so than when we record counselling sessions and then review the filming on the course. It's great, because we all find ourselves in that vulnerable position of being the one in the hot seat, so it doesn't feel too shaming to make mistakes. In one message I drafted I actually said, 'If I were you ...'. We all had a laugh about that.

RESEARCH FICTION, AND THE BENEFITS OF 'WRITING CURES'

The grandmother in one of Samoan novelist Sia Figiel's stories tells her granddaughter to write things down to forget them:

> My only advice to you is: Don't Write Anything Down! It's the easiest (and surest) way to forget things. Writing things down does that, Malu, you know? And you'd don't wanna do that girl.

> (Figiel, 1999: 13)

This wisdom is supported by Western scientific evidence, most notably by social psychologist James Pennebaker:

> One reason that we believe that expressive writing has been effective is that it serves as a life course correction. Occasionally, most of us benefit from standing back and examining our lives. This requires a perspective shift and the ability to detach ourselves from our surroundings. If we are still in the midst of a massive upheaval, it is virtually impossible to make the corrections. [...] There are times when we are forced to stop and look back at our lives and evaluate what issues and events have shaped who we are, what we are doing, and why.

> (Pennebaker & Chung, 2007: 37)

Beginning in the mid-1980s, Pennebaker's initial randomised controlled trials were with groups of students who were asked to write down their experience of a traumatic event which they had never told anyone about (Pennebaker & Beall, 1986). The exact wording of the instructions might be useful, as reproduced in an article written over 20 years later:

> For the next three days, I would like you to write about your very deepest thoughts and feelings about the most traumatic experience of your entire life. In your writing I'd like you to really let go and explore your very deepest emotions

and thoughts. You might tie this trauma to your childhood, your relationships with others, including parents, lovers, friends, or relatives. You may also link this event to your past, your present, or your future, or to who you have been, or you would like to be, or who you are now. You may write about the same general issues or experiences on all days of writing or on different topics each day. Not everyone has had a single trauma but all of us have had major conflicts or stresses – and you can write about these as well. All of your writing will be completely confidential. Don't worry about spelling, sentence structure or grammar. The only rule is that once you begin writing, continue to do so until your time is up.

(Pennebaker & Chung, 2007: 6)

One group was asked to repeat this exercise each day for the three days of the study. Meanwhile, the control group was asked to write about trivial topics on all three days of the experiment. Self-reports indicated that writing about previously undisclosed, emotionally upsetting experiences, although sometimes, and briefly, painful at the time of writing, produced long-term improvements in mood. With the student group who wrote about their thoughts and feelings, illness visits to the university health centre were also found to be far fewer than for the control group participants. The benefits of what has been called 'the writing paradigm' have been subject to several meta-analyses (Sloan & Marx, 2004; Smyth, 1998). Perhaps most startling to Western scientists were the clear physiological advantages of expressive writing indicated in subsequent studies across different populations: for example, reduced blood pressure, positive effects on blood markers of immune function, reduced symptoms of asthma and arthritis.

These links between mind, body and spirit would not have been at all surprising to the Samoan children and their grandmother in Sia Figiel's novels.

CONCLUSION

For Philip, when he decided to train to become a therapist, the personal journal writing part of the course was 'easy'. Anita has no idea why she's asked to keep this personal journal and resents the time it takes. She was attracted to CBT training because it has a sound scientific foundation for therapeutic intervention, not to practise journal writing. Jo has found some of the personal journal writing she's been asked to do on her counsellor education programme surprisingly useful, but also exposing. She doesn't like to think her tutors will read it, nor anyone else she knows from the course.

There are many reasons why any practitioner or student in the talking therapies would benefit from keeping a personal reflective journal. Writing is like a form of mindful meditation. This kind of writing means slowing down, focusing in the here-and-now and accepting what is going on in your mind and body. The implications for self-care in an occupation which can be stressful are clear, and there are accompanying benefits for clients.

Write!

2.1 How will you safeguard your personal development and writing?

Commit now to a system that will work for you – password protected files? Locked drawer?

2.2 First impressions

Personal development in therapeutic practice and training takes many forms. When you first walked into your selection interview, or the very first meeting with your therapy group, you would have been observing physical characteristics, mannerisms and all of the non-verbal signals we take in when forming first impressions of new people. Similarly, those people are doing the same thing, assessing cues about your identity from your voice, your appearance and other indicators of cultural positioning. One way of making this decoding explicit is to write about the kind of impact new people have on you.

Think of a recent experience of meeting new people. It could be in a work setting or at a social occasion. Write down your immediate impressions of one person you met there for the first time. This is a kind of descriptive writing that can make visible a complex set of skills which are honed in therapeutic practice. For example:

> Cheryl said she had turned 80 that year but looked younger. Maybe it was because of the way she moved. She was slim and light and seemed to have no difficulty in getting in and out of her seat or walking across the room. She was deaf in one ear and tended to crane her head to look directly at the person she was talking to. At one point she made a joke about this and seemed generally to be able to hold her own in conversation, telling stories in a bright, smiling way. Her voice didn't seem that old either. I noticed she wore a locket on a gold chain and three-quarter length trousers made of heavy linen. There was a floral scent that came in with her.

2.3 Response to keeping personal reflective journals

The psychological therapies are not the only discipline where reflective journals are required. Teachers, social workers, nurses and other health professionals value reflective practice and keeping a reflective journal is required as part of professional development. Perhaps you've experienced being required to keep a journal before. What was your response? 'Airy-fairy', or a vital way to get through the day?

Write down your immediate response to being asked to keep a personal journal as part of your training. A couple of sentences is fine.

Don't censor!

Nobody else will read this writing unless you give permission.

3

Preparing for the Adventure

Essential theory

Philip: I don't know about reflective and reflective writing. The jargon puts me off. It takes me into my head, whereas doing the writing takes me into all sorts of places.

Anita: I've done one of those tests and I'm not the reflective kind. So there's not a lot of point me trying this reflective journal stuff – I'm much better off just getting on and doing it. I'll do something to satisfy my tutors; I'm sure I can invent some worries to interest them.

Jo: Well I've read that you can do one of those personality typing tests on different occasions and get totally different readings. One day you might be cast as totally non-reflective, and then next – that's exactly what you are. Those things only test how we are at the time: humans are multi-faceted beings – different things at different times.

Reflective writing is a personally questioning process. Perhaps it should be called *flexive*; reflection being a mere mirror image with no sense of development or change, whereas *flexion* means 'alteration, change, modification' and 'a bend, curve, and a joint' (Oxford English Dictionary).

In preparation for an adventure which creates 'alteration, change, modification', this chapter looks at why we need to write rather than just think and discuss, and the specific nature of journal writing. Writing intended to disturb habitual ways of understanding can feel uncomfortable at times, but this temporary instability is an essential and ultimately positive element; change cannot take place without it.

Further issues needing attention before we start the journey are discussed and clarified. Who is this self who is both reflective writer and reflective reader, as well as reflective interlocutor with colleagues about issues raised? And what do we understand narrative to be in this context, and the nature and role of the narrator?

Reflective journal writing encompasses two major processes: reflection and reflexivity. Generally, this book makes no practical distinction, but knowing what they both are is useful. This is clearly and straightforwardly explained, as are the values and principles which underpin the whole reflective and reflexive endeavour.

WHY WRITE?

Writing is powerful communication: perhaps even more so than speech, as it does not disappear on the breath. Every utterance is communication between interlocutors. But no one initially listens to writing except the quiet accepting page, which creates a record. The etymological roots of the word 'record' are 're', meaning again, and 'cord' meaning heart (OED). Recording is getting closer to what is in the heart. The writer is their own first reader, their own primary interlocutor. So writing, in the first instance, is a private recorded communication with the heart of the self.

Expressive and explorative writing is really a process of deep listening, attending to some of the many aspects of the self habitually blanketed during waking lives. Some of these aspects we ignore at our peril. A therapist wrote for the first time in a confidential, carefully facilitated group; after she'd read her writing to herself, she wrote: 'Hell, did I write that? Was that really me? You can't pick something safe with writing, like you can with role-play. I suppose it's because you're not listening to yourself as you write. Writing takes you out of control' (Bolton, 2001).

'You're not listening to yourself *as* you write.' No, while writing, the page offers no judgment at all. But there *is* a future interlocutor: writing with a white pen on white paper would not have the same effect. You listen to yourself *after* you write, when you re-read your own writing. Writing creates tangible footprints which can and probably will be followed, but interlocution is postponed. There is no immediate reaction of head-nodding, smiling, frowning, grimacing, no immediate response of questions, affirmation, shouts or screams. The process of gaining insight is three-staged: first the dash onto the page, then re-reading to the self, then the sometimes emotional reading and sharing with a carefully chosen confidential other (or others). Writers have authority: nobody else is in control, though it takes some a long time, or even never, to realise this.

All this sounds so purposive, yet to be effective this writing has to be undertaken in a pure spirit of enquiry. Explorative enquiry is process- rather than product-based: seeking answers to perceived problems or *to get published* will not create useful or communicative texts. Attempting journal writing purposively would be as much use as therapists knowing in advance what clients should explore.

Shakespeare's sonnets were perhaps a 'way of working out what he's thinking, not as a means of reporting what he thought' (Paterson, 2010: 3).

Many professionals begin by arguing they don't need to *write* their stories. But once a story has been written, read and discussed, they understand how an artistic process can significantly develop their perceptions and understanding. To enable dynamic change as in the examples below, the story has to be communicated: written, read, reflected upon, shared.

WHAT AND WHY *JOURNAL* WRITING?

Journal writing uses personal, explorative and expressive processes, similar to creative writing's first stages. Each writer works according to their own interests, concerns, wants and needs. Authority and control always resides with writers, to re-read, share with appropriate others or not, store unread, or possibly destroy therapeutically.

The emphasis is on a process of satisfaction and interest to writers, and possibly a few close colleagues, whereas literary writing is oriented towards products of as high a quality as possible (e.g. poetry, fiction, drama), generally aimed at an unknown readership.

Journal writing is an adventure into the unknown of our own knowledge, experience, memories. Because we don't know what we will find out: *we have to learn by not knowing.*

Writing allows us to let go of the certainty we normally feel in our lives: who we are, what we think, feel, know. We do this to allow ourselves openly to explore whatever needs exploring in a process of *certain uncertainty.*

We are the world's best authorities on our own experience and so will never write the wrong thing (uncomfortable sometimes, but never wrong). It is the *content* we can't get wrong; the grammar, however, might often be very wrong, and this does not matter at all. In order to tell us what we need to know, this writing has to take free-rein: *it is in letting go that we find our direction.*

Journal writing uses a philosopher's method of constant enquiry. Each response in our journals leads to yet more questions, in a process of *unquestioning questioning.*

The best thing about journal writing is that it's exciting and enjoyable, just like any adventure or philosopher's enquiry. Yet what we learn has the power to change our lives for ever: for the good. Journal writing is *serious playfulness.*

Why journal writing works

Writing provides simple, quiet, private, focused, recorded forms of reflection, of paying proper attention to one's own self. Humans are fabulously complex beings:

we know, remember, feel far more than we realise. Yet much of this is stored inaccessibly, especially at times of stress or, most particularly, trauma. Writing can encourage our closed internal doors to slip ajar. Material the other side of these doors is sensitive and vulnerable: care is needed over appropriate ethical boundaries and principles.

Our minds are rather like London's Royal Opera House in Covent Garden. Most of the time we live and work in the auditorium – that lovely crimson and gold space – unaware that behind the stage curtain there are vast spaces unknown to us, where all the workings of the Opera House go on: three massive stages, countless rehearsal spaces, practice rooms, offices, canteens, costume, scenery stores and so on. It takes specialist enquiry to gain admittance to the essential areas beyond the wings of the stage.

Writing helps gain admittance to our mind's vital and huge backstage areas because issues seemingly impossible to share with another person can be shared relatively fearlessly with a piece of paper which never gets bored, angry, distressed or shocked, and its potential impeccable memory is impersonal. I say 'potential' as writing can be ripped up, burned, flushed away: just creating it without re-reading helps. Writing can be read and reflected upon, perhaps developed, redrafted, perhaps later shared with a trusted confidential other or group. Writing's privacy makes it qualitatively different from conversation, which will be remembered idiosyncratically, people cannot be asked to forget what they have heard.

Thinking is also private, but it's hard to focus, and even harder to remember reliably. Recording by tape or CD has to be associated with hearing one's own voice, which many dislike, and requires mediating technology.

Writing can be a private communication, first with paper and then with the self. This privacy can enable exploration of areas unknown prior to writing (examination of troublesome emotions, memories, sticky issues perhaps). People write often with no planning, forethought or real clarity of what is landing on the paper. The process is physical: the being writes, sometimes as if without the cognisance of the mind. Allowing words to fall onto the page and then seeing what's there can feel like playing around (Winnicott, 1971), like dancing or singing.

Stress can make it hard to voice problems and fears. Many, conversely, need to express ups and downs far more than colleagues, supervisors or other students have time or patience for. Paper and pen are endlessly patient, present, and never judge.

Expressive and explorative writing also helps gain permission beyond the stage curtain because it comes more directly from the body, via the hand. Our mouths are also part of our bodies, but talking is more likely to be censored by the controlling forces in the mind. Ted Hughes said: 'The progress of any writer is marked by those moments when he manages to outwit his own inner police system' (1982: 7). That police force (or Opera House usher) will be on duty far more with speech than with writing. He or she is much less on the lookout for the written word.

UNCERTAINTY

Undertaking this writing is straightforward, but as you must have guessed the theory behind it is complex. Going behind the curtain (slipping past the mental police/usher; allowing yourself simply to write what tumbles down your arm to your writing fingers) takes the writer into a liminal space (*limen* being Latin for *threshold* [Shorter Oxford Dictionary]). This psychological threshold is a transitional place of uncertainty where normal assumptions and stable understandings are questioned and sometimes overturned. It is a powerful educative state, where learners open themselves to possibilities, create space for dynamic new knowledge and understandings to enter. Such a force for change can of course feel uncomfortable, however – sometimes very uncomfortable in the short term.

> There is a tide in the affairs of men.
> Which, taken at the flood, leads on to fortune;
> Omitted, all the voyage of their life
> Is bound in shallows and in miseries.
> On such a full sea are we now afloat,
> And we must take the current when it serves,
> Or lose our ventures.
>
> (William Shakespeare: *Julius Caesar* 4(3): 218–224)

The 'full sea' on which you are 'afloat' is that of education. To be unwilling to cross the threshold, scared of taking the opportunity of the uncertainty of liminal places like personal expressive and explorative writing, is to 'lose our ventures'. As with all meaningful ventures, it can feel at the time a bit like being taken over by a flood.

THE SELF AS WRITER AND READER

We now turn to examining: who is this 'self' we're exploring and expressing? Reflective journal writing is underpinned by a view of the self as complex and plastic, in a process of constant change which the writing facilitates positively. This reflexive focus upon the self as 'something to write about … is one of the most ancient Western traditions' (Foucault, 1997: 233).

> Most of our energy goes into upholding our own importance. This is most obvious in our endless worry about the presentation of the self, about whether or not we are admired or liked or acknowledged … If we are capable of losing some of that importance, two extraordinary things would happen to us. One, we would free our energy from trying to maintain the illusory idea of our grandeur; and, two, we would provide ourselves with enough energy to … catch a glimpse of the actual grandeur of the universe.
>
> (Castenada, 1993: 37)

> Our deepest fear is not that we are inadequate. Our deepest fear is that we are powerful beyond measure. It is our light, not our darkness, that most frightens us. We ask ourselves, Who am I to be brilliant, gorgeous, talented, fabulous? Actually, who are you *not* to be? … Your playing small doesn't serve the world … We are all meant to shine … And as we let our own light shine, we unconsciously give other people permission to do the same. … Our self perception determines our behaviour. If we think we're magnificent creatures with an infinite abundance of love and power to give, then we tend to behave that way, and the energy we radiate reflects those thoughts no matter what we do.

(Williamson, 1996: 167, 190–191)

Williamson and Castenada both address conundrums about our selves, though their statements appear to be contradictory. I think, however, that they both mean the route to leading fulfilled lives and helping others is via allowing ourselves to be ourselves. Not only to recognise our 'one wild and precious life' (Oliver, 1992: 54), but to enable ourselves to let it shine without striving either to hide its light or to allow artificial brightness.

People narrate a range of stories about themselves (as parent, doctor, teacher, patient perhaps, or from different points of view); each aspect of their situation constructs a slightly different story, a slightly different self. And the narratives change over time, as situations change. People could therefore be said to be made up of multiple changing selves, rather than a unitary *true self*. In constructing and re-constructing stories about lives and work, we could be said to narrate ourselves in writing. This narration and re-narration can be critical processes: actions, perceptions, assumptions, values, taken-for-granted roles and point of view are open to question and rewriting.

Montaigne is said to have begun the fashion for writing about oneself in his essays. His style of writing was to give himself up to doubt and uncertainty and what he felt was his predominant quality – ignorance. He paid attention to the simple feeling of being alive in the present moment (Bakewell, 2010). Virginia Woolf said his rule for doing this was to 'observe, observe perpetually' (1969: 78), similar to the Zen Buddhist search for mindfulness. 'Zen masters spend a lifetime learning [the ability to just *be*] … only after their teacher hits them with a big stick – used to remind meditators to pay full attention. Montaigne managed it after one fairly short lifetime, partly because he spent so much of it scribbling on paper with a very small stick' (Bakewell, 2010: 37, 38). Reflective writing is still trying for what Montaigne achieved through the writing of his essays in the 16th century.

WHAT IS NARRATIVE?

Narrative has a central role in reflection, from the everyday mulling over of events to sophisticated reflexive writing processes. Communicating and thinking about experience in story form is so everyday that we are mostly unaware of doing it.

Narrative (along with metaphor) is the human strategy for making sense of things. We are story-making creatures, telling stories to help understand issues, thoughts, memories, ideas, feelings, actions, constructing our identities thereby (Sartre, [1938] 1963). Each person is also part of others' narratives, and is therefore moulded by these as well as the narratives of their society and culture (see Adler & McAdams, 2007).

A narrative is an account of a situation which is narrated, that is, told. In this book we use the terms 'narrative' and 'story' interchangeably because we are interested in their role in our lives, rather than linguistics. A story is a discrete unit with beginning, middle and end, though it articulates with other narratives. It also has distinct characters who do and say things, is set in a place of some sort, and happens over a period of time, though sometimes this time can be very short. Something always happens in a narrative: the situation at the end is different from at the beginning, though this development might be subtle. The 'something' which 'happens' might be psychological, spiritual, physical, social or cultural.

Life-as-lived does not come in neat story form providing meaning, but is all bits of story middle, muddled together. We give life meaning by storying events afterwards. We create narratives about experience, generally unaware we are doing it. We reformulate life experiences with story form when we retell them either to ourselves in private thinking or to others. Story form gives a sense of order, a progression of events leading to some sort of change and some type of conclusion (Sartre, [1938] 1963). Narrating a story teases a single comprehensible strand out of the huge complexity of our experience of life. Our stories are not always useful to us, however, even if it feels they are; they can even be damaging. Some accounts of our lives, or of the lives of others which impinge upon us, merely reinforce a view with which we are stuck and which might be dysfunctional or worse (Hitler's story of the Aryan race and the Jewish race is an extreme example).

Narrative plays a large part currently in Western people's understanding of their selves in personal and professional lives and social and cultural worlds. 'Perhaps a push toward narrative comes from [Western] contemporary preoccupations with identity in times of rapidly shifting populations, national, international, and neighbourhood borders … Individuals must now construct who they are and how they want to be known, just as groups, organisations, and nations do' (Riessman & Speedy, 2001: 429).

Taking critical authority over personal narratives by personal reflective writing can be significant for the development of the self as person and professional. These narratives do more than impinge culturally, socially, politically and professionally: they are positively formative of the person.

ROLE OF THE NARRATOR IN WRITING

A considerable proportion of reflective writing is expressed in narrative form: the story form is a powerful vehicle. All narratives have a narrator. This seems absolutely obvious; it is less obvious *who* the narrator is. Every account – fictional, biographical, autobiographical, case study, historical – is presented from a point of view (perspective). This viewpoint can be personified as the narrator of the story.

Communicating and thinking about experience in story form is so everyday, we are mostly unaware of doing it. We are even more unaware of how we structure these accounts, particularly the point of view from which they are told. Yet becoming aware of the narrator of each narrative, the perspective from which it is told, has significant benefits. The learning gained from reflective writing can be significantly developed by focussing upon the nature and character of the narrator in each story. A dynamically wide range of different types of narrator are possible.

People get stuck in habitual stories of who and what they are, when and where they belong, how their life is going, and why situations and other people are as they are. Creatively writing narratives with a critical awareness of the role of the narrator can help to disrupt habitual day-to-day stories, enabling perception from a range of perspectives. Reflective writing uses artistic methods to question from outside the frame of the painting which is day-to-day life, rather than aiming to create art.

In autobiographical telling, the everyday vehicle of reflection, the narrator is straightforwardly the self, the author of the story. Creating narratives separate from ourselves, told by a narrator other than the autobiographical 'I', can offer a distance on experience. A fictional narrator gives a different point of view from my own, therefore widening my perspective on the situation, character or place. An author can write from the perspective of many different narrators at different times.

The *narrator* has a critical role in stories; storyteller/writers gain greater authority when they are aware of which narrator is being used. Reflective writers begin to realise they can choose their own narrators, writing stories in a range of different ways from the perspective of consciously chosen narrators, such as from the point of view of other actors in the event: colleagues, patients, clients, students, relatives, friends. Each narrator projects a different (sometimes surprisingly divergent) perception of the self, society and culture, and can help clarify the ethics of a situation (Bolton, 2009). Writers can be encouraged to become critically aware of the narrators of the life stories they write. Learning from the subtle differences given to stories by switching narrators can be a way of taking authority over the narration of one's stories and therefore taking greater responsibility for one's own life.

For example, Antonio Munno, a family doctor (GP), experimented with alternative narrators in fictional narrative writing to clarify his understanding of patients' perspectives, developing his professional perception and therefore his professional conduct. He used the letter-writing form valuably, and bravely examined his own feelings and prejudices.

EXAMPLE
A complaint that changed my practice

The family asked to meet me. Their daughter had recovered from meningococcal septicaemia, and they wanted to know why I hadn't diagnosed it when they saw me that morning six weeks ago at the GP surgery. A few hours after I had treated her for an upper respiratory tract infection, her parents noticed a rash on her legs and took her straight to the accident and emergency department, where the seriousness of her condition was recognised.

The letter of complaint arrived a few weeks after she was discharged: How had I missed the diagnosis? And how was it that the emergency doctor who had seen their daughter at home a few hours before me had also dismissed her illness?

My stomach wrenched with anger and frustration. Can't they see? That's the whole point: two doctors a few hours apart both made the same clinical judgment that this was a viral illness. There was nothing that morning to indicate meningitis or septicaemia. To the family, the fact that two doctors had failed them compounded their criticism of the quality of care they received: to me, that double failure showed the difficult reality of naming an illness that often declares itself only with time. [...]

As the date for our meeting drew closer, that black churning bitterness was still there, and I realised I had to do something. [...]

I decided to try one of [Gillie Bolton's] suggestions and write the story of the family's complaint from the point of view of the parents. The first line came easily: 'She nearly died you know. Our daughter nearly died.' At that point my perspective on the complaint changed. I felt the parents' fear, and I understood their terror. They had taken their ill child to a doctor and had trusted him to keep her safe. They needed a doctor to walk with them, support them, and to give meaning to their fears. The child got worse and nearly died. They lost the doctor; they could have lost their daughter.

The complaint wasn't about diagnostic skills or statistical probabilities but about a family trying to make sense of the horror of nearly being ripped apart forever. By thinking about the complaint from the family's point of view, I understood that my role in the meeting wasn't to defend but to listen.

(Munno, 2006: 1092)

Munno was able to engage with this event from different points of view. Employing the parents of his young patient as the model for the narrator of a version of this story enabled a wider and clearer understanding from their point of view. This gave insight about the impact of actions, and of cultural or social forces. Cecil Helman, also a family doctor (GP), reinforces the value of this approach:

> The art of medicine is a literary art. It requires of the practitioner the ability to listen in a particular way, to empathise and also to imagine – to try to feel what it must be like to be that other person lying in the sickbed, or sitting across the desk from you; to understand the storyteller, as well as the story.

(Helman, 2006: 1)

Confidentiality

> If privacy is life's most precious possession, it is fiction's least considered one. A fictional character is a being who has no privacy, who stands before the reader with his 'real, most interesting life' nakedly exposed. We need never see people in life as clearly as we see the people in novels, stories and plays; there is a veil between ourselves and even our closest intimates, blurring us to each other. We know things about Gurov and Anna (characters in a Chekhov story) – especially about Gurov, since the story is told from his point of view – that they don't know about each other, and feel no discomfort in our voyeurism. We consider it our due as readers. It does not occur to us that the privacy rights we are so nervously anxious to safeguard for ourselves should be extended to fictional characters.
>
> (Malcolm, 2003: 4)

Reflective writing which uses, for example, a patient (or client, student, colleague) as the model for the character who narrates the story might seem to cross a privacy boundary. Yet these people will never know that a reflective writing story character has been based on them. Or if, for example, the parents of Munno's patient found out about his writing, they'd probably feel profoundly grateful as it enabled him to approach them ethically and empathetically and with his espoused values utterly consonant with his values-in-practice (Bolton, 2010). It is not themselves as people who are exposed thus 'nakedly', it is the writer's own understanding and perception of them, and this is always done carefully and respectfully. Reflective writing work is undertaken privately, and discussed only with carefully chosen confidential peers or tutors.

Omniscient, and reliable/unreliable narrators

Some literary stories are narrated by one of the characters (e.g. Daniel Defoe's *Moll Flanders*; autobiography), or by different characters at different stages (e.g. Mary Shelley's *Frankenstein*); all early novels were narrated thus. More recently many fictions, such as Eliot's *Middlemarch*, are written from the perspective of the 'omniscient narrator'. This being, the *omniscient narrator* created by the author, narrates the story from outside and knows everything: every character's motives, inspirations, thoughts and feelings, social and cultural forces, what happened before and what will happen after.

A power of fiction lies in its ability to give readers entry inside characters' hearts and minds, to know the story's future outcomes, and the impact of the past. Fiction readers follow plots fizzing with ethical dilemmas, their interest held by the amount of inside knowledge divulged at key points.

There can, however, be no authentic *omniscient narrator* of autobiographical life stories. In telling or writing life stories (written from the perspective of the autobiographical 'I'), there is no outside authority to take the reflective practitioner by the hand through the maze of their own ethical dilemmas.

In fiction there are reliable (and unreliable) narrators. Completely reliable or unreliable narrators belong in fiction, like omniscient narrators. An example is Ann Kelley's unreliable heroine Gussie (2007), who tells of living heroically with heart disease. Her story is consistently optimistic, resembling Victorian moral tales of unfaltering bravery in the face of suffering, with no reference to existential pain, terror, physical pain, distress.

In writing about life experiences autobiographically, my narrator self is likely to be more or less reliable or unreliable as in life, and certainly not omniscient. We do not know ourselves or how other's think and why they behave as they do very well, or we would not need to undertake reflective practice. It is possible, however, to choose the way the story is told, for example as close to reliable as possible, or as close to unreliable (Bolton, 2008). Reflective writers have experimented with unreliable *fictional* narrators as an explorative strategy (Bolton, 2003).

Family doctor (GP) Mark Purvis was unaware how deeply his life and work was affected by his brother's death in a road accident when he was nine, until he wrote a poem about it from the point of view of his child-self. His child-self was the narrator of the story, and a pretty reliable one: the poem reads heart-wrenchingly true (Bolton, 2010). Having written the poem and shared it with his small confidential professional development group of colleagues, Mark was then able to discuss this life-changing event with his family, for whom the issue had been taboo. He was then able to explore what he learned from all this with his work partners. He began to understand how his unacknowledged personal distress had stood in the way of treating dying children and dealing with bereaved parents. With the support of colleagues, enlightened by the illumination of the poem, he was able to move forward with this part of his work.

We learn our life story narrators are not given, that we can, to an extent, choose more responsibly how to tell our stories, or allow writing to choose for us, just as Mark found himself writing in the voice of himself as a young child, often a wise or illuminative narrator.

> Every society needs a barefoot Socrates to ask childishly simple (and childishly difficult!) questions, to force its members to re-examine what they have been thoughtlessly taking for granted.
>
> (Matthews, 1980: 95)

Further examples are:

- A medical student wrote in the voice of an angry child in a consultation, helping her see how she might talk to him in a way he could understand.
- A manager wrote what a dominating senior colleague might have been thinking (as 'thought bubbles') at key moments in a meeting: some were surprisingly unconfident, giving the manager future coping strategies.

Writers can learn to choose their narrators, therefore take greater authority and control.

Internal mentor

The wise aspect of oneself is a significant narrator. An aim of reflective journal writing is for people to find their own power, to develop their own self-reflective and self-therapeutic authority. A child cancer patient wrote a story of a pop star giving his child character sound and comforting advice. This star was his archetypal trustworthy and kind authority figure or internal mentor (Bolton, 2011). An adult cancer patient wrote dialogues with and gained strength and wisdom from his internal 'spiritual father' (Bolton, 2011).

This wise 'subpersonality' (see Rowan, 1990) model is in keeping with the way people across cultures create personifications or models for areas of the self which seem to be present, yet inaccessible. Examples are: ego, id, and superego (Freud); God and Satan (Christianity); The Tao (Taoism); the Delphic Oracle (Ancient Greece); shamanic lands of healing (shamanic religions). In different ways, different cultures apportion atavistic power to these areas or beings. Authority is vested in individuals (e.g. psychoanalyst, Pope, sage, Pythia, shaman) who appear to have access, and thus the ability to offer wisdom, insight, strength (personal, political, social, cultural).

Poets, composers, playwrights, painters, sculptors seem to have been another type of powerful and venerated magical intermediary, perhaps throughout history and prehistory. Shakespeare, Beethoven, Michelangelo, Hepworth, Nijinsky are all examples of gifted people wielding artistic keys to open frustratingly closed doors, allowing readers, audiences and viewers glimpses inside. In reflective writing people can find their own shaman–artist 'subpersonality'.

Internal critic

There are negative 'subpersonality' narrators which can be powerfully influential, and hard to recognise and tackle. Some, which have been called the 'internal critic', habitually tell stories to the person's detriment, for example: 'I made a blunder yet again ...'. Reflective journal writing can help such people find more positive and constructive narrators who don't just mete out blame and guilt but might tell the same story, for example: 'That didn't go very well, but circumstances were difficult and I think I can see how I can learn from the disaster'.

Writing can also help those who conversely employ consistently self-justificatory narrators, repeatedly refusing to see situations as learning opportunities.

EXAMPLE
Negative self-justification

A professional found he had a negative self-justificatory subpersonality narrator who said things such as 'My new staff member is as bad as the others'.

He was able to play with different perspectives in writing and found a constructive 'subpersonality' narrator who approached it thus: 'If *all* my staff are obtuse and obstructive, perhaps I need to think about how I ask them to do things?'

He found it hard, however, to perceive his dominant but unhelpful personal narrator, seek positive ones, and start to use them habitually: learning new skills is easier than unlearning old ones.

Here, reflective writing did offer insight and support; development was difficult instead of impossible.

> O chestnut-tree, great-rooted blossomer,
> Are you the leaf, the blossom or the bole?
> O body swayed to music, O brightening glance,
> How can we know the dancer from the dance?

(Yeats, 1962: 128)

Yeats, in his wisdom, asks us to consider how can we know the narrator from the narrative? They are inextricably a part of one another. Each narrator will tell their story according to their nature: there is no other way to gain the insight which such narration can offer.

REFLECTION AND REFLEXIVITY

Reflection and reflexivity try to take the veil off everyday working and private life. Together they aim to make the extraordinary seem ordinary: comprehensible and clearer. Together they also aim to make the ordinary seem extraordinary: ordinary elements of life can often pass unnoticed, yet they can be of great significance. Being able to focus upon these ordinary elements as if they are extraordinary can uncover this significance and enable insight and therefore development.

Reflection

Reflection is focusing upon our world and our relationship to it, for example how we impinge on our clients; what their perception of us might be; how what we say and do influences the ways other people (colleagues as well as clients) respond to us. How what they say and do influence what we feel about them and how we respond to them. Reflection is therefore a looking *outwards* towards others, our environment and culture.

Reflexivity

Reflexivity is a focus *inwards*, a dialogue with the self. It is a critical enquiry into our own thought processes, prejudices and habitual assumptions about such things as power and authority, professional role, diversity, and the match between values and principles used without conscious awareness in practice (tacitly) and those which are stated consciously (espoused).

To be reflexive, the enquirer has to find a way of standing outside themselves. This is a paradox, as no-one can literally observe from outside themselves. This is why this book gives so many exercises and strategies such as playing with metaphor, writing about oneself as if one were a stranger, examining personal beliefs and values (see the Write! exercises at the end of this chapter) and so on. These are innovative and creative, and therefore frequently enjoyable to undertake; for this reason they can help writers slip behind the Opera House curtains of their minds.

When I say *critical*, in this context I mean a focused enquiry process into personal and professional experience in order to ask a series of questions. *Critical* in this context does not have the negative connotations it carries in everyday language, but is a process of critique.

The self-questioning of reflexivity is also aided by narrative writing. Questions can be directed at a narrative, once it has been written: who is the narrator of this story?; what was my role in this?; how did I respond and how might I have responded differently?; what does this narrative show my values-in-action (tacit) to be?; what does it indicate about my taken-for-granteds and assumptions?; what does this narrative tell me about my role, as perceived by myself as well as perceived by others? and so on.

Being aware of, and even at times choosing, the narrator of the stories we tell and write of our lives is also a powerful reflexive process. These are imaginative uses of fiction to help us to stand outside ourselves reflexively (for more about reflexivity, see Chapter 10; Bolton, 2010; and www.uk.sagepub.com/bolton).

Ghosts and shadows from the past

When you look at an old painting in a gallery, sometimes the oil paint is very thin with age, and you can see where the artist painted a previous picture on the canvas and it's showing through. This showing through is called *pentimento*; canvases were very expensive so were often reused, or perhaps the artist changed his or her mind how they wanted the painting to be. It can be confusing: the sky above the horseman has flying ghostly figures; the woman has six arms like an Indian goddess.

This is like the person whose present actions are over-influenced by the past. A woman professional who was once a pretty girl still simpered when asking others to do something for her. She didn't realise her present mature self (aged 68) needed to be painted strongly over the coy child. Normally there is no way for such a woman to recognise that her little girl pentimento is making her behave inappropriately as an adult woman. Our pasts affect us in ways of which we are unaware. This professional was confused by her colleagues' negative responses, and had developed only unhelpful defensive strategies for dealing with them. Her colleagues couldn't tell her what the problem was, and she did not have a good enough friend to do so. Writing an account with the particularly negative colleague as narrator, she came face to face with the unsuspected problem. It wasn't easy to change a habit she'd had for so long, but it was well worth doing so.

The ability to stand back from the painting which is the self, to perceive the pentimento, is a feat in itself, and leads to uncomfortable but valuably developmental liminal spaces (part way between the present picture and the past one). Discovering ways of painting appropriately and strongly over the out-of-date unwanted image is even more complex. We do not easily step out of our frame and view ourselves critically; reflexive writing exercises making conscious use of which narrator is telling the story can help perceive the pentimento and find out how to cover it over permanently. Then the painting might develop a lovely patina of age, adding appropriate depth and intensity.

VALUES AND PRINCIPLES

Expressive, explorative, reflective journal writing needs boldness based on trust in the process, and respect for the writer-self. My journal is private; it's very, very occasionally read by one other as well. I can say what I like, when, and how I like. The boldness this sort of writing requires is also based on self-respect. This in turn is based on a generosity to myself: the gift of time, materials and focused solitary attention, and a putting on one side the sense of my own inadequacy. A willingness to believe (or perhaps willingness to suspend my disbelief) that all those different aspects of myself which writing explores say things that are OK for me to hear. They're mine. They're me. The foundations below, one journal writer said, 'helped me consider and appreciate the value and quality of my life and experiences'.

Trust

Trust in explorative and expressive writing can reduce self-consciousness, allowing writers to tap into their strong wise creative sides. Whatever you write will be right for you at that time. Although possibly initially unclear or lacking in understanding, we are the world's best authorities on our own experience and so cannot write wrongly about it. Journal writers trust they will not be laughed at, despised, disbelieved or shouted at by the paper. This can enable the expression of experiences, thoughts and feelings difficult or even impossible to share directly with another. Writers can furthermore explore areas about which they are unclear or unaware of before commencing, allowing forgotten memories or unarticulated theories to surface. This aspect of reflective writing is creative, which has a unique insightful illuminative power different from cognitive reasoning work; wise Pooh (Milne, 1958) understood the difference:

> 'Rabbit's clever,' said Pooh thoughtfully.
> 'Yes,' said Piglet, 'Rabbit's clever.'
> 'And he has Brain.'
> 'Yes,' said Piglet, 'Rabbit has Brain.'
> There was a long silence.
> 'I suppose,' said Pooh, 'that that's why he never understands anything.'

> (Milne, 1958: 274)

Self-respect

Willingness to explore beliefs, actions, values, identity, is respect for personal integrity. Writing can give confidence we have something vital to communicate, and can say it well, enhanced by knowing it is only for us to read, at least initially: there is no teacher-reader waiting to correct. We therefore communicate respectfully with ourselves, tackling inevitable hopes, fears, hesitations. Examining a range of different elements which make up ourselves (e.g. destructive inner critics and wise internal supervisors) can help personal integration. An unselfconscious integrating certainty gained from respecting ourselves in all our diversity can allow insightful openness and creative uncertainty.

Responsibility

We are fully responsible for everything we write and our response to it, even when facilitated. We have full authority over our writing at every stage, including re-reading to ourselves and possibly sharing with confidential trusted readers. Writing fiction can, for example, offer significant insight (see Munno, 2006, above). Such authors gain clarity into others' perceptions, or other possibilities. In taking full responsibility for our actions we gain freedom to understand, explore and experiment with inspirational playful creativity. Too often we expect doctors, therapists, insurers, lawyers to take responsibility for our anxieties and problems. Deep, yet tentative private personal enquiry has gone out of fashion, but not in reflective journal writing.

Generosity

We willingly give energy time and commitment to those with whom we work, and to our own personal and professional development in a spirit of enquiry. This giving enables us to gain inspiration and experience from others, and from our own enhanced self-understanding.

Positive regard

We write about family and friends, colleagues and students, clients or patients. Any feeling can be explored within the privacy of writing, both for cathartic release and in order to understand and discover appropriate ways to act in the future. We can express and explore a range of memories, thoughts and feelings, yet still retain positive regard for these other people. Writing can even enhance positive regard by shedding light on negative experiences.

CONCLUSION

Writing can enable 'a glimpse of the actual grandeur of the universe' (Castenada, 1993), and remind us not only that we have an 'abundance of love and power to give' (Williamson, 1996: 167), but also offer strategies how to do it. This chapter has introduced a range of equipment we need in terms of understandings to write reflectively and reflexively.

Chapter 4 now turns to the adventure itself: how to start writing.

Write!

3.1 Finding out more about yourself

Use the beginnings below to ask about yourself. Write as much or as little as you like – spend 3 minutes or 30 – it's impossible to get it wrong. Write without thinking. In fact, try not to think at all until later. No-one else will read this unless you expressly wish them to.

- I am ... .
- I know ... .
- I think ... .
- I believe ... .
- I remember ... .
- I feel ... .
- I want ... .
- I wish ... .
- I can ... .
- I wonder ... .
- I hope ... .
- I was told ... .
- I promise myself I will ... .

Such note- or list-making can be done again and again; different responses might be discovered at different times.

'I should ...' and 'I ought ...' are absent from this list, as are other dogmatic self-instructions. Only a positive, genuinely enquiring attitude will inspire useful, interesting responses. *Should* and *ought* and their ilk cause locks to jam, keys to rust, easing oil to turn to water and door-handles to snap.

3.2 Finding out more about your life

Abstract to concrete

- Make a very quick list of words which describe your life; do it as much off the top of your head without thought as possible. These might, for example, be *happy, sincere, complex, supportive, helpful, kind, energetic* and so on. Then choose one word and write it at the top of a fresh page.
- Now list as many images for your word as come to mind, like this:

  - Kind is a ray of sunshine on a gloomy day.
  - Kind is pink.
  - Kind is turning a beetle over when it's stuck on its back, legs waving.
  - Kind is a cup of tea after a long day's work.

- Re-read your list when you begin to run short of ideas. Reorder them and think about relationships between items. This might give further ideas.

3.3 Finding out more about a client's point of view

Think of a person (client or colleague perhaps) you don't find easy to deal with. Think of a particularly difficult time with them.

- Note down the important elements of the situation, or even better, write the story out fully.
- Write what they were thinking about you at every important moment during the event. Write these entirely from their point of view, like cartoon thought bubbles.
- Turn it into a dialogue with you responding to every thought.
- Now do the 'Image and Word Picture' exercise (Write! exercise 4.7) with the same person.

3.4 What can your name tell you?

Write your names at the top of a clean page in their normal order, which might be: given name, middle names, family name perhaps. Write whatever comes into your head about any aspect of them, in note form, for 5 minutes. This might be memories from a long time ago, or things you've read about the meaning of your name. You can't write the wrong thing: put it all down – you might surprise yourself.

3.5 How might you describe your life?

- Imagine that your memoires are being published in paperback. Write a draft title and back-cover blurb describing the book.
- The memoires of a colleague/friend you admire are being published similarly. Write a draft title and back-cover blurb describing the book.

3.6 How are you feeling now?

If you are a weather or a season, what weather or season are you? Not what do you prefer, but what are you at this moment? Write describing in detail the weather you feel you are most like at this moment.

4

Starting Out: How to Write Reflectively

Practical, straightforward help on starting to write

Speech is silver; silence is golden.

(Proverb)

Silence has a bigger vocabulary.

(Fanthorpe, 1996: 3)

Like all newbies I was haunted by the prospect of the blank page before me staying blank, but the almost mystical unlocking process created by which those simple words 'Write anything that comes into your head for 6 minutes' was, and indeed remains, baffling. Hard to believe, but that acts as the key to access parts of our thinking that most of us seldom use. It's almost impossible to convey to the uninitiated.

(Brendan Boyle, General Medical Practitioner (GP))

Philip: How do I start writing in the journal? I usually find somewhere where I feel comfortable – somewhere outside is good if the weather's OK. There are less distractions and I make sure my phone is turned off. Usually, I don't think, I just write. The words appear on the page, whatever's there goes down on to the paper. I prefer handwriting – much slower with the felt tips I like to use, but that seems to help somehow.

Anita: I went to the library and found some resources on writing and therapy. One book said: just write and write – writing it out, whatever it is. It seemed so negative – I got more and more depressed and miserable about it as all my miseries and anxieties came out. Mostly what I'm worrying about stays at the back of my mind – it's to do with clients and practice – I'm afraid I'm doing the wrong thing and damaging the client, afraid I'm going to make them feel worse not better, because I'm getting so anxious about it all.

Jo: The book I read says only do that sort of 'splurging it out' for six minutes, and then do a very specific exercise, which is more like a game. So the game takes over and kind of provides its own momentum and content. So you don't go round and round the old miseries so they get worse, and you do find you've got lots to say. And some of it's quite surprising.

Journal writing has the power to help people understand themselves, each other, their relationships with each other and their world better. It draws on the imagination and deep memory as well as logical cognitive thought. This can affect self- and world-views because it works through experience, exploration, creative expression and other non-cognitive processes rather than instruction. We multi-task, rush from care to concern, sit through mediated entertainment, suffer being limited to the checkable and accountable by quality control. Our minds and bodies, however, can be unshackled from the 'to do' lists, from the desperate need to be seen to achieve and produce, from constant e-mails, telephones, mobile/cell phones. This journal writing is undertaken in silence, or at least the quiet of no talking. As the poet U.A. Fanthorpe (1996) has pointed out, it is here that things can really happen without distracting babble. This sort of writing is a process of intense listening to what we really know, feel, remember, think.

This chapter discusses starting and developing journal writing, offering examples and exercises to explicate the subtle human communicating modes of narrative, detailed accurate description, experimenting with point of view, image (particularly metaphor), and in the case of poetry, rhythm and repetition. It explains how, when, where, with what materials, and with whom resulting writing might be shared ('Why write?' was the subject of Chapter 2), and how to tackle certain blocks. It discusses possible redrafting processes, sharing writing with others, and some underlying principles of journal writing.

This book supports you to write both reflectively and reflexively. The interesting but complex distinction between the two is explained briefly in Chapter 3. Effective, enjoyable, life and work enhancing journal writing does not, however, rely on knowing which is being undertaken and when. Distinctions are not made here, or elsewhere in this book, between reflection and reflexivity: we take the processes of reflective journal writing to include both appropriately (for more about reflexivity, see Chapter 11; detailed critical explanation is offered in Bolton, 2010).

Psychological, social, cultural and spiritual insight can be achieved appropriately and gently when we give ourselves permission to allow writing to help us explore experience and express feelings, memories and knowledge. Effective learning is like successful lambing, to ensure a steady supply of wool to keep us warm. Lambing requires a safe place away from predators and cold winds, patience, skilful support if necessary, good pasture to ensure rich mothers' milk, sunshine, and a big hilly securely walled field for lambs to run and jump in to strengthen limbs and lungs.

A range of writing strategies are helpful. Ted Hughes called them games to outwit the controlling inner policeman (1982). Each can offer access to a different element, and their use also ensures lively and positive journal writing which is unlikely to get stuck, repetitive or destructive. This chapter and others contain widely diverse exercises for approaching personal and professional issues from side angles, for example, image exploration. Tackling difficult issues obliquely, such as by the way word pictures can create insightful new relationships between the thing and the word picture (image or metaphor), can provide potential avenues towards otherwise unapproachable areas.

This chapter explains and gives examples, including free-flow (as in the initial 6-minutes introductory writing), cathartic (shouting anger with a scarlet pen), reminiscence (*that* client!), logical cogent thinking (listing and weighing pros and cons), symbolic image exploration (metaphor, dreams), fictional communication with a significant other (unsent letters, dialogue), communicating with different aspects of the self (dialogues with the 'internal mentor', my angry self), fictional stories (a relatively safe-feeling way to explore certain events, such as with clients) and more.

The *personal development writing* process is simple, though memories, thoughts and feelings raised are complex and can be uncomfortable or even painful. It can be likened to a search for treasure where fearful rivers need to be crossed and dragons slain, or an intense and wonderful romance laced with quarrels and misunderstandings.

BEFORE BEGINNING WRITING

Writing materials, time and place

Materials can make a difference. Most people like nice paper, notebooks, sharp pencils or good pens, and coloured paper and felt tips are not only for children. Good materials are a pleasure and indicate respect. A social worker spent time buying a leather folder and fountain pen, a nurse found a shocking pink book and pen. Some, however, find second hand paper and a ring binder give permission to be scruffy and tentative.

Here is a partially-sighted therapist journal writer:

> I used a personal shorthand, consisting of abbreviations, some actual Pitman shorthand and what, I think, is a bit like the text messaging method – missing out vowels and using, for example, 'U' for 'you'. All this was in capital letters.

> I think now I might use my laptop, with earphones so no one else could hear the screen reader. The wonderful thing about this would be that I could then use speakers and the computer would read out to everyone what I had written. When it comes to re-reading my writing later, I have found listening and transcribing my reflections an additional force in the creative/therapeutic process. *Hearing* what I am writing as I type it seems to add another dimension to the process: about acknowledging two different and equally valid forms of writing, I think. (Linda Garbutt)

For people with mobility, where they write might make a difference: the leather folder and fountain pen man drove miles to a country park and did amazingly different writing on a lakeside bench than he would have done at his computer. And when to write: the middle of the night or first thing in the morning can be great, according to your body clock.

THE CONFIDENCE TO START – REALLY START

Writing uses words, our everyday communicating medium. Requiring only basic literacy skills, paper and pencil, writing is simple and cheap. A stumbling block can be negative memories of spelling, grammar and construction taught with an authoritarian confidence-destroying red pen. This chapter contains many ways to reduce these fears and guide you to begin to enjoy the freedom of writing without performance anxieties. Explorative and expressive writing is private, to be read initially by the writer alone, then possibly shared with one or two carefully chosen others. All that is needed is willingness to:

- have a go at open exploration and expression, alone in creative golden silence
- let go of previous inhibitions about *rules*; if grammatical accuracy is needed, redrafting is straightforward later
- trust the process and respect both writer and reader: oneself
- give oneself the gift of the small amount of time and energy required
- be willing to face some uncomfortable feelings and memories, knowing that writing is gentle and paced and will only present the manageable, and anyway can be stopped at any time and the right person to talk to found if necessary.

Starting to write is enjoyable, with initial unassuming steps. We write one word at a time, seeing where it leads:

> How do I write? One word at a time. The first sentence feels like the tip of a thread. I pull it very gently. Another sentence. And again I try, teasing out phrase after phrase and hoping that the thread will not break. It is as if before me there is an invisible garment of which only one thread can be seen. Each day I draw it out a little further.

> (Williams, 2008: 75)

Encouragement and support are helpful, especially initially, as is empathetic interest combined with lack of surprise, shock or untoward interest at anything written or divulged. Even writing nothing is not a failure, but an indication that the time or place is not right.

Key to success is perceiving writing as flexible, versatile, straightforward, enjoyable and private. And with no purpose other than personal exploration and expression.

- You can choose what and how to write.
- Everything you write will be right: because its an expression of your own experience, knowledge, memories, and you can't get such things about yourself wrong.
- The writing belongs to you; you need only share what *you* wish to share.
- It's yours! You are in charge of where it's kept, and who reads it or doesn't.
- No-one will talk about it without your permission.
- Grammar, spelling and so on *do not matter*: they even get in the way and can be sorted out later if wished.
- It needs no special form or structure.
- Books such as this offer abundant suggestions as to how and what to write.

HOW TO START

Six minutes free writing

This opening strategy is a beginning for every journal writing session. It gets the pen or pencil moving over that space, daunting to every writer: a blank page. It can note and temporarily store safely some of the muddle of thoughts which can otherwise dominate. It can capture insights or inspirations which seem to spring from nowhere; these can then be developed in the ensuing writing. Many have called it the *splurge method*.

Put the pen on the page and write with no forethought, planning and certainly no awareness of grammar or form. A list might come out, or seemingly jumbled odds and ends; our minds often jump about before we find a path through. Whatever it is, it will be right. It need never be shared if you don't wish, and need never be re-read: it's completely private.

The painter Paul Klee described himself as sometimes 'taking a line for a walk'. He put his brush, charcoal or pencil on the canvas, just to see where it went. We can do the same with words. In this most basic writing method, the 'six minute write', words take themselves for a walk along the page. Reading them afterwards, you find out what they've said. This follow-the-flow-of-your-mind key to all writing is the secret of the first stages of much poetry, fiction, playwriting, autobiography and memoire, as well as journal writing. We can borrow their initial stages. Here is I.S. describing her first 'six minute write' exercise, followed by an example of the exercise by Juhani Ihanus:

> As someone who is approaching a big birthday I have started to wonder where my life is going and ponder some of the choices made and lessons learned. I wrote some thoughts about these which were too personal to share (and we didn't *have* to share, which was good) but were certainly helpful to me. I think there is something about seeing life choices and dilemmas written down which condenses them into universal themes, for example passion versus stability or the drive to inclusion versus the urge to stand alone. Having done this and summarised some fairly deep existential issues in 6 minutes flat I felt strangely free, as if by naming them I had divested them of some of their power.
>
> (I.S.)

> Birth is a day shrilling lucid the most animal step out never recurring unparalleled throats changing stories … I don't know what will follow what people here are becoming should one or not at once I ask writing births get confused differently correctly moving to a bush and a bunny it is not until now that there is roughness on the tongue a hoarse throat again I reach out for a melody without any ear for music that is not poetry or it is frozen but a gentle aria kisses the frozen sea so rarely writing the hand numb whatever is lacking no clock not now.
>
> (Juhani Ihanus)

Juhani has really allowed himself to write absolutely anything on the page, letting go of everyday assumptions about writing rules. The meaning of much of this is opaque to a reader who knows nothing of him or his thought processes. It was, however, significant and very valuable to him; and this is the only function of 'six minute writes': to be of significance to the writer and the writer alone. I.S.'s account above of her writing experience made it clear to us how illuminative it was.

This writing can illuminate like a bolt of lightning. And having written, it can feel like lightening yourself of a heavy load. Sometimes you will find it bland and uninteresting; next time, though, it might illuminate. Forget all rules of writing you ever learned – full stops, paragraphs, spelling, verbs, handwriting, proper ways of beginning and ending. Don't worry about anyone else being able to understand it: *you* are the only person who is going to read it to begin with. There's plenty of time later to sort out grammar and make more sense for someone else if you want, and to cut out or alter bits you'd rather another reader didn't hear.

- Take whatever materials you feel like today: experiment with what works best for you.
- Choose where to sit: under a tree, at the kitchen table, somewhere miles from home or office. Listen to what you feel like doing.
- Choose a peaceful time when you *know* you will have at least 20 minutes, *uninterrupted* and *alone*.
- Make yourself comfortable in whatever way is right for you.
- *Write* whatever comes into your head for six minutes *without stopping*, without re-reading, as far as possible without thinking about it. Don't sit and think *at all* before you start: put the pen or pencil on the paper and start writing, in mid-sentence if necessary. Allow your writing hand to do the thinking for you.
- Your mind hops around, so well might this writing. Write *whatever* is in your head: descriptions; shopping lists; moans about traffic, weather, children, colleagues; an account of something that happened to you; last night's dream; work or dinner plans – it doesn't matter what it is. Don't stop to question anything: write without thinking.
- Since you don't think in sentences or logical sequences, neither might this writing. Only include punctuation, correct grammar and spelling which occurs naturally. *Follow the flow* for 6 minutes.
- If you get stuck rewrite your last sentence, or look up and describe the first thing you see.
- You will never write a wrong thing. You are the authority of what is in your head, no-one else: you can't get it wrong. And no-one else is going to read it anyway, unless you expressly decide otherwise later.

There are other ways of experimenting with this writing:

> I got us to do another 6 minutes, but this time using the paper differently – covering it with their thoughts in any way other than the usual top left-hand corner down in lines to the bottom right. Chris wrote from the bottom upwards which made him laugh and appreciate breaking out of the usual way of doing things. Franco wrote in a compact way across the left-hand corner of his page, got fed up with that and then trailed a single line off across the page. Winston wrote in a column down the left hand-side of the page, across the bottom and up the right-hand side. He was transported back to school days by the doing of it and enjoyed the challenge of different content sparked by the exercise and the spatial aspect of fitting what he wanted to say into the pattern that he was producing.

> (Judy Clinton)

On a different occasion Judy asked the group to write their Six Minutes in nonsense words, which was also successful. Here a personal writer describes their first six minutes:

> Arriving for my first reflective writing experience 7 years ago I had no idea what to expect. I suddenly found myself properly empathising with some of my phobic/anxiety patients. I was terrified! What had possessed me to enrol?
>
> It was incredibly reassuring to discover that you do not need any writing skills at all. By what seems to be simplicity itself, we were led into a process of unlocking memories, thoughts, reactions, experiences by acting as a catalyst, sowing seeds, stimulating us to truly reflect on our day-to-day experience as family doctors – and how that affects us ourselves. Each session starts with a blank sheet and we write anything that comes into our heads for 'six minutes'. Like all newbies I was haunted by the prospect of the blank page before me staying blank, but the almost mystical unlocking process created by which those simple words 'Write anything that comes into your head for 6 minutes' was, and indeed remains, baffling. Hard to believe, but that acts as the key to access parts of our thinking that most of us seldom use. It's almost impossible to convey to the uninitiated.
>
> (Brendan Boyle)

Journal Writers can stay with this *splurge* method: writing moans and complaints, cathartic outbursts or reflective meanderings which might superficially seem to go nowhere but are often perceived to contain valuable insight when re-read. Splurge writing requires no beginning and end. It is all middle, and can be picked up and put down at any time or in mid-sentence. Writers can then fruitfully move on to any of the following writing strategies.

WRITING STRATEGIES

Lists

Lists seem undemanding, everyday, yet can be extraordinarily illuminative. No sentences, no paragraphs, and the form is all middle with no beginning and end. Try choosing a word from the 'six minute' writing, any word, at the top of the page, and list whatever comes underneath. Or write the word in the middle of the page and allow all words and phrases to cluster over the page from this central word. If you can't choose a word from the 6 minutes, open a book at random and pick a word – cookery, novel, poetry, text book or work related. Here follows an exercise which can remain just a list or could become a much longer piece of writing.

Activity: Listing exercise for debriefing

The journal can be used to debrief after a session with a client. Start by going through the can-opener questions – which Kipling also found invaluable ('What and Why and When/And How and Where and Who', 1902: 83) – to start self-questioning, which might open up the situation. Develop your own questions, which might resemble these:

1   Where and when was the session, and with whom?
2   What was the presenting problem?
3   Why do I think X came to see me?
4   How did he/she take responsibility for themselves in the session?
5   How did we tackle negative things positively?
6   What elements were noteworthy?
7   What appealed to my sense of humour, or was fun?
8   What was a surprise?
9   What do I feel I could have done better?
10   Why do I feel the way I feel now?
11   What did you think and feel, Internal Mentor? Please write me a letter!

Lists can of course be more focused, such as: Things which irritate/exhaust/lighten me; Things I find difficult to understand; Why do I like this client? There can be as many subjects as writers. A simple list can resemble cogent poetry of sincere opinion and feeling (as in Write! Exercise 4.1 at the end of this chapter, for example).

Description

Describing accurately helps focus attention on detail and nuance, a cornerstone of reflection. It is often part of other writing, such as narrative, fiction or poetry. Observation and description can also be useful while waiting for the deeper focus of that day's writing to emerge. You can pick a client, a colleague or someone else, your working room or an aspect of it, an object you keep on your desk – anything – to try to depict (try Write! Exercise 4.2).

Judy Clinton uses writing after every session to help give her insight into her demanding job. You can see how she wrote herself through straight description to feeling empathetic and keen to help them. This regular description of her clients, which enable her to muse upon the significance of their presenting appearance and behaviour, significantly supports her in developing attitudes and strategies to 'help them lead a happier and more fulfilling life'.

The first guy to arrive, older than the rest (34), arrived about ten minutes late. He was amiable, polite and headed straight to get a drink and disappeared for some time (drink+fag), by which time client number two crashed through the door in a whirlwind of activity and voluble swearing. He grinned a welcome at me and sat down to have an animated chat with Mr Fag about the latest drinking bout he'd been on. The two engaged in this manner for a bit while I observed, not at all clear as to how I was going to handle this one. Clearly the second arrival had a great deal of talent for abusive language and an ability to become paralytically drunk, and a disconcerting knack of winking one eye which I couldn't decide if it was intended or merely involuntary. In drifted number three client with a cloche type hat pulled firmly down over his rather bleary looking blue eyes and a large glinting stone immersed in his ear. I continued to observe while they 'caught up with the goss'. When a break came in their talking I jumped in to ask them why they were there and so on, as I had done with the morning group. …

It was a very tough day and in many ways a humbling one for me. These people are floundering in a society in which they haven't the language, the skills, the character, the support or anything else. No wonder so many of them turn to crime, become mentally ill or otherwise become destructive. They need help in so very many areas of life, but most of all, they need to feel that they matter to someone and that there is some way forward for them into a happier and more fulfilling life.

(Judy Clinton)

Narrative

Humans are narrative-making creatures; creating stories is our way of making sense of things. Working with clients and colleagues constantly raises queries, anxieties, creates exhilaration, stress and causes re-examination of values and assumptions. Writing the story of an event can enable significant issues and questions to become apparent, and greater sense to be made (see Write! Exercises 4.3 and 4.4).

Explorative reflection

Six minute splurge writing is the best example of this sort of writing. It can also be focused: perhaps starting with a particular issue needing reflection. Or sentence stems can set off a valuable train of thought (or sometimes a narrative) (see Write! Exercise 4.5).

Word pictures (image and metaphor)

A staple of poetry and prose, metaphor focuses upon significance: what things mean to us, remind us of, what they stand for in our own particular universe. The significance of one thing is carried over to another. Abstract words like 'anxiety' or 'love' are difficult to grasp; the image of being harried by wolves is readily graspable, as in the metaphor 'anxiety was a wolf pack at my heels'. Adrienne Rich spoke of 'the great muscle of metaphor, drawing strength from resemblance in difference' (2006: 2). We perceive beyond things, look and listen inside ourselves to help understand ourselves, situations, pasts, hopes and fears better; to do this we need to perceive beyond the *thingness*, *itness* of things (what wolves are really like is immaterial here), to focus upon metaphorical realities (its what wolves make us think of which matters).

Writers do also focus on the *thingness* of things, carefully observe and describe how a particular client carries themselves, their way of speaking, aftershave they use and so on, in descriptive writing using all the senses, as explained above. A writing skill is to perceive depth, to switch between perceiving metaphorically and literally: 'all that is real is in constant contact with magic and mystery' (Diaghilev, 2010: 17) (try Write! Exercise 4.6).

Letters and dialogues

Dialogues or letters never to be sent can be written to and from alive or dead people, injured or hurt body parts (see Bolton, 1999), and aspects of the self (e.g. inner child). Direct communication with an internal *you* can enable venting, or discovery of feelings, thoughts or memories. A really good interlocutor for such letters or dialogue is the internal mentor (see Write! Exercise 4.8). Here are two examples: the first is a pair of letters to and from 'the most compassionate person we could imagine', and for the second, the exercise was to write about an event and then write a letter to yourself from your internal mentor about the event.

> Dear x,
>
> If you were best able to help me you could explain why my parents set me up to fail in life, didn't want the best for me and are still threatened by any sign of my success. You could explain this in a way that allowed me to still love them. You would help them to talk to me (really talk) and facilitate an open dialogue of the kind we are never likely to have … What part of me was in those unhelpful inter-actions too? I need to know that in order to truly learn from it. After this you'd hug me and hold me and we'd go for walks seeing the woods and the flowers and the streams … After all this I'd know that you had always been there for me and would always be there for me. I'd know not to grieve that which felt curtailed

(relationships, career goals, choices not taken) because I am now in a better place and the very best is yet to come.

Reply from x

Firstly let me say how pleased I am that you are thinking these things and locating these difficulties where they belong-outside of yourself. I have always thought of you as a shining star full of promise and potential. Don't let others zap it! We don't choose our family and in some ways you got a poor deal but it's made you who you are. They didn't act any better because they couldn't *be* any better. They were young, feckless, dogmatic and damaged. They look back on some of it with something akin to regret but admitting that is a different thing. Pride is important to them and prevents the apology you often feel you need … There are a variety of ways to be sorry just as there are a variety of ways to be strong, but then you already know about that.

Having written these I felt like a load had been lifted from my mind.

(I.S.)

The third-person narrative was so long that I cannot reproduce it here. It was about a very punctual man, who dared to make only a few very cautious imaginary leaps in his daily walking and shopping routine routes and who finally met a bunny under a bush, chasing the bunny (which represented his disorder) away, thus missing the encounter with his animal other. The friendly letter from his internal mentor reminded him of the possibility to allow minor irregularities as a starting point for more exceptional journeys through the mindscapes. The mentor recommended that the man would take the bunny as his guest and let it play its own games. At rare moments they could also join and train together some initial unprecedented leaps.

In my 'six minute' writing (above), I already had the 'animal step'. It is of importance that the 'bunny' first appeared in the six minute writing and continued its life in the third-person narrative where the bunny was a disorder (a nuisance) for the man (perhaps also representing his disorder). Originally, for me, there was a natural experiential continuation between those two writing exercises, the latter exercise building on the former and enriching the experience to unforeseen directions.

(Juhani Ihanus)

These are all *unsent letters.* I.S. makes it clear how significant the writing was to her. Using the letter-writing device enabled her to say things to herself she couldn't otherwise have said. Juhani uses a metaphor – a bunny as an animal other – to help him understand something about a client. Letters or e-mails to be sent can be practised before a satisfactory version is created and sent – always a useful strategy, particularly for dealing with an angry response, for example.

FORMS OF WRITING

Journals use all the above methods as well as the following forms.

Fiction

Fiction is for experimenting and playing 'what if?' and 'might have been'. Writing from the point of view of another, for example, a client (such as in Write! Exercise 4.3); writing from the point of view of a wise observer (Write! Exercise 4.8 for example). Try rewriting the story of an event switching genders, so if you are a male counsellor try writing an account of a session with yourself female, or a female client as male; or try recounting the story of a disastrous event as successful.

Poetry

Poetry's short lines and succinctness can contain great feeling, and so often written at a time of emotional need. Rules of grammar, spelling and use of English can be twisted innovatively or even invented as the writer wishes. Rhythm and sometimes rhyme often develop naturally. Both these help to make poetry memorable, and deeply satisfying because they bring us closer to the rhythm of our own and our mother's hearts, and other rhythms of the world such as the restless restful sea or ocean. Poetry can be an expression of feeling and experience and need not be in the least 'difficult': it can be seen as writing which doesn't reach the right-hand page margin and disobeys rules. Quite often list exercises (as in Write! Exercises 4.1 and 4.6) end up as poems, as do many involving metaphor (and see Write! Exercise 4.7).

WHAT HAPPENS NEXT

Writing remains unchanged, unless revised. Writers re-read their material to see what they've written: an intense listening and responding. Sometimes they are not ready to re-read: storing writings unread can give essential waiting time. Sealing writing into an envelope can have further power: research has shown that descriptions of regretted decisions, sealed thus, decreased negative feelings about the decision. Research control groups showed unsealed envelopes and descriptions of insignificant events to be ineffective (Burkeman, 2010: 91).

Redrafting

Reworking writing can be illuminative. Writing keeps an accurate record, and can if desired be restructured, added to, have material removed or altered; it can even be rephrased to express an opposite opinion or point of view. Writing is plastic in this way, unlike audio- or video-taped discussion or monologue. Redrafting can help clarify vital images, as the experience, emotion or memory is captured as accurately as possible in apt succinct words and images. Neither speech nor thought can be redrafted thus. Redrafting is re-recording, getting closer to what is in the heart all the time. Not all journal writers redraft: the insight and development gained from the initial writing is sufficient for many reflective journal writers.

Sharing writing with others

Reading and discussing writing confidentially with a carefully chosen other(s) can encourage writers to recognise and own what they have written about, and help develop the writing. An aim is to express and share the writing itself, so reading the actual words, rather than paraphrasing, enables interlocutors to relate to the unique qualities of the piece of writing, which will be different from its spoken equivalent. Despite being not-for-publication, explorative writings are often clear, powerful expressions of deep human experience. Reading such material with writers, sharing their journey, is a privilege and can often be enlightening to colleagues. This confidential writing and discussion can furthermore sometimes open issues up, helping prepare them to be talked about with significant others.

> I immediately had a sense of total trust in my fellow small group members and felt honoured and humbled as we began to share our writings over the subsequent hours.

> We work in small groups of 5–6, and listening to each other's writings is the most fantastic way of recharging your batteries in the company of like-minded peers. I cannot recommend it too highly.

> (Brendan Boyle)

Overcoming blocks

Some, new to writing, feel nervous or inadequate due to old associations with being a writer or student. Yet this is not like writing for publication, or academic assessment. There is no teacher with a stern correcting pen, and no requirements of proper structure, form or grammar. And it can be done in different places with different materials and at any time of day or night. Gilly Pugh reflected how a writing exercise (about an event as a *fairy story*) was 'incredibly freeing. ... Suddenly I don't have to be clever, I just have to tell a story' (see Bolton, Field & Thompson, 2010). The initial six minute writing described above is designed to get the pen flowing as uninhibitedly as possible.

Rosalind Adams, who works with children and elderly people, struggled to learn this authority and ownership of her own writing: 'By far the most precious thing I've learned about writing is the skill to open my heart to my notebook. It's a simple skill but it took a series of workshops to enable me to get the full benefit of this sort of writing. I can now write what I truly feel and I regularly surprise myself with what appears on the page' (www.rkawriting.co.uk).

We can only open our hearts to those we utterly trust, such as the accepting page. Giving this trust might not come easily, and might take 'a series of workshops', but it is worth struggling for. Some, however, distrust family, friends or colleagues, fearing the wrong person might read their writing. One nurse took her journal with her everywhere, such was her anxiety. Two novelist friends arranged for their personal journals to be destroyed unread if they died suddenly, though they were not worried enough to stop writing. Strategies for the storage of writing can help. I (Gillie Bolton) think no-one would want to bother to decode my handwriting; my scribble would probably be rather boring to anyone else.

PRIMARY PRINCIPLES FOR REFLECTIVE WRITING

Power

Writing is powerful; in many ways more so than talk. People need support, encouragement and subtle direction while they are discovering this. The individual writer is the only one with power over their own writing. Many beginning writers think that someone else wields power: an old schoolteacher in their head; the facilitator of the course; the reader; publishers. Each writer owns their own writing and has control and power over it.

Paradox

Once people really start writing a journal they often feel bewildered by paradoxes, by the way life suddenly seems no longer so predictable. Writing gives insight; in so doing it can seem to strip away some safety and predictability. It doesn't create these paradoxes, it enables people to perceive them in a way they hadn't previously. Sharing writing carefully and confidentially with peers, supervisor or tutor can enable these insights to be useful rather than destabilising.

Privilege

Writing, working with others in gaining insight through writing, sharing the writing of others in order to develop their understanding of their own lives is a tremendous privilege.

Write!

Start each writing session with the 'six minute' writing method described in this chapter. Then move on to one of the exercises below. Re-read your writing carefully yet openly and uncritically to yourself privately before thinking if you wish to share it with anyone else. You might add in new words, take some out or otherwise alter it slightly as you re-read. Remembering you have five senses can be a useful redrafting element.

4.1 Why?

- Make a list, each item beginning with 'Why …' (e.g. Why am I lucky enough to have a great professional partner/colleague/client/supervisor?; Why doesn't that client listen to me?; Why does the moon change nightly?). See if you can get up to 100 by writing fast without thinking at all.
- As a variation, you could do the same exercise, this time beginning each list item with What?, Who?, How?, Where? or When?
- Re-read your list with attention, adding or altering any; write any answers you like.

This list might be the beginning of a poem itself. You could, however, extend the writing:

- Choose one or more from your list to write more about, in an open, free way, perhaps searching for answers.

4.2 Observation, and point of view

- Write a detailed description of your workspace (consulting room, counselling/therapy room, office, study). Include what you feel about it.
- Now write as if from the point of view of a client coming into it, or a colleague. Describe their impressions, thoughts and feelings.

4.3 Narrative, and point of view

- Write about an experience with a tutor, teacher, mentor, therapist, counsellor or perhaps someone who taught you a great deal even though they weren't in a teaching/therapeutic relationship with you. Try to write about the first occasion which comes to mind without questioning why that one has come: it might seem insignificant, for example. Its significance will become apparent when you've finished writing. Tell the story as fully as you can, including details.

(Continued)

(Continued)

- Now write about the same occasion again, this time from the perspective of the other person, so the other person will be 'I' and you will be she/he or Sally/Tom (or whatever your name is).

4.4 People in your life, and their point of view

- Think of a time in your experience with a client, student, patient of yours, or perhaps your child. Write a letter to that person, reminding them of the occasion: tell them about it in detail, anything that occurs to you.
- Now write the reply from your client/student. Let them write to you telling you their impression of that occasion and their relationship with you.

4.5 Getting in touch with yourself

Complete the beginnings below in a way appropriate to you. Write as much or as little about each as you like, or perhaps only one or two. You might return to it again and again. Offering a straightforward way of being in touch with your self, they might prompt you to write differently at different times.

- It is ... .
- Now ... .
- It started when ... .
- How about ... .
- If only ... .
- What if ... .

4.6 Getting in touch with your thoughts, feelings, ideas

- Make a list (write down the first things that come into your head); write a couple of sentences about each:

  - an old thing
  - a new thing
  - a borrowed thing
  - a blue thing.

- Now write a list of:

  - an old smell or taste
  - a new colour or something else you've seen
  - a borrowed memory (something a parent or partner told you about perhaps)
  - a blue piece of music, picture or building.

- Now write a list of these:

  - an old emotion
  - a new feeling you've never felt, or only felt recently

- o an emotion you experienced in another (for example a child's delight)
- o a blue feeling.

This list might be a poem in its own right.

You might like to expand or develop your list or poem. Or perhaps it reminds you of a significant memory of an occasion; write about it as fully as you can. Include as many details, and refer to as many senses as possible. This might be part of the poem, a separate poem, or a narrative.

4.7 Understanding others better

- Think of a person you know well, and would like to reflect more deeply about.
- Put their name at the top of a page.
- Write, with no pre-thought, a list of phrases expressing your impressions, thoughts and feelings about them, as long a list as you can (remember they need never see this).
- Now write another list:

    - o If your person were an animal, what animal would they be (what animal would they be, not what animal do they particularly like)?
    - o If your person were a colour, what would they be?
    - o If your person were a child's toy, what would they be?
    - o If they were a cleaning material, what would they be?
    - o Invent more categories yourself (e.g. a food or drink etc.).

- Now write a letter telling them you are thinking of them, and asking a question.
- Write their reply, responding to your question.
- Now write another list of word pictures, similar to the above; this time write as if you are the other person describing you. What animal might they think *you* are?

4.8 Finding your own wisdom

- Write a letter to the wisest, kindest, most helpful person you can imagine; make this person (or being) up, (it doesn't really work if you choose a real person, even if they are no longer alive). In your letter, ask their advice about a particular issue in your life, which might be a time when you were really in a confusion, unde-cided, unsure of yourself, feeling others did not understand you perhaps, alone, or possibly anxious or depressed. Or you might ask for general support or advice.
- Now write a letter to yourself from your Internal Mentor, suggesting how you can learn from this past experience.
- Or you could write this interchange as a dialogue, as if it were a playscript.

5

Writing to Identify Prejudice

Culture, assumptions and stereotypes

> Counselling and psychotherapy, wonderful inventions of the modern era, are mostly based on the idea that each of us is a unique individual and that individuals can change.
>
> (McLeod, 2009: 33)

We take a view that individual genetic inheritance, psychology and each individual's social world all play their part in making up 'ourselves'. Identity is fluid and can change, as can the social or cultural soup we live in.

This part of the chapter explores some of the ways in which we shape and are shaped by that cultural soup, and the inequalities which are also in the mix:

> The powerful mechanisms which make people sensitive to inequality cannot be understood in terms either of the social structure or of individual psychology alone. Individual psychology and societal inequality relate to each other like lock and key.
>
> (Wilkinson & Pickett, 2009: 33)

In creating Philip, Anita and Jo, we represent three possible points on the continuum of ways of working in writing about the self, and in counselling and psychotherapy.

Traditional concepts of the autobiographical self are critiqued by the narrative turn in psychology (Bruner, 2004). The self in relation to others is perceived as contested, negotiated and dependent on such constructs as gender, ethnicity and class.

> Perhaps a push toward narrative comes from contemporary preoccupations with identity in times of rapidly shifting populations, national, international, and neighbourhood borders ... Identities are no longer given and 'natural'. Individuals must now construct who they are and how they want to be known, just as groups, organisations, and nations do.
>
> (Riessman & Speedy, 2007: 429)

The taken-for-granted and 'grand' narratives of psychodynamic, cognitive behavioural and humanistic theories are disputed (McLeod, 2009: 223) by narrative approaches; local social, cultural and environmental knowledge is honoured (White & Epston, 1990); and the language available to us is seen to be socially and culturally constructed (Speedy, 2008).

Mainstream approaches have become more 'politicised' in recent years, however. Ethical frameworks require examination of justice and equalities. Prejudice has been the subject of enquiry in many ways in counselling and psychotherapy, including the need to consider discrimination on the grounds of class (Ballinger & Wright, 2007), race (Lago, 2006) or gender (Enns, 2004). Homophobia and other forms of oppression by majority or dominant groups tend to intersect with race and gender. Knowing how to develop anti-discriminatory practice it essential (Lago & Smith, 2010).

The personal and the political interconnect. Working across cultural boundaries may have been part of your CPD (Diamond & Gillis, 2006), and issues of professional power and social justice might also have arisen in personal and professional development groups, whatever the orientation of your practice (Levinson, 2010; Proctor, Cooper, Sanders & Malcolm, 2006). Reflective writing enables you to see and critically analyse your own attitudes and experiences at work.

Identity, the way we are, varies over time and depends on who we are with. The language we use to describe ourselves tells us a lot about how social relations operate, and the words available to describe who we are must be subject to how we were brought up. Whether you agree with these views, what is clear from the Greek and Roman writings we can still read and which connect us back to ancient times is that we can track changes in how we think, feel and behave by writing autobiographically.

> The self as something to write about, a theme or object (subject) of writing activity ... is one of the most ancient Western traditions.
>
> (Foucault, 1997: 233)

Seneca the Younger, a Roman stoic philosopher, wrote letters as a mentor to younger generations, advising regular introspective writing about thoughts and behaviour as a moral duty (Seneca, 1969). Self knowledge is the goal.

Try this: So who are you?

Try tuning in to some everyday expressions about 'self' such as:

- I haven't been myself since then.
- She was beside herself.
- How are you in yourself?
- He tends to withdraw inside himself.
- Get a grip on yourself.
- I'd like to get back to my old self.

Everyday sayings about 'self' tend to assume a 'core' of personality traits. Some theories of counselling and psychotherapy take the view that the self exists as stable and coherent, capable of reason and insight.

Counselling and psychotherapy have long been critiqued as individualistic and ethnocentric (Chantler, 2005; Moodley, 2007). Some indigenous cultures value a holistic approach to the talking therapies, however: where the physical, the spiritual, the psychological and the social work together. The same is true for non-indigenous people who have embraced a holistic position. Individuals differ in the extent to which they identify with their culture's values and norms. This chapter explores some of the complexities of individual identity and connections with the wider cultural world, including prejudice and discrimination.

Some indigenous world views about the self emphasise interdependence rather than independence. For example, it might be considered a sign of immaturity or even instability to be assertive about personal rights. Instead of independence, good mental health might involve closer connections with family and community. Inner feelings and thoughts might be less important and cultural identity more important, that is, family networks, language, access to the social, spiritual and economic resources connected with the extended family and tribal group.

This extract from a conversation between Jo and Anita illustrates some of these ideas. It began as an interview for an assignment Jo had to complete for her psychotherapy course.

CONVERSATION BETWEEN JO AND ANITA

From: Jo

hello Anita, and really good to hear your news.

Of course I remember when you used to come and stay! Back in the day you came and slummed it in the city with Lee

[*Anita's sister*] and the rest of us. I had no idea you were training in counselling and psychotherapy – it's a long time since we shared that house, and over the years Lee and I have lost touch. We were all doing different degrees and took different directions when we left university. I suppose it's bound to happen. Lee was doing science like you. How is Lee and the rest of your family? I'll look forward to catching up when you come and stay.

You won't believe this but I'm also on a therapeutic training course and doing my placement in a community agency. I love it, and just hope I can get some paid work at the end of it. There are so many questions I'd like to ask you about CBT and what it's like to work in a multidisciplinary team.

Looking forward to seeing you

Jo

From: Anita

Hi Jo

OK, that's great – I'm glad that date suits you.

Actually I did know you were doing therapeutic training because I saw a letter you wrote in the therapy journal. That's partly why I wanted to get in touch again – and how I got your e-mail address. Yes, it'll be great to catch up.

See you next week and thank you

Anita

ANITA AND JO SITTING IN JO'S FLAT

Jo: You know I've got this assignment to do – the interview thing – and you said I could interview you when you came to stay – could we spend an hour on it now? It would be great to get it out of the way.

Anita: Sure. Let me get that cup of coffee first.

Jo: Did you get a chance to read the consent form and everything?

[*Anita nods.*]

Jo: Hmmm – how do you turn this recorder on – is that it? Yes, OK to start now then?

Anita: Yes, I'm ready.

Jo: How did you get into training to be a therapist?

Anita: You'll laugh. I've always been a listener, you know, with a family like mine, how could I be anything else?

Jo: [*smiling*] I know how much one of your sisters can talk, that's for sure. But why CBT?

Anita: There was a special push to recruit people to study overseas. You know, psychotherapists are in short supply where I come from. So, there was a scholarship, and it was after I'd graduated, and I thought why not? In medical centres where I've been doing my placements here, CBT is really the only kind of therapy that anybody's heard of. It suits me too, logical, scientific, evidence-based. The only bit I don't really go for at the moment is the Personal and Professional Development group. It's just pretentious ramblings. I want to start making a contribution, not puffing myself up with words. It seems so selfish! OK, rant over, I just don't know how all these self-therapy exercises and journal writing will help me become a more effective therapist.

Jo: It sounds important and maybe we could talk more about it – is there anything else you don't like?

Anita: It's complicated. Spirituality is completely missing on our course, and it feels like a very big gap. Our belief at home is that spirituality can't be divided from mental and physical health. The support of the whole family is really important too – the extended family, the ancestors even, not just the immediate brothers and sisters and parents. So, when some of the others in the group start going on, sobbing all over the place about what's going on for them as an individual, I just don't know ... It all seems so empty to me. I put my thoughts in a bubble and watch it float up to the ceiling. I've been told I'm quiet in the group – they should see the thoughts in that bubble! I get so angry when I write in the journal I have to keep, my heart starts thumping, honestly it can't be good for me.

Jo: No wonder you have your doubts about it. ... so what's your favourite part of the course?

Anita: The placement I suppose. I really like working with the people at the surgery. And then we're all in this group supervision, all the trainees from different therapy courses who work at the surgery. I'm the only one doing CBT. The group facilitator is amazing – so calm and supportive – even when people have a go at her. Everyone's opinion is valued. I noticed a massive difference, for example, between the ways a cognitive behavioural therapist works and everyone else in the group. They are all on person-centred or more integrative training courses. They seem to emphasise their own feelings within a therapeutic situation. I realised in one session how harsh I sounded, not talking about feelings and the effects of the therapy on me. It's got me thinking about empathy. One of the people in the group is really against the medical model, a bit like you, she goes on about the language CBT people use, outcome measures, treatment, diagnosis and all that. [*She smiles at Jo*] – she's probably another sociologist like you ...

Jo: Watch it – invitations to dinner can be withdrawn you know!

Anita: So what else do you want to know?

Jo: There are loads more questions I'd like to ask you. We don't have to do it now though.

Anita: Have you heard of cultural flex (Ramirez, 1991)? We have this module called 'Counselling and diversity'. At first I didn't go because I thought if all they're going to talk about is working with people from different cultures, what's the point? I am from a different culture. The majority of people on my course are white. It's like asking fish to be aware of water. They don't even notice their own assumptions. But then, I heard that they were also covering sexuality, age, social class and religion, as well as race and ethnicity, so I started to go. We've had some great sessions with outside speakers from local agencies, especially those working with refugees and people in drug and alcohol work. Some of the speakers have been very critical of the way the CBT literature mostly operates in a political and social vacuum, but I think that's changing (Levinson, 2010).

Jo: We have a similar module called 'Anti-discrimination in Counselling Practice' (Lago & Smith, 2010). Sometimes the classes get really heated with people crying and shouting. It seems that when we talk about race and gender in particular, it is hard to communicate, hard not to bring up all kinds of wild feelings. Oops! I shouldn't be talking so much in this interview. I'm going to switch the recorder off.

[*Jo gets up and turns off the recorder.*]

Jo: But you see I feel so strongly about it – the individual is being blamed for what is a political and structural issue. We have to question how people are 'Othered' ...

Anita: What? What is 'Othered'?

Jo: It's about how we all see ourselves as the norm, but in obvious and sometimes very subtle ways some groups are always more powerful than others, more 'normal' than others – for example, women in the UK are much more likely to be diagnosed with depression than men. Does that make women more neurotic or is society mad? It's about who is at the 'centre' in terms of power and influence, and how we deal with differences in society.

Anita: But then for me ethnicity and race are so much more important.

Jo: Of course – there are marginalised groups in lots of different ways, marginalised by gender, class, religion, sexuality, disability – and as far as I can see, counselling and psychotherapy have mostly been used by middle-class, white people in the UK anyway.

Then there's all the labelling – I'm horrified when I hear people from other orientations talk about clients at the agency where I work, labelling them as personality disordered, anorexic or whatever. I don't want to identify the person as the problem, the problem is the problem. Look for change in terms of internal, psychological processes in the person and you are automatically implying that there is a deficit in that person. In your course, how do you think about this whole idea of self? I mean it's so complicated.

Anita: It's one of the things I really don't like about my training. It is so individualistic. I sometimes wonder if I should have done family therapy, but CBT is what everybody's heard of if I want to get a job either here or at home. Anyway, at least there's an evidence base and it is scientific.

Jo: That depends – what do you mean by evidence? Have you ever read any of the sociologists who are critical of the medical model?

Anita: No, why should I? Counselling and psychotherapy fits with medicine as a discipline – it's about healing the mind – so psychology, yes, but not sociology.

Jo: Oh my word. Let's eat – can't argue on an empty stomach!

INTERVIEW WITH PHILIP

One of Jo's course assignments is to interview two students or practitioners from counselling and psychotherapy programmes as different from each other as she can find. She has been able to meet Anita face to face and to record part of their conversation. She then interviews Philip online:

Jo: Thanks for agreeing to do this. Are you OK with the confidentiality agreement and consent form and so on?

Philip: I think so, yes, flying by the seat of my pants but that's alright. I'll have to go out around 10 this evening to go to work, so that gives us about an hour. Is that long enough?

Jo: Of course. What do you do at work?

Philip: I work as a security guard – nightshifts. It helps to pay for the course I'm doing.

Jo: Ah, sounds good, how did you get into that?

Philip: I used to be in the Army and it's easy to get into security if you've got connections. One of my mates contacted me. It's quite well paid. I don't like the nightshifts though.

Jo: Yes, I do some shifts at a call centre for the same sort of reasons – it helps to pay the rent and the course fees, doesn't it. Would it be OK to begin then? So how did you get into therapy training?

Philip: That's a long story – how long did you say we've got?

[*They both laugh.*]

Jo: Well, you know, just start and see what happens – is that OK?

Philip: If anybody who knew me back in the Army had any idea I'd gone to university to study counselling, they'd have never believed it. I dropped out of school for a start, and *counselling* – I was the worst for mocking it, even when my brother was going through a divorce and went to Relate with his wife, well she was his wife then, I was so ignorant. Anyway, once, on a tour of duty, something happened and I went to see the Chaplain ... [*pauses*] then when I left the Army and became a civilian again, and my mother died and a few other things went wrong and the whole thing fell apart. The GP put me on antidepressants, of course, and suggested I signed up to see a therapist who worked in the GP practice. ... and before that certainly ... [*pauses*]

Jo: Let me know if you want to stop any time, you know.

Philip: No, it's all right, I'll skip forward. I didn't want to go and see this woman of course, but my wife said if I didn't go, she would go – out of the door that is, and out of the marriage. So I went. The counsellor I saw had been in the police force. She understood – it was the first time I'd been able to tell anybody about some of the things I'd seen in the Army. Going every week kind of gave me something to get up for – so, to cut a long story short, after about a year when I was still on the sick, I started a part-time counselling course at the local college. You know, 10 weeks, introduction, no previous experience or qualifications required. It was fantastic. I learned more, read more, wrote more in those 10 weeks than I had ever done before ... Met some amazing people, all kinds of people ... [*pauses*]

Jo: So how ... and that was how you got into the degree?

Philip: Yes. One of the tutors suggested I should apply. He'd marked some of my essays and reckoned I could do it.

Jo: Why a person-centred course?

Philip: This same bloke, the tutor who suggested I went to university, taught part-time on the degree course as well, so it was easy to choose, in a way because it chose me. I knew him, this tutor, trusted him. And I liked him. Anyway I don't think I could have taken that risk, you know, done that level of training in any other kind of course at that time. I couldn't have stomached being bossed around. They walk the talk, the tutors on the person-centred course, they don't come across as the big experts, telling you what to do. The way that people change, I really agree with the person-centred ideas that it's got to come from the person themselves. I can see it in my diaries and journals, I can follow it through, even from when I was at school.

Jo: Wow – you've kept a journal for all that time?

Philip: Yes, the only good English teacher I ever had started it with us in junior school and I've kept it up. People used to take the p#@! – the Michael – but even in the Army, I used to find time. Some of it I've burned. One of the best bits of our course for me is the Reflective Journal group.

Jo: What do you like about it?

Philip: We're all so different, people from all sorts of backgrounds, and in that group we've got so close. There's only three of us men, and that was hard at first. But when we started reading out parts of our journal writing, I realised how wrong I'd been about some of the women who seemed so confident, so sorted.

Jo: Philip, I can see we're going to have to finish soon or you'll be late. Can I ask one more question?

Philip: Sure, I've quite enjoyed this interview actually. I wasn't sure what to expect, but it's been good to think back to how I got into this.

Jo: So, what is your least favourite part of your training course?

Philip: Hmmm, I'm not sure. It used to be filming ourselves in counselling practice. It made me so self-conscious, knowing that other students and at least one tutor would watch it afterwards and ask me questions. Now I am used to it. We do it every week. No, I think there's nothing I don't like – maybe some of the jargon ... but the tutors have a laugh with us about that. They treat us like adults – well, we are – but, you know, they don't come the big, arrogant, expert thing. They are genuine. It is how we're taught to work with clients too. We stay with the person, moment by moment, following, like in a dance.

In the Reflective Journal group, I'm not saying it's been all calm and controlled, but if there is some tension, it *is* brought up and talked about. That's the congruence part. People have got up and walked out, we've nearly all cried, screeched at each other, and had massive rows. It's been amazing. I would never have believed I could do it.

Jo: Yes! It's like that in our personal development group. People are so open about expressing their feelings. They hear their own voice ... anyway, sorry I'm getting carried away. Thank you again for doing this. If I can ever return the favour let me know.

Philip: No problem – as I say, I've enjoyed it. I've never written about that time when I first went to see the therapist at the GP practice in my journal, and this has made me think it's about time I did.

SOCIAL CLASS

Reflective journals can help develop sensitivity to working with others who are different from ourselves or what we consider to be 'the norm', for example by gender, age, race, religion, class, sexual orientation and disability. Self-writing can also develop awareness of our own cultural identity and inequalities in society (see Exercise 5.1 at the end of this chapter).

Philip: Where I grew up, on a council estate in the Midlands, we were all just looking to get a job, but there weren't any. I got out through the Army. Once that was no longer my life, and I started courses at the college, I could see how class still divides this country. Whether you say, mam, mum, mom or mummy doesn't just depend on whether you live north or south of Birmingham. Class is everywhere, the British disease. It's what you wear, eat, watch on TV, spend your money on, and that's before we even start to look at which school you go to and where the power lies in this country. This is where I get angry. It puts years on me watching the news and seeing how it's still so biased – how many people in the current government, never mind the Cabinet, went to private schools?

Anita: I suppose I only knew about working-class people in England through watching soap operas like *Coronation Street*. Coming here to work and to do the course, a lot of this class thing has made more sense to me. Different accents, for example, seem to place people. And of course it's different for me – before I even open my mouth, the first thing people see is brown, then that I'm a woman. I have a non-English accent, of course, but often British people can't place it. They see I'm not white and then they notice my accent. Certainly fitting into any of the categories labelled middle-class or working-class, it doesn't seem to matter really, does it? Colour first, and then my gender – and that is what seems most important to me now I'm living and working here.

Jo: I'd certainly put gender first I think, it was a feeling I had very early on at home that the boys were treated so differently. It sounds petty, but even now when we all get together, the boys are never expected to lift a finger. So you could say I was provoked, or, as my brothers would prefer it, called myself a feminist and just got mouthy. It wasn't until I got to university that I realised the class differences. The five of us shared a flat – one guy actually brought grouse and pheasant back when he went home for Christmas! He had a double-barrelled name but I would never have known he'd gone to public school, never mind Eton (he disguised his accent very well). I know sometimes I feel uncomfortable when I'm working with clients who have never had the chance. Born poor, and very likely to remain poor.

Philip: The students' cafe is OK, but every now and then, I go into town and into a pub that's very quiet at lunchtime. I find a table at the back, order a pint at the bar and a sandwich and sit down. For an hour I just read the newspaper. Fantastic. White sliced bread, cheddar cheese and raw onion were made to go together with best bitter.

Gender

Philip: I never like being in the minority and I never have been until I started at University. It's even worse on this counselling programme. Some of the women on the course want us to work in separate groups, but that would leave three of us men on our own. What's the point of that? It seems extreme to me.

Anita: Hmmm – you two are going to be having a punch-up in the car park if we're not careful ...

Jo: I don't think I'm as extreme as I used to be. A few years ago when I was reading radical feminists like Andrea Dworkin and arguing that all men are rapists, then I might have been called extreme. I used to go on marches – I was really involved. But now, I hear people talk about feminism as if it's all over and done with and I can't keep my mouth shut. Sometimes it'll be a little-known thing, nothing that hits the headlines here. For instance, a woman I know, who's still active, sends me e-mails, global reports, the results of big surveys from the World Health Organisation and that kind of thing. It's desperate stuff. Shocking statistics about the incidence of rape and murder, sexual violence, and gender differences in income across the world. Sexism and feminism – sounds so old-fashioned doesn't it. I see some of the group on the course frown when I mention the F-word, or when I point out some of these inequalities. I will stop talking about sexism and other dirty words like feminism when discrimination against women stops.

As the conversations between Philip, Jo and Anita reveal, different theoretical positions lead to different stories about identity and power in counselling and psychotherapy. Since the beginning of the feminist and civil rights movement in the USA, much attention has been given to considering the usefulness of available psychotherapeutic theories for counselling clients (see Exercise 5.2).

Race and ethnicity

Mainstream approaches in counselling and psychotherapy have sometimes been critiqued for being colour-blind and monocultural. The complexities of understanding cultural differences and a growing awareness of the inadequacies of some approaches to counselling and psychotherapy for black clients and people of colour, and for therapists from different ethnic and racial groups, have led to change. These changes are reflected in the emergence of a vast literature on cross-cultural and multicultural counselling in the last quarter of the 20th century (Pedersen, 1997; Ponterotto & Pedersen, 1993). In turn, multiculturalism has been critiqued, a healthy development indicating that theoretical approaches to counselling and psychotherapy are certainly not moribund (Moodley, 2007).

Philip: I wondered why some of the Asian guys I used to work with never went to the pub. They were from Pakistan, so couldn't drink alcohol of course. It got so heavy, that whole race and religion thing, as redundancies and closures went on. Now I realise it's all right for me to say that, because I'm white. I have the choice whether to pick up on racist comments, for example, or not.

Anita: It's funny you know – nobody ever knows quite what I am. Sometimes they think I'm from South America, or maybe the Philippines, somewhere exotic. I get tired of explaining. So far only one client has asked not to work with me. She asked for a white therapist.

Jo: In Birmingham there was a time when signs outside boarding houses used to say 'no Blacks, no Irish'. My dad told me.

Religion

Philip: We were asked to complete a questionnaire, a survey that some students in another course were doing. It was about counselling and spirituality. I can see how the core conditions, empathy unconditional positive regard and congruence, are in line with Christian beliefs. I just don't like churches. I don't have a religion. I believe in people.

Anita: In the Pacific, religion comes first. I'm not saying I agree with everything I was taught, but it is such an important part of who we are. The only part of our course which gets anything like spiritual is when we do mindfulness exercises.

Jo: There's a joke, well a kind of joke, where I come from that you take in religious prejudice with your mother's milk. It is part of the reason I moved away. I just didn't want to live with that conflict anymore, day in, day out.

Age

Philip: Some of them on the course, they could be my grandchildren. I used to think there should be a minimum age, that entry onto counselling courses should be limited to the over 30s. Some of them judge me – I judge them too. What is it with these trousers they wear that they can hardly sit down in? There you go you see – us and them/they. I'm the oldest on my course by quite a bit. Some of the younger ones, and I mean the ones who are under 30, they haven't got a clue what I'm talking about at times. One girl – sorry, woman – did voluntary work somewhere in South Africa straight after dropping out of university. She worked with people, mostly women and their children, who were dying of AIDS. She comes across as ditsy – her word – but I realise she's not. We've done some counselling sessions together now and she's very good. Maybe age isn't so important.

Anita: I know where I'd rather grow old, and it's not here in the UK. Quite apart from the cold and wet – you've got to keep moving in this climate, it's not for old bones – it's how I see old people being treated here that really upsets me. The respect I see given to the older women back home, in particular, is so different. They have a central role, a part to play in any family or community meeting. In fact, nothing can start without them – it's great. I suppose at the moment I feel pretty well in the middle, and age doesn't seem to play a very big part in therapeutic relationships. I certainly don't get any feedback on my age from clients at work, and nobody's asked for an older therapist so far.

Jo: Recently I've come across some life story work – the idea of recording old people's lives seems such a good thing to me. There's so much that is being lost in my parents' generation, their experiences during world wars, rationing and all that. In my family some want to tell their stories and some don't. What I have noticed is the stigma attached to going outside the family to talk about problems, and very little provision for older people in counselling and psychotherapy. It would be very valuable to offer counselling in their homes, for example.

I'm just moving into that age where I've become invisible as a woman. Mind you, I was always a tomboy: never really happy in a skirt, so I never caused a big stir out on the street. In fact, it's quite a relief really to be invisible – it's not such a huge shift.

WHAT DO WE MEAN BY 'SELF'?

Traditional theories of 'self' in counselling and psychotherapy draw from ancient philosophy as well as psychological theories. Freud in particular borrowed from Greek mythology with references to Oedipus, Eros and Narcissus, for example (Freud, [1933] 1973). Different theories use different images of the self as well as a different vocabulary to describe human development. Freud's writing about inherent personality traits, conflicts and the unconscious is clearly different from narrative theories where the self is essentially fluid, and ideas about the unconscious and fixed personality traits are not recognised. Therefore, images or pictures of the self only make sense if seen from a particular theoretical standpoint. The image of digging deeper into the self is useful in psychodynamic thinking, as is the idea of the self resembling an iceberg with only a small part of the 'knowable whole' lying on the surface. The comparison of the self with a faulty machine, which needs repairing, makes sense from a cognitive behavioural point of view.

The image of revealing the 'true' self as if through the peeling back of the layers of an onion is more appropriate to humanistic theories of the self: Carl Rogers' work describes a sense of personality traits that are essential and core, a whole self progressing through developmental hopes towards an actualised self.

Damasio (2000), from a neuroscientific point of view, comments:

When we talk about the self in order to refer to the unique dignity of the human being, when we talk about the self to refer to the places and people that shaped our lives and that we describe as belonging to us and as living in us, we are talking, of course, about the autobiographical self. The autobiographical self is the brain state for which the cultural history of humanity most counts. (pp. 229–230)

CONCLUSION

The focus in this chapter is on writing about your experience of culture: social class, gender, age, race, religion, ability and disability, sexual identity. By increasing your awareness of where you are in relation to these identity markers, you will deepen the possibility of spotting discrimination in practice and be able to work against it.

Write!

5.1 Which social class were you born into?

Social class is about more than relative wealth and poverty.

> Over time, crude differences in wealth gradually become overlaid by differences in clothing, aesthetic taste, education, sense of self and all the other markers of class identity.

> (Wilkinson & Pickett, 2009: 28)

Does social class make any sense to you in your culture?
    If you can recognise social class as part of your identity:

- Make a list of the ways in which your position in terms of social class is made visible by what you wear and what you eat.
- How have these indicators of social class changed during your life, if at all?

5.2 Gender

Complete the following sentences:

- What I like about working with male clients is ... .
- Lesbian clients are ... .
- What I like most about working with female clients is ... .
- I am most comfortable with female clients who ... .
- When I work with gay clients I ... .
- I would never work with male clients who ... .
- I find myself wanting female clients to ... .

5.3 Gender and the family

> In Western industrialised societies, the assumption of a mother, father and their children living as a unit persists, although this model of the nuclear family is often now not the 'norm' in developed or developing countries. Different kinds of family groups are beginning to appear more and more in the media, with soap operas featuring same-sex couples, extended families and all kinds of blended families and so on. Certainly patriarchy and gender roles within the

---

family have been challenged by feminism for over 50 years. Some of those arguments continue and, arguably, have made an impact in counselling and psychotherapy.

(Wright, 2009b)

Complete the following sentence stems; they work best if you write quickly without thinking too much:

- A man's job ... .
- A husband's role is ... .
- My mother and I ... .
- What gets me into trouble is ... .
- Women are lucky because ... .
- A good father ... .
- A girl has the right to ... .
- When they talked about sex, I ... .
- A wife should ... .

Now write your own sentence stems!

5.4 Narrative naive questioning

- If your belief is that a husband is in charge of his wife, how does that affect your relationship?
- If you believe that husband and wife are interdependent, how does this affect your relationship?

5.5 Stereotyping – How do you perceive yourself as being stereotyped?

To stereotype is to form a fixed mental impression. The word 'stereotype' comes from the pre-digital printing industry and was a method of producing cast-metal printing plates from a mould, usually made of paper or some other material.

Describe your experience of three stereotypes that you have had to deal with in your life. For example, you might want to look at stereotypes based on the colour of your skin, how you look, your hairstyle, the clothes you wear, your accent, the car you drive, your role in the family.

5.6 Demonstrating your awareness of prejudice and oppression

Demonstrating professional competence often requires a written statement. Some professional bodies require therapists to develop an awareness of the nature of prejudice and oppression and an awareness of issues of difference and equality.

Think about those times when you have become more aware of your own attitudes and prejudices. Write a letter as if from a very wise and generous mentor who is describing how you have worked to overcome those attitudes. The letter includes specific instances of your anti-discriminatory practice.

PART TWO

NAVIGATION

6

With Company or Travelling Alone?

Writing with others, whether in writing groups, online or to an imagined audience

Like a mindfulness meditation, a Quaker meeting full of silent waiting and wondering, a star-filled clear night sky, the writing gifted me transcendence from the ordinary. It let me hear what had been inaudible.

(Morag Cunningham)

Philip: On a Wednesday afternoon, we take turns, choosing sections from our journals, reading, listening and commenting. I don't mind reading out some of my reflective journal to others in the personal development group. In fact hearing the words out loud seems to add something. Sometimes the responses from other students are really valuable, such as when I miss the spiritual dimensions that some in the group always bring up.

I've started taking particular sections from my journals to supervision. It saves time. Reading out loud what I've written about counselling with a particular person, for example, often provides 'aha' moments. It's as if there's a starting point for our supervision session much further downstream, almost like listening to a recording, bringing the client and the work into the supervision room for reflection. When I read my notes out loud, the feelings that come up in that work with clients can surprise me – very strongly. I think I would miss some of them without this writing and reading in supervision, as well as some of the thinking that is much clearer once it's been written.

Anita: The trouble is when I started writing about how I see the world, my personal schema, it felt like I was betraying the family. We don't talk to anybody outside the family about those things. It's like when we were asked to introduce ourselves in the first few days of the course. I had to laugh.

What would the group have thought if I started with the greeting I would use at home? Naming my mountain, my river, and the way I am identified by them. I am my mountain because my mountain is my ancestor, with me wherever I go. This is when I know I'm very foreign, very different.

We've done some creative therapy classes and everything I make and do looks very different too – the other students comment on it. In one session we used modelling clay and then made masks. It's enjoyable but I can't imagine doing creative therapies in the GP surgery where I work. When we wrote about the clay models and the masks, I found I was writing a letter to the auntie I'm named after. So, is this reflective journal writing? Can that be right?

Jo: At first I was cautious, a bit inhibited in how I wrote on the social network. After all I don't know these people. But now the connection I feel with some of the group on the network, some living on the other side of the world, is stronger than most of my friendships here. I've never met Tom face to face, for example, but feel very close to him. It is amazing. I feel like they're not judging me. I have friends and family I can talk to – I'm close to my sister, especially, but I feel freer online, I don't feel I'm burdening people and won't bump into them at parties, or in the supermarket. I know I'll never meet some of them. They are living continents away but they know more about me than some of my family here.

Sign of the times maybe, but it's almost as if something hasn't happened until I see it on the social network. I tend to check it first thing in the morning and then just before I go to sleep at night. I feel isolated if I don't log on regularly during the day.

This chapter is about connecting with others by sharing your writing. As you might already know, your reflective journal writing can enable you to be alone when surrounded by people, and conversely, when you decide to communicate, your solitary writing will enable others to read your thoughts and feelings and see how they resonate with their own. The importance of choosing very carefully how you share your writing has already been emphasised.

Moving now from journeying alone in writing, we focus in this chapter on three different kinds of company you might choose to travel with:

- *The All That Is or the spiritual:* We look at what the African-American novelist Alice Walker calls The All That Is or The Great Mystery and using some ways of writing to connect with the spiritual.
- *Digital communication:* Using the Internet to connect with others in writing is now a way of life for bloggers and people using social networks. Consider the paradox of sitting alone in front of a screen while connecting with the world.
- *Writing groups:* To share self-writing with a trusted, confidential group in counselling and psychotherapy training groups, group supervision or in creative and therapeutic writing workshops.

Chapter 5 focused on how reflective writing enriches the supervisory relationship. Writing before, during and after supervision is another creative way of sharing your writing and choosing your company on the journey of reflecting in writing in counselling and psychotherapy.

WRITING TO THE GREAT MYSTERY

For some indigenous cultures, spirituality cannot be divided from mental and physical health. All things including the landscape, the sky and the sea have spirit. The spiritual body and physical body are joined. Writing in a secular, individualistic way, which is dominant in the Western psychological sciences, might be quite alien.

> I worked at the University of the South Pacific in Fiji for a couple of years, practising and teaching counselling. For those years I had been living and working with people whose languages and cultures were as different from mine as could possibly be imagined. English, the colonial language, was our common language. Sometimes, students and colleagues would be speaking to me in their third language, English, which was also the medium of education in some of the islands. (Jeannie Wright)

Activity: Mother tongue

A major advantage of writing as opposed to speaking is using your first language, in spite of not speaking the same first language or mother tongue as your therapist or client. There is considerable evidence that being able to externalise thoughts and feelings is beneficial, whether orally or in writing.

- How many languages do you speak?
- Which is your mother tongue?
- Which language are you using for your reflective journal writing?

DIFFERENT WORLDVIEWS

The Maori are one of many indigenous cultures in the world where family and community and interdependence are more highly valued than independence, that is, the collective not the individual is the central frame of reference. Patricia Grace, an award-winning Maori novelist, writes about a soldier, Tu, who finds he can write about unspeakable wartime experiences that he has survived physically but not wholly intact psychologically, nor spiritually. He has kept diaries from the point of leaving home to sail and fight on the other side of the world and which started out as:

> Simple recordings of times and places, jottings to do with my journeys and experiences of the war, which for me took place in southern Italy. Brief scribblings and a few musings is what I started out with, as you'll see. But the notebooks came to mean much more to me than just somewhere where I could doodle the date and place names. … So, though I've thrown out almost everything else extraneous to my occupation of space on this planet, the notebooks are still with me.
>
> (Grace, 2004: 12–13)

Although part of a large, extended family, Tu is isolated with his wartime experiences where many of his close family and friends died.

> It's been said that I wrote while in dugouts and trenches with bullets flying overhead, in sewers and drains, hidden vineyards while the vegetation was being strafed six inches above our heads, guts up in mud, in night trenches in the snow. It's all a load of rubbish. I wrote mainly during rest times, during waiting times. … I wrote in hospitals and on board ships. I wrote when I felt like being alone. (p. 276)

Paradoxically, writing can be used as a way of withdrawing from the world, being alone, as well as connecting with it. Tu waits until after his death to share his notebooks and diaries with his family, by leaving them to the next generation, a nephew and niece.

Your worldview

Most of the major theories or 'forces' in psychology of the 19th and 20th century were developed by white men, either European or American. The focus tends to be secular rather than spiritual. The aim of most therapeutic work, influenced by Western theories in psychology, is on changing the individual, and on affirming the independence of the individual. Independence in Maori society, for example, could be viewed as a weakness and a source of illness (Durie, 2010). Culturally appropriate goals for many Asian clients might also need to put individual needs secondary to the needs of the family and the community. The African saying *Ubuntu*, 'I am because we are', similarly places a focus on collectivism.

Multicultural counselling theory takes the view that counselling theories are not universally applicable. Here is an example from working in the South Pacific:

> A middle-aged student from the Solomon Islands consulted the counselling service for help with stress at exam time. He believed he was bewitched, and was waiting for the end of the semester when he would be able to travel back to his home to consult traditional healers there. Meanwhile he had been diagnosed with depression by doctors at the student medical centre and prescribed antidepressants. Respecting his views about traditional healing and, at the same time, offering some help with anxiety and time management was the focus of the work. (Jeannie Wright)

Depending on your own position and sense of cultural identity, some of the writing suggestions in this book might make more sense than others. Many theorists and practitioners now acknowledge important differences between indigenous and Western conceptions of health and well-being, searching for ways to integrate and honour indigenous 'non-scientific' ways of healing (Moodley & West, 2005).

If you have started keeping a journal, you might be able to see where your worldview tends towards the secular or the spiritual on some kind of continuum, the individual or the collective, the value of independence or the inter-dependence. We suggest that identity is fluid and ever-changing.

INDIVIDUALISM AND COLLECTIVISM

Changing inner thoughts and feelings as the goal of counselling and psychotherapy has been contested by some 20th- and 21st-century theorists. David Epston and Michael White, for example, influenced by family therapy practices, originated what has come to be called 'narrative therapy' (White & Epston, 1990). In addition, individual change may appear to be beneficial for a person, but might deny the collective experience of some cultures and therefore create tensions and contradictions for that person.

One student from the Pacific Islands described going home to her village after years of living in urban Australia. She had become used to living in her own house, with her own room, and had developed a way of writing about her experience by blogging. Going back to her village meant giving up the idea of privacy. There was no time at all when she was alone. She tried writing a journal late at night or very early in the morning, but found that she was interrupted and had to explain what she was doing and why.

Similarly, important features about indigenous cultural identity and values, described in terms of the relationship with the land and the natural world, the spiritual, the ancestors and the meaning of time, are sometimes alien and hard to hear by Western ears. bell hooks, an African-American activist and writer, says 'Like all the books I have written, it comes to me from places dark and deep within me, secret, mysterious places, where the ancestors dwell, along with countless spirits and angels' (hooks, 1993: 7).

A Chinese first-generation immigrant, a client in career counselling, explains how she would involve her whole extended family in decision making, rather than she as an individual working in isolation to decide about her future career. She is conflicted about the changes in her life and the differences she notices in this new country she now lives in. In our counselling meetings she becomes extremely upset, and that too adds to her distress, because part of her cultural values is that strong feelings and emotions should be avoided and certainly not expressed with a stranger. Writing in her first language before and after our counselling sessions is acceptable to her and, she says, very helpful.

The Chinese novelist Xinran uses the image of an over-full heart to express the power of writing: 'Writing is a kind of repository and can help create a space for the accommodation of new thoughts and feelings. If you don't write these stories down, your heart will be filled up and broken by them' (2003: 229).

Activity: Unfilling your heart

- Think of a time when your heart felt 'filled up'.
- Write a letter to yourself about that time without holding back.
- Notice the images you use to express feelings.
- What are you going to do with this letter?
- Write a reply.

THERAPEUTIC THEORIES AND SPIRITUALITY

The major 'forces' in Western psychology would use different kinds of language to pose and answer questions about spirituality or the transpersonal dimension in counselling and psychotherapy (Rowan, 2005). Humanistic approaches would refer to the 'actualising tendency' as the fundamental drive of the transpersonal and the creative (Fairhurst, 1999); Jungians might refer to the collective unconscious and transcendent function of the psyche; spirituality might not be associated with cognitive behavioural practice, however, cognitive behavioural theorists have recently embraced the Buddhist-based practices of mindfulness. Christine Padesky, a colleague of Beck's and, foremost, contemporary cognitive therapist suggests that:

> Cognitive therapy is compatible with religious beliefs as long as the therapist is sensitive to and helps the client explore fears that therapy will be inconsistent with religious faith.

(Padesky & Greenberger, 1995: 50)

Morag Cunningham, a therapist and teacher, writes about her own experience of how writing allowed time to grieve:

> The research paper with its use of 'self' as 'data' legitimised the hours on my computer. Allowing myself the luxury of time to write in fact allowed me the time to grieve, the time to make peace with myself and accept my own imperfect ways of dealing with my loss. It also allowed me to connect with a community of people who were grieving like me …

> I have long known that writing is therapeutic, that it has the potential to bring about change, to relieve, to console, to clarify, to embolden.

I have long known the theory, taught it, preached it. In my last life, I encouraged hundreds of adolescents to explore themselves on paper, to delight in the written word, to create their own truths, to interpret the truths of others. In this new life I encourage my clients to write the letters they do not need to send, to run with the metaphors, to journal the dreams.

I was however profoundly surprised by the intensity of this, my own reflective writing experience. It has been spiritual in many senses. Like a mindfulness meditation, a Quaker meeting full of silent waiting and wondering, a star-filled clear night sky, the writing gifted me transcendence from the ordinary. It let me hear what had been inaudible.

DIGITAL COMMUNICATION AND THERAPY

Living on the far side of the world from family and friends, several times in my working life, has meant embracing technology. I still write letters, and I love that lightweight air-mail paper, like blue onion skin. I send postcards and use the telephone, but communication for me has been revolutionised by the Internet. Some of my friends log on to Facebook the minute they wake up. Maybe I am the wrong demographic to love social media, but I have always been able to see the therapeutic potential of the Internet since being introduced to it in a so-called developing country, Fiji. (Jeannie Wright)

The use of the Internet and digital communication is developing so fast that terminology becomes out of date very quickly, and no doubt some of the language in this section will sound dated even before this book is published.

Social networks, e-mail and blogging

Finding someone or some people to share your self-writing with needs care. As in finding a therapist, especially if you are training in counselling and psychotherapy, these people need to be trustworthy as well as accepting, curious and sensitive. 'Blogging is like keeping a diary under your bed, only the whole world knows it's there' (Tan, 2008: 6).

Perhaps if Patricia Grace's character, Tu, had been living in the digital age rather than during the early 20th century, he might have started blogging on his return from the war. At the time of writing them, his diaries become a kind of sanctuary, similar to some of the experiences of social networkers.

The value of sharing some of your experience in writing has been celebrated in many ways, some of them connected with collective ways of fighting and recovering from social oppression. In the 1960s and 1970s, starting in the USA, women began to form 'self-help' groups, using writing and other therapeutic activities (Ernst & Goodison, 1981; hooks, 1993).

In the 21st century, social networking and the power of blogging have come to the fore as different forms of self-help.

> I was initially very apprehensive about a global audience, and I purposefully had only readers I didn't know in actual life as I found I would self censor what should have been a streaming flow of consciousness.
>
> ('Jenny' in Tan, 2008: 15)

Using one of the social network sites or blogging as an easy way to keep in touch with friends and family is now commonplace in some parts of the world. AOL reported in a 2005 survey that almost 50 per cent of bloggers saw their online writing as a form of self-therapy. Blogging has been called 'social writing' and described as 'an online journal or diary organised typically in reverse chronological order', while social networks are a kind of 'digital commons' (Tan, 2008).

Sharing writing through the Internet has become one form of online therapy. I (Jeannie Wright) was first asked to work with a client using e-mail when I was counselling in Fiji at the University of the South Pacific in the 1990s. A member of staff, a woman whose marriage and family relationships were causing her great distress, e-mailed me to ask if we could work online. She feared for her life if she was seen entering the counselling centre by her husband or any of his family. It is clear that the sense of anonymity and, some would say, illusion of confidentiality created by internet communication is one reason why some people choose to work therapeutically in this way.

From: Jo
To: Jason

The manager and my supervisor at the agency have asked me to e-mail you about your induction as an online coun-selling volunteer. I've been volunteering here for a few years now and they've asked me to meet you next week before you start working with clients. I have been a mentor before, and can also remember how nervous I was when I started working online! If there are any specific questions you have already, you might want to make a list so that we can cover the main things you want to know in our meeting. Don't worry though, I'm not going anywhere, so we can keep e-mailing, phoning or whatever works best once you have started with clients.

See you on Tuesday, Jo

> **Activity: Online and e-therapy**
>
> - Take 5 minutes to imagine you are Jason.
> - What questions would you have to put to Jo?

E-therapy

After leaving Fiji, I went on to develop online counselling as staff counsellor at Sheffield University, working with staff of all ages, from all departments, porters and professors. Sharing writing using e-mail made absolute sense to me, and, clearly, to some of the staff who used the online service. It was my view that online counselling, using e-mail, can be like a continuation of or another medium for writing therapy, and using e-mail to work therapeutically still feels that way to me.

(Wright, 2002)

We were very careful with encryption in the early days of online counselling in Sheffield (it is possible to encrypt e-mail messages using software available now on most word-processing packages which scrambles the words and can only be deciphered using a password). We also developed an early code of ethics and practice at Sheffield, but I realised early on that I missed physical presence, the richness of hearing someone's voice tones change, noticing their non-verbal signals and most fleeting facial expressions, a perfume. Ironically, given the very disembodied experience of online therapy and supervision, I have continued to be part of the technological way of working, both offering and receiving supervision online, for example, but using voice-over-internet phone as well as e-mail now. (Jeannie Wright)

As more sophisticated ethical codes for online counselling have developed (Anthony & Goss, 2009), some of the risks of internet communication have been acknowledged and addressed. If you are part of the phenomenal growth in social networking, you will certainly have considered the potential dangers of photographs of you appearing on insecure sites. There you are, unaware of the photographs being taken, at a party maybe years ago, in a state that you would not want your current employer to witness. Celebrity slip-ups in online communications seem to feature regularly in the media.

Sherry Turkle has researched identity in the age of the Internet, arguing that the explosion in digital communication has gone too far. She gives examples of parents pushing a child on a swing with one hand and texting with the other hand, and of family meals where parents and children are all online while sitting round the table. She suggests that we now have to redress the balance and decide how we want to use and/ or be distracted by technology. If you don't want your words read, or your photos seen, don't write them up or post them up on the Internet: that feeling of being anonymous is an illusion. If you are a totally committed social networker, or very cautious about using the Internet for personal communication, use your own judgement to weigh up what even the social media experts are now calling a mixed blessing (Turkle, 2011).

On the other hand, illness blogs in particular have flourished, as writing on the Internet provides a way to come to terms with traumatic events. Blogging is more than just writing. It also enables social connection, and a greater sense of control, both of which are vital for well-being. If you want to look at different kinds of illness blogs, try www.wordpress.com. You will find 18-year-olds blogging about life with liver cancer (http://theknockoneffect.wordpress.com) and older people who have just had surgery and who want to let friends and family know how they are without having to telephone. This is a wonderfully creative use of personal writing and digital communication, the benefits of which cannot be overstated for those who are isolated by illness.

Totally outside of the formal and relatively controlled world of counselling, psychotherapy and supervision, forms of technological self-help have been developed. 'Jenny' is a regular social networker and blogger; for a number of reasons, such as having young children on her own, she finds digital connections convenient in reducing her social isolation:

> I think that if you felt isolated in some way, perhaps you are in difficulty with a personal relationship, or are experiencing discomfort in your job, knowing that there are others in your same situation can help alleviate the concept it's only you that is coping ... I have found that people tend to think in isolation, so to 'discover' you are not alone can make you feel better.

('Jenny' in Tan, 2008: 11)

Activity: Isolation

Think of a time when you have felt isolated. Write a dialogue between yourself and a totally accepting, nurturing presence starting with:

- How are you?
- How have you been?
- Start the writing with 'Dear ...' and your name.
- Then write the reply.

SHARING WRITING IN GROUPS

Groups have huge potential energy for the good of the individuals and group as a whole. People learn from their tutors and facilitators; they learn far more from each other. What is learned can be surprising: everyone brings expectations, hopes and fears which, combining with unspoken elements, create hidden curricula.

What a facilitator thinks the group is doing may be dynamically different from what participants take away with them.

There are two functions for journal writing work within a group. One is to write during the session, the other to share writing which might have been done in session or previously. Undertaking writing exercises within a group session is conducive for many (though a few find it constraining). Facilitators can suggest insightful and fruitful exercises to do in session; this can help the pen to flow if you have to write to a set time with others doing the same around you. It's all too easy to waste time instead of getting down to it in one's own time and space, though a positive suggestion is to set an alarm clock, say for 20 minutes: you must stop writing by the time it pings and so have to get going once you've set the clock.

Skilfully facilitated confidential group work can offer a sufficiently safe environment to explore personal writing and to develop its potential. Peer readers can help writers understand their own images and perceived connections, so they can see what their writing is telling them; they can also offer positive critique and suggestions.

Personal writing ideally goes through a set of dynamic stages, for which group or paired work offers the ideal process. Pieces are written within the group, or brought; then they are read silently to the self and altered, expanded or adapted before being read to the others and discussed, keeping within boundaries previously decided by the group. Group members might suggest alterations or offer new pieces to be written. New or redrafted pieces can then be brought back to the group on another occasion, and the cycle starts again. Reading to oneself silently and thoroughly before reading to others is a vital stage – writers often don't really know what they have written until they read it.

> Writing doesn't always help. It may just reinforce obsessive thoughts and fix them. Writing in the group helps me with this because I learn ideas and more imaginative ways of writing. (Participant)

Every one of those thoughts and ideas needs and deserves an audience who are willing to listen attentively, ready with positive responses. We need to feel confident that our story is of importance to others. This means the group being willing to listen carefully and empathetically to the twists and turns of each member's writing, so they can intuit how to respond appropriately. This whole process can be positive and enriching of both the person and the writing.

Gillie Bolton ran a writing workshop for the counselling service at Sheffield University where I (Jeannie Wright) was working (see Bolton, 2010, 2011). There must have been about 20 of us, including some of the part-time counselling staff I had never met before. It was in the first year of coming back to Britain from working in Fiji. Getting my kids back into school, me back into work and finding a place to live had been hard. I hated the cold, dreaded the traffic and had not had/made time to pause and reflect on this transition. This writing workshop, quite unexpectedly, opened the door to a space where I could start that emotional process on paper.

The workshop must have been in the early evening, straight after work, and lasted maybe three hours. It was held in the staff club in an upstairs room overlooking a very busy dual carriageway. Gillie introduced us to the way she uses writing in small groups, and then gave us all some shells picked up from the beach. I first remember holding the shell close to my face, feeling its cool smoothness and smelling, maybe in my imagination, that salt–sea rush. I held the shell to my ear and wrote:

> Hold the curved, cold cone shell to my ear
> It's irresistible
> I can hear the Pacific
> No, it's the rush hour roar on the Western Road
> Glimpse the shell-white waves exploding on the reef
> No, it's bits of crisps on the carpet
> Is that the salt, the coconut oil, frangipani?
> No, it's yesterday's oven chips and stale beer.
> When fine, white sand falls onto my paper
> I'm lost,
> Stop the sob.
> Can't cry here.
> Outside a wailing siren.

(Jeannie Wright, 1999/2000)

We did read out some parts of our writing in groups of three or four. What stands out to me from that first experience of a writing group was the silence. All the others in the room disappearing as I wrote, and yet knowing they with there, in a companionable kind of way. Silences too between people reading. We didn't do much talking; some discussion at the end of the evening. I remember slowly finding words to try to express what had just happened. After the workshop I wrote to Gillie about that writing experience:

> After six months, I had thought I'd reached a different sort of acceptance of place and felt shocked when I wrote this by the depth of the grieving and the imme-diacy of the list of 'I miss'.

If you have experienced those 'aha' moments, personal revelations in small 'self-exploration' groups, you will understand the power of writing groups. Confidentiality is key in creating the safety offered in such groups. Combining that facilitated group experience with expressive and reflective writing can extend the opportunity for self-knowledge. Here are some other reasons:

The experience of a (journal) workshop is like entering a sanctuary ... a pro-tected situation, safe from the outer pressures of the world in which an individual can quietly reappraise their relation to their lives. The procedures that are followed through the workshop give them a methodology to use ... the presence of others in the workshop, each exploring the individuality of their own life history, builds an atmosphere that supports and strengthens. (www.intensivejournal.org)

CONCLUSION

You may decide that some of your writing will never be shared with anyone. It is essential that you choose which parts of your writing you want to show to other people. In this chapter we have suggested some ways of connecting with other people in writing.

Writing to a higher power, whatever that might mean to you, is one way.

Using the Internet to connect with others, both in writing and using other media, is another.

Writing groups, which might be part of the group work you do in your particular therapeutic practice, provide another possible connection.

Write!

6.1 Spirituality

Draw or write in response to these questions:

- What is your relationship with spirituality?
- How much is spirituality a part of the landscape of your life?
- What types of spiritual experience have you experienced in your life? Have any of these experiences taken place during counselling or similar work?
- In what ways do you draw on spiritual practices (e.g. meditation, prayer, yoga, use of sacred objects) in preparing yourself for, or coping with the demands of, counselling work? (McLeod, 2010: 43)

6.2 Writing to the Great Mystery

Some people choose to write letters to God. A famous contemporary example is in Alice Walker's novel, *The Color Purple*, where Celie follows the instruction 'You better not tell nobody but God. It'd kill your mammy' (1982: 3). Alice Walker refers to God as The Great Mystery or The All That Is.

- Find a place where you feel as close as possible to The Great Mystery. It might be a beach, leaning against sand dunes listening to the waves, or in a park with children on the swings, or it might be in a place of worship.
- Music might be important to help you connect with the spiritual. Put it on now.

(Continued)

(Continued)

- Write a letter to The Great Mystery or The All That Is, whatever that might mean to you.
- Decide on a time limit before you start – maybe 20 minutes, maybe less.

6.3 Unsent letters

Writing letters that are not intended to be sent is one strategy to externalise a problem. Writing letters to God could be seen as a form of unsent letter writing. Looking at things from a different point of view through letter writing is a central part of some therapeutic practices, especially narrative therapy (Crocket, 2010; Payne, 2000).

- Write a letter to someone you are currently feeling uneasy with.
- Start the letter with 'Dear' and their name.
- Allow yourself to say whatever you want to say, because this letter is not going to be sent and you can decide to destroy the writing if you wish.
- Then write the reply.

6.4 Writing to withdraw

- Reflect on a time when you've used writing or drawing to withdraw from the world.
- Where were you?
- What was the situation you were withdrawing from?

6.5 Masks: collage and writing exercise

- Find a large paper bag, big enough to represent your face and your head.
- Using photographs, collage or drawing, attach to the outside of the bag things that represent or create the mask that you habitually use in social situations. These are aspects of yourself that are easy to reveal and share with others.

How much of ourselves do we hide? From the rest of the world? From ourselves even? The silent unspoken.

(Figiel, 1999: 14)

- What does the mask you have made hide?
  - From the rest of the world?
  - From yourself?

On the inside of the bag are aspects of yourself that are not easy to reveal or share with others.

- Using photographs, collage or drawing, attach to the inside of the bag things that represent aspects of yourself that are private.
- Make some notes about your reflections on creating this inside and outside piece and what it conceals and reveals.

(a)

(b)

FIGURE 6.1 Masks

© Liam Wright-Higgins. Reproduced with kind permission.

(Continued)

(Continued)

6.6 Genograms

Genograms are part of the family therapy tradition and have been used as a visual way of understanding family patterns (Ivey & Ivey, 2002). You will need some large blank pieces of paper and some pens or pencils, or a digital platform, whichever you prefer; some photos or pictures of your family and friends will also be useful.

Create the genogram

- Look at the paper or screen as a visual representation of your culture and your community within that culture.
- Place yourself within the community, maybe in the centre or wherever seems appropriate. Draw a symbol or use a picture to represent yourself.
- Add your family members and friends. Use appropriate symbols or pictures and place those closest to you, for example, as close as you can to you at the centre.
- Choose the most important and influential groups you belong to, for example spiritual groups, sports groups, clubs, work groups.
- Draw connections between the focus (you) and the friends and family members and community groups so that the importance of these connections is apparent. For example, use double lines or heavier lines to indicate the most influential groups.

Search for narratives of strength

- Think about a person or group as you look at your genogram. Who has had a strong positive influence on you? Close your eyes if it helps, and focus on an image in your mind that represents an important positive experience with this person or group. Write it down.

Search for narratives of difficulties

- Choose an individual or group within your genogram who has had a strong negative influence on you. Visualise an image that represents an important negative experience with this person or group. Write about how you overcame this negative experience.
- What does this genogram tell you about your cultural identity?
- Creating a genogram and thinking about narratives of difficulty and of strength can be a powerful exercise. If you're feeling vulnerable, lonely, unsure about your own judgement or simply prefer to work in relationship with others, finding some people or a person you can trust with this exercise is the next step. Perhaps you might decide to talk to a counsellor or supervisor.

6.7 Writing online

- Some readers will be experienced in online counselling and supervision. If that is the case, write a list of what you most miss about working face to face.
- What impact might this have on your decisions about ways to share your writing?
- If you are not a digital native, and if you have never worked online in therapy or supervision, write a list of your dislikes or fears about e-therapy and online supervision.
- How would you feel about sharing your personal writing online?

7

Writing the Past

Autobiographical memories

Looking back to speak forward.

(Proverb)

Philip: We did an exercise in a personal development session where we were asked to draw ourselves at the age of eight and write about what we'd drawn. I hate anything to do with art. Always bottom of the class in art. I took some chunky crayons and a big piece of paper and just started scribbling. I used brown and green and the house we used to live in was on the page. The others in the group were quiet, nobody was looking around, all heads down writing and drawing. I felt nervous in case we were asked to show the drawings to the group, but that was not part of the instructions we'd been given, so I carried on. When I did talk to the person next to me about the drawing, I realised that I had drawn myself as a child in isolation – there was no one else pictured.

I had a dream recently which stayed with me for a long time. It's been recommended that we keep a record of our dreams and I've started doing that. Sometimes all I can remember is the feeling. This dream was full of fear. I recognised the office of the agency where I'm working but I didn't recognise any of the people who were there. One of our group on the course has had a complaint made against her. She's been suspended from the course and her placement is under investigation. It's made us all very jittery.

Anita: OK, everyone's got to look back to when they were eight years old. I chose a piece of black paper and drew the mountain in the winter with the snow shining in the sun. Using chalk was messy but I soon felt like I could enjoy this. My sister and me were outside the house, playing with balls and then on the trampoline. I was still drawing when we had to stop and choose someone to talk to about what had come up for us.

When I woke up this morning I was drenched with sweat. I'd been dreaming that I was having a baby but I couldn't do it, couldn't give birth. I was lying on a high narrow hospital bed, the kind I've seen in maternity units, and there were people all around me. Some of the people I recognised. Two were some of my old teachers who were always very critical. I sat up on this high couch and looked at them and that's when I woke up.

Jo: We were asked to draw ourselves at the age of eight. I drew school. It was a safer place, especially the library. Because I was a library monitor I used to go to see Mrs Hall at lunchtimes and stack the books into piles according to the category they belonged in. I drew her in those straight trousers and cardigans she used to wear. Sometimes I used to want to lie down and sleep there – it was quite warm and quiet in the library.

It's not always possible to remember my dreams but I'm starting to write them down as soon as I wake up. They turn into drawings too. I keep paper by the bed. Getting up and logging on isn't the same. Then I read out what I've written, as if it's happening now, in the present. So, for example, I'm up high, overlooking a river and then I'm jumping from boulder to boulder but the gaps are getting wider and I'm frightened of falling. I'm still feeling frightened when I wake up and for the first part of the day that feeling stays with me.

The aim of this chapter is to explore the past in writing. With an emphasis on psychodynamic and radically different narrative theories and practices, this chapter invites you to look back and find out what you can learn about the present and the future from the past.

Working at your own pace through this chapter, seeking support when you need it, will bring you most benefit. Creative therapies tend to surprise us; it's impossible to know what will emerge. So unless you have already been able to work extensively in counselling and psychotherapy or in some other way on childhood memories and experiences, it's worth making sure you have the support you need in place before working through the suggested activities and writing exercises in this chapter.

From the psychodynamic treasure trove of theories, we begin with Freud's theories of the unconscious (Freud, [1915] 1991) as a repository for aspects of mental life beyond direct awareness. Writing exercises also include exploring attachment styles, and working within the therapeutic frame. We also consider how to write about dreams, which Freud famously described as 'the royal road to the unconscious'.

From narrative therapy, influenced by social constructionism, comes the idea that there is no inner 'self' that is knowable (Burr, 2003). The stories we tell about who we are and about our experiences connect us to the wider cultural soup we live in. Stories are the way in which people make sense of their experience; narrative ways of working with clients, such as re-authoring stories and externalising, are not just techniques but suggest a different way of understanding what counselling and psychotherapy are and could be.

THEORETICAL FOUNDATIONS

Psychodynamic counselling and psychotherapy

Freud's theories, originating in Vienna in the late 19th century, have been called the beginnings of Western psychology, and a central influence on Western society. Concepts such as the ego and id, free association, defence mechanisms, Freudian slips, and the significance of dreams have informed popular culture and the arts from grand opera to soap opera. Freud's work is clearly an important influence in counselling and psychotherapy as well as in many other academic and applied disciplines (Jacobs, 2006). In particular, psychoanalytic theories have had the most to say about sexuality (Butler, O'Donovan & Shaw, 2010: 177).

Understandably over time, some of Freud's ideas became out of step with current thinking, for example theories about women and sexuality have been critiqued since the beginning of second wave feminism (Mitchell, 1974). Contrary to some of the stereotypes of psychoanalytic psychotherapy and traditional psychodynamic therapies, some practitioners and well-known psychodynamic authors represent a radical political stance. Feminist Susie Orbach's work on the social pressures on women in Western societies to be thin and for their bodies to fit a certain ideal is well known (Orbach, 2009).

The psychodynamic approach to counselling and psychotherapy includes many different schools of thought. The activities and writing exercises in this chapter are based on three key assumptions: that we are usually not conscious of the true nature of our emotional problems, which have their origins in childhood experiences; that present distress is caused by repressed conflicts in the past; and that unconscious material emerges indirectly in creative activities such as writing, in dreams and fantasy, as well as in the therapeutic relationship (Clarke, 2000: 177).

The idea of creative and autobiographical writing as a 'holding space' is another important psychodynamic concept (Winnicott, 1971). We suggest that journal writing can provide a safe place to 'let go' freely, using the boundaries of the page/screen and sometimes a set time allowed for any particular writing exercise.

The significance of early experience is essential to psychodynamic thinking. Jung, in his later years, began writing an autobiography, looking back to his childhood:

> It has become a necessity for me to write down my early memories. If I neglect to do so for a single day, unpleasant physical symptoms immediately follow. As soon as I set to work they vanish and my head feels perfectly clear.' (1963: vi–vii)

The novelist Virginia Woolf, writing in the early 20th century, talks about how writing fiction allowed her to let go of an obsession with her mother who died when she was 13 years old:

> It is perfectly true that she obsessed me, ... then one day walking round Tavistock Square I made up, as I sometimes make up my books, *To the Lighthouse,* in a great, apparently involuntary rush. One thing burst into another ... but I wrote the book very quickly; and when it was written, I ceased to be obsessed by my mother. I no longer hear her voice; I do not see her. ... I did for myself what psycho-analysts do for their patients. I expressed some very long felt and deeply felt emotion. And in expressing it I explained it and then laid it to rest. (1985: 90)

Virginia Woolf was clearly aware of the relatively new practices of the modern healers called 'psychoanalysts', her brother Adrian being one. She compared results of her creative writing with what she knew of psychoanalysis at that time. Psychoanalytic and psychodynamic therapists aim to help clients, or patients, achieve insight and understanding about past experiences – conscious and unconscious – and how these recalled experiences relate to their current problems. Some of the central assumptions of psychodynamic work are that these insights into the past can then be translated into the present and, in Virginia Woolf's words, 'obsessions and problems can be laid to rest'.

The psychoanalyst Karen Horney (1942), an early advocate of self-analysis, suggested that it was possible to discover some of the fault lines, defences and vulnerabilities in our own psyches. Disorders, psychoses and neuroses are very much a part of the language of psychodynamic and psychoanalytic therapy. Freud recommended therapists return to therapy regularly throughout their careers to decontaminate from contact with damaged psyches in their work with patients.

It is likely that part of your practice and therapeutic training will pay some attention to abnormal psychology and the American Psychiatric Association's *Diagnostic and Statistical Manual of Mental Disorders,* now in its fourth edition (1994). If awareness of mental illnesses has not been part of your practice, it may be useful to check how the various neuroses and psychoses have been categorised, even if your particular approach resists the idea of diagnosis, individual deficit and the medical model. See Exercise 7.10 at the end of this chapter.

Attachment theory

Developed initially as a critique and in response to theories of psychoanalysis, the attachment perspective in psychotherapy says that the way we narrate our life stories reflects how we view the world. First developed by the British psychoanalyst John Bowlby and his associates, beginning in the 1950s, attachment theory has much to say about the autobiographical self. According to Bowlby (1988), if childhood goes well there are predictable emotional and relational results:

> If it goes well there is joy and a sense of security. If it is threatened, there is jealousy, anxiety and anger. If it is broken, there is grief and depression. (p. 4)

Bowlby examined how the earliest relationships in a baby's life shape their capacity for stable relationships and attachments in adult life. These theories are contested. Over 20 years ago, Professor Mason Durie, a psychiatrist, teacher and researcher based in Aotearoa New Zealand, critiqued the ideas at the very heart of attachment theory, and the underlying individualism of Western psychology. It would not be 'healthy' for a Maori or indigenous person living according to traditional customs to become 'a person in their own right'. Collective ways of living emphasise the role of the extended family in well-being, and possibly others in the community, such as ministers and traditional healers.

Becoming aware of cultural beliefs and values is difficult because those cultural 'truths' are so deeply ingrained that they appear to be 'natural'. Cultural and social assumptions are the most difficult to enquire into and question: the last to become aware of water are the fish that swim in it. Most of the exercises in this chapter offer different ways to move away from the cultural 'norms' we take for granted. Exploring relationships in the family of origin is one place to start. Relationships in our early years are of enormous significance from a psychodynamic and attachment perspective.

Try this: Who looked after you?

Reflect for a moment on who looked after you when you were younger. It may not have been your mother or your father but possibly someone in your extended family who was your major caregiver.

Maria, studying for a counselling degree, writes:

> I had been seeing a counsellor for over six months and had not been able to remember very much at all about my life before I was 10 years old, before we came to live here in the UK. I started to do some sewing with some other women

who have young children and suddenly remembered Auntie Ruth, my father's sister, who had always looked after me before I went to school. My mother was at work and my father had already left to come over here to look somewhere for us to live. Auntie Ruth was always sewing, making clothes and quilts. It makes me feel very sad that we lost all of her when we moved here. No photographs, none of her sewing, nothing.

Attachment theories and brief attachment-based intervention

Attachment-based theories suggest that the way we react to difficulties in adult life may take us back to pain or trauma in childhood (Holmes, 2001). Attachment theories also suggest that how we form and maintain close relationships in adult life may be foreshadowed by different experiences of close relationships in childhood. Attachment research has also found interesting connections between 'narrative style' in adolescents and young adults, and childhood attachment experience.

The British psychiatrist and psychotherapist Jeremy Holmes has developed valuable ways to work with attachment theory in practice, including the use of an adapted form of the adult attachment interview, first developed by Mary Main and her colleagues. There are many versions of the adult attachment interview (Holmes, 2001), essentially a psychodynamic means of assessment aiming to 'surprise the unconscious' into revealing itself by asking detailed questions about relationships with parents and significant others, and about separations and losses. People who have experienced secure attachments, according to the theory, can talk about their past in a coherent, collaborative way, with continuity between relationship patterns in childhood and those of later life. It is recommended that you seek out some support before working on your early life in any depth.

Whether or not you accept recent developments in attachment theories, consider reading some of Jeremy Holmes' work on the secure base and attachment theory in psychotherapy. A full account of the development of brief attachment-based intervention (BABI) is in Holmes (2001: the appendix on pp. 151–165 is a good place to start). With detailed instructions and handouts for BABI clients, the following extract outlines the aim of Holmes' approach:

> The overall aim of the therapy is (a) to start to understand how the overwhelming need for security and self-protection may at times be self-defeating, and expose the client to the very dangers which she is trying to avoid, and, (b) to begin to strengthen her sense of secure attachment so that she will be better equipped in the future to cope with the problems with which everyday life presents us.

(Holmes, 2001: 153)

Transference and counter-transference

Transference is the process of transferring early experiences of relationships to the present, and particularly in the context of therapy. One of the goals of psychodynamic counselling and psychotherapy is to prevent clients repeating early patterns of behaviour in current relationships. In psychodynamic and particularly in psychoanalytical approaches, managing transference is a major part of successful therapeutic outcomes. In addition, the counsellor or psychotherapist must be able to explore the unconscious nature of counter-transference, that is, the therapist's response, whether positive or negative, to their clients. Differentiating between counter-transference reactions that are triggered by client transference and those that are projections of unresolved personal conflicts are central to reflective practice and clinical supervision in psychoanalytic and psychodynamic approaches. Traditionally, training courses in psychodynamic counselling and psychotherapy have required students to undergo lengthy personal therapy during the period of training, partly to develop this ability to manage transference and countertransference.

Alice (pseudonym chosen by the author), a psychodynamic psychotherapist, provided the following fictitious example based on work with several clients:

> He just left, leaving me feelings I can't make sense of. There's an echo of sexual tension between us. He openly flirted with me again today. It would have made sense had I felt irritated, even offended! After all, much of what he says is a dissonance within me. 'I am a chauvinist and I am proud of it!' One of his punchlines widely framed in a seditious grin. I was giving way or giving in, responding permissively to his flirtations. What was happening here? What madness was this? I ached for the shelter of supervision!
>
> Is there therapy in my permissiveness?
>
> Today, talk about white women being too argumentative and high maintenance. He sounded angry, resentful. I reflected on his anger. He laughed. His joviality seemed shallow – a cover-up I thought. I reminded him of his choice to work with a white female therapist.
>
> Client: Ah! You're different!
> Therapist: How do you know?
>
> So much for supervision as I wandered aimlessly, on the edge of revealing my experiences of his flirtatious battering. I feel uncomfortable broaching the subject. How will he take it? With a joke? His usual dismissive stance when we approach some level of therapeutic intimacy between us? He seemed flat when he left today. No sexual tension. Was I missing it? No. But I was missing something, reaching out for it where there was only space.
>
> I really don't know what to make of my feelings.

Flirting again, almost relentlessly. Today I was wrapped in a sandstorm. I tried to cover my eyes with parts of my desert garment. The sand found a way in, my eyes objecting shedding gritty tears. Sand blasting my cheeks. It stung like mad, piercing, abrasive. Nowhere to run for cover. I tried to find him squinting in the storm to see if he too struggled like I was. He mentioned his ex-wife today. For the first time I sensed a vulnerability between us. At first she was the love of his life then she became the 'white bitch' who 'stripped' him of everything he had.

Client: I bloody trusted her, didn't I.

I think we have finally found an oasis, plenty of water and even fig trees for shelter. Safe from sandstorms. I felt he gazed momentarily on himself. He knew the way! When he is ready he will share what lay beneath his flirting. This is mellow permissive me sighing in relief. For just a while I will stay with him in this shelter from the storm.

Activity: Writing about transference and countertransference

- What is your reaction to this piece of writing?
- Pause and allow yourself time to gather together some words in response to reading Alice's account of her reactions to a particular client.
- Reflecting on practice in this way takes honesty, and may feel too exposing. Of course it is always possible to destroy this kind of writing if you choose to.

FORMS OF WRITING

Dreams

The interpretation of dreams in Western therapeutic cultures is associated with psychoanalytic psychotherapy. Jung critiqued and developed Freud's work on dreams, introducing the idea that the dream could be related to the person's everyday life (Jung, 1998).

In many cultures, dreams are used as a valuable guide to finding solutions to problems. The examples of Philip, Anita and Jo's dreams, outlined at the beginning of this chapter, provide some examples of how dreams might inform and be informed by waking thoughts and feelings.

Activity: Recording your dreams

Keep some paper by your bed so that you can record your dreams over the next few weeks.

- Catch down the story of the dream as fully as possible with as many details as possible; rather than writing a rational series of events, go for images, feelings, people in your dreams.
- Notice if you are active or passive in the dream.
- Elicit the essence of the dream by ignoring details if you feel yourself losing track.
- Catch the feeling, your sense of atmosphere in your dream.
- Draw or write – whatever works for you.

FIGURE 7.1   Dreams
© Liam Wright-Higgins. Reproduced with kind permission.

For more on writing dreams, see Bolton (1999: ch. 6).

Some people say they don't remember their dreams. Visualise yourself waking up and recording a dream.

It's worth asking yourself to dream, and to remember what you dream, before you go to sleep.

You might try retelling your dream out loud, as if it's happening right now, and noticing your thoughts and feelings as you retell the dream.

Try keeping something to write or draw on by your bed. That way, if you do wake up with some image floating in your waking mind, you could capture it before it disappears. Recording a dream as quickly as possible is important; the memory of most dreams fades quickly.

Writing poetry

Like dreams, poetry is not bound by the rules that limit expression. There are times, such as love affairs, loss and death, when people want to read, possibly even write poetry. And running with the rhythm and rhyme that poetic language creates tends to work particularly well when everyday language is not enough. Grammar has no power in poetry.

Poems use word pictures and symbols rather than the everyday structure and form of prose. bell hooks, the black American activist and critical theorist kept diaries from an early age, as a narrative of resistance, as writing that enables us to experience both self-discovery and self-recovery (hooks, 1999: 5). Writing for her was a sanctuary, a safe place, but not without feelings of humiliation and shame about what she confronted which, at first, forced her to destroy what she had written. The exception was in writing poetry. She never destroyed poems because there was nothing revealed in her poetry, about the 'me of me' (hooks, 1999: 10). On the other hand, the kind of poetry people doing therapeutic writing may develop might express 'the me of me' very powerfully.

Memoirs, autobiographical memory and narrative approaches

Autobiographical memory is mysterious. Even with recent advances in neuroscience, there is very little understanding about the mind, which has been called the most complex known thing in the universe. The unconscious may contain repressed and potentially conflicted material, which some writers have compared to a locked box. We take a much more fluid approach to the unconscious, not as something static and closed, but as a source of creative fantasy, autobiographical memory, daydreaming and imagination.

On the basis of recent research, human memory is not now regarded as just a recording device, like a DVD recorder (Damasio, 2010). Writing your autobiography involves both memory and imagination. It might be difficult to know what is real, what is recalled, and what is fantasy. We reconstruct memories based on previous experience as well as the immediate episodes we've just lived through. In therapeutic relationships recollected episodes from memory are explored and discussed. We suggest that autobiographical writing can play a similar part in self-analysis or self-practice (Wright, 2009a).

Activity: Autobiographical writing

Whether or not you have already started to write an autobiography, see what comes to the end of your pen or onto the keyboard in answer to the following questions:

* What are your earliest memories?
* What parts of your life story have resonated with client stories recently?
* How far do you believe that what happened to you in the past shapes the way you might think, feel and behave in your present therapeutic work?

For more on autobiographical writing, see Exercises 7.1 and 7.2 at the end of this chapter.

NARRATIVE APPROACHES TO TRAUMA

When people are in crisis, they are often described as 'losing the plot'. Traumatic experiences may be beyond words. There is a need to tell the story at the time, when the person is immersed or even overwhelmed by the experience, as a kind of letter to the world, to use the poet Emily Dickinson's phrase. Yet there may be dangers, and a resistance to remembering brutal past events and experiences, even if purging or externalising them brings relief.

Creative activities which draw on alternative intelligences to the cognitive, particularly non-verbal activities like drawing and using photographs tend to be rich in connecting us with past experiences and memories. Word pictures can work in the same way. Here is novelist Carol Shields comparing forgotten memories to stalagmites and, in an even more startling image, describing desires scattering like cockroaches. This is the power of metaphor, the kind of writing which can be used to make abstract ideas concrete and even uncover secrets and disturbing memories:

> Certainly writing is a search that may, like psychoanalysis, lead us into secret labyrinths where thoughts we had never suspected are discovered, where ancient and forgotten fears thrust themselves like stalagmites into consciousness, where we catch glimpses of desires so evanescent that they scatter like cockroaches before the light.
>
> (Shields & Howard, 2000: 9)

Traumatic memories may be suppressed, for a variety of reasons. Soldiers, like Tu in Patricia Grace's novel (2004) mentioned in Chapter 6, may vow secrecy about their experiences, which means that on their return to civilian life they are unable to talk about their experiences. Resulting problems such as mood swings, depression, alcoholism and other addictions and broken relationships can lie in the wake of such secrecy. Memoirs written years later by soldiers from the Second World War and Vietnam War who are now in their late 60s and even 80s play an important part by 'writing out' traumatic experiences.

Kim Etherington, a practitioner and life story researcher, writes:

> Memory is not necessarily a factual, coherent or linear record of something that actually happened. Rather it is a process of bringing together parts of our experience to create a coherent and organised whole.

> (Etherington, 2003: 32)

bell hooks destroyed her journal writing for years, but eventually wrote a memoir about her childhood which was her way of accepting the past. She writes, 'I no longer need to make this journey again and again' (1999: 12).

Kim Etherington asked a group of people to write about traumatic experiences in their life and how they had come through them, in some cases transforming their lives:

> By writing our stories we become agents in our own lives. We claim a voice that previously may have been silenced by potentially marginalising traumatic experiences which are culturally denied. (2003: 20)

Narrative approaches take a different view of mental health problems, based on contesting 'the language of deficit' (Gergen, 2001). Rather than using the interpretation of past experiences to label a person as in some way 'disordered', narrative approaches resist the view that the person is identified with the problem. The problem is the problem. A person might describe themselves as 'depressed', 'obsessive' or 'fixated' according to more traditional therapeutic language, and would work with a narrative therapist to re-author these stories, searching for strengths, often not just in the individual but in their cultural resources.

Most people in most cultures grow up with folk stories or knowledge of myths and fables, although in the digital age the oral telling of stories has been replaced by the electronic media. It is now possible to choose to access any number of films, novels, soap operas via the Internet or other media, where images of different life stories are presented. Kim Etherington is also widely known as a life story researcher:

> Since I was a small child I have written poetry as a way of soothing myself, and making sense of my experiences, using images, metaphor and language to express thoughts and feelings. … looking back now I realise that the stories were all about me. Nobody told me to do this; it was as natural to me as talking to myself – which I'm told I did repeatedly as a small child. As a counsellor I have always encouraged my clients to keep diaries, write stories and poems too. Sometimes they discover, by this means, a part of themselves of which they had been unaware: a creative, inventive, imaginative, feeling part of themselves. (2000: 17)

Two of Kim Etherington's former adult clients, Mike and Stephen, brothers who had been sexually abused from childhood through to the age of 18, agreed to collaborate in reclaiming the story of their recovery: ' – ... and they have survived, indeed they have done more than survive – they have flourished. They want people to know *how* they survived, what helped, what they needed, what resources they found both within themselves and externally' (p. 15).

During therapy, Mike and Stephen kept diaries, wrote letters to themselves and to others. Their account includes a fairy story about their grandfather, who had abused them both, unbeknown to the other. The story begins in the traditional way:

> Once upon a time there lived two little boys in a little house, in a little village, outside a little town. They lived with their mother and father and were very happy. Nearby lived several aunts and uncles, and all their little cousins, and best of all, their grandfather. (p. 23)

Group activity: Re-telling trauma stories

Kim Etherington offered this workshop at a conference in Britain (Etherington, 2004). It combines individual reflective writing and drawing and a small group exercise.

- Choose a trauma experience from your adult life that is meaningful to you. (Kim used as an example her experience of the birth of her first child.) If you cannot recall such an experience, you could think about a traumatic experience you have witnessed in therapeutic work.
- Focus on the experience, perhaps by using focusing or mindfulness ways of coming into awareness.
- Draw any image that comes to mind.
- Take your time.
- Write any words that come to mind.
- Look at what you have drawn and what you have written and give yourself time to reflect on what you see.
- Note feeling words you may have overlooked and add them to the picture. This might take some time.
- Ask yourself the following questions:

  o When is the first time you heard of this kind of trauma (e.g. childbirth)?
  o What were the circumstances?
  o What was it like for you?
  o How old were you?
  o Where are you in the memory?
  o What do you feel as you recall?

(Continued)

(Continued)

- o What do you think as you recall?
- o What kind of beliefs were formed in response to this experience?

- Consider aspects of your identity, for example gender, age, race, religion, ethnicity, social class, sexual orientation.

  - o How did they shape the formation of those beliefs?
  - o Would you say this is still what you believe?
  - o Has anything changed and why?

Talking with others in a small group

- Have you talked with anybody about this experience of adult trauma?
- Is anything still unspeakable? If so, write 'I have not spoken about it because ... .'
- Have your responses to the trauma influenced your sense of identity? If so, how?
- Think about your professional life. What is your professional relationship with the type of trauma you are considering here?
- Discuss what this experience today has alerted you to in relation to the trauma.
- Consider what this might mean for your work.

SEXUALITY, COUNSELLING AND PSYCHOTHERAPY

Talking about sex and sexuality can raise anxieties in clients and therapists. There are no 'right' answers and, as is often the case, one of the advantages of reflecting in writing is that it is possible to choose to be entirely private about your reflections until you are ready to destroy or share your writing. Identifying the family, cultural and social influences on experiences of sex and sexuality at different times in your life can cause questions to emerge about all kinds of assumptions about the 'normality' we take for granted.

Activity: Cultural messages about sex and their effects

What are the messages you have received about sex from different sources in your culture? These sources might include, family, peers, religion, school, the medical profession, sexual partners, the media?

(Butler et al., 2010: 164)

- What effect have these cultural messages had on you and your work as a therapist?
- Think about where you live and work. What kind of relationships do you see around you (e.g. single mothers/parents, nuclear families, extended families, decisions not to have children)?
- What is the most typical family unit in your cultural context?

It is also useful to check out the assumptions clients hold about the family, sex and sexuality. Becoming aware of the cultural and historical contexts that influence sexual behaviour can also be enlightening.

FICTIONALISED ACCOUNTS OF THERAPY

Several experienced and well-known therapists have recently written fictional accounts of therapy sessions. You might want to look at Susie Orbach's (1999) stories of the intimate relationships between therapist and client; Phil Lapworth's (2011) 'Tales from the therapy room'; or Irvin Yalom's bestselling stories and famous collaboration with the client and writer called Ginny (Yalom, 1989; Yalom & Elkins, 1974).

Whether or not you work within a psychodynamic, narrative or pluralistic framework, you will recognise the human complexity of what happens in therapy in these accounts. The same might be true where film, television and other media have attempted to represent the therapeutic relationship. You might decide to write fictionalised pieces about some of your clients and some of your own experience of therapy.

CONCLUSION

For some people, understanding the roots of their current problems or vulnerabilities means looking to the past. This chapter discusses how what happened to you *then* might shape the way you think, feel and behave *now*. In the next chapter the explorations continue into landscapes of present time.

Write!

7.1 Childhood memories

As a child:

- To whom did you turn when distressed, ill or tired?
- Who did you feel understood you best as a child?
- What was your most frightening situation or moment as a child?
- How did you get comfort when frightened?

(Holmes, 2001: 155)

7.2 Photographs

Choose a photograph of yourself when you were a child. As you look at the picture, capture your thoughts and feelings in whatever way seems most expressive to you.

(Continued)

(Continued)

- How old are you in the picture?
- Who's with you, or are you on your own?
- Where was the photograph taken?
- Do you know who took it?

On paper, this activity might sound simple. Whenever we look back to childhood, however, painful memories and feelings of loss and grief can come up for some people. Make sure you have some support in place.

7.3 Drawing and or writing: fictionalising stories

Using a device like a fairy story or any kind of third-person narrative (using 'he' or 'she' rather than 'I'), write an autobiographical memory from your early life – a happy or unhappy memory, it's up to you.

Start with 'Once upon a time', as in a fairy story, and decide how long you want to take for this activity.

The fictionalising of memories can distance the experience, and allows you to invent a new ending: you are in control.

As with other activities in this chapter, make sure you have some support in place, whether through therapy or supervision, should this writing and drawing become distressing or feel overwhelming.

7.4 Drawing/painting and writing: early memories

For this drawing, you will need paper and colour pens, or a screen if you prefer.

- Draw yourself at age eight, or any early age you can remember, in a particular place, with others or alone.
- Where are you?
- Who else is in the picture?
- What has surprised you, if anything, about your thoughts and feelings as you look at your picture?

7.5 Roles in the family

Our earliest experience of living in a group is usually through family life.

- Think of the time when someone in your family of origin got angry.
- Who was allowed to get angry in your family of origin?
- How did gender roles play out in conflict?

7.6 Reflecting on dreams

It may also be useful to write about your memories of important or especially powerful dreams you've experienced in the past.

What are the themes or patterns you notice? You could re-write one of the dreams from the point of view of one of the characters.

Gestalt practitioners would suggest becoming one or more of the symbols in the dream and dialoguing with them.

Jungian practitioners might suggest continuing the dream in to the present and future.

7.7 Create a lifeline

Warning! This exercise can be very powerful and it is important to do it in a private place where you feel relaxed and not rushed. Your lifeline need not be seen by anyone else until you are ready. It is for your own use. It may be that you want to discuss your lifeline with a therapist or supervisor.

If you are creating a lifeline as part of a counsellor education group, it is likely to take at least two hours. If you are working alone, you could decide on how much time you want to dedicate to this exercise, taking breaks when you feel like it.

- Draw a lifeline beginning where you think best, looking back to the past.
- Draw peaks to represent high times of fulfilment and happiness.
- Draw troughs to represent low and difficult times.
- In between those extremes, there might be flat lines, representing times when life was more like plateaux.

This exercise is commonly used in personal development work in counselling and psychotherapy education, and in practice. If you are asking your clients to reflect on their lifeline, it is essential to have undergone this process yourself (McLeod, 2010: 24).

This exercise need not be about your earliest memories of childhood, and the line can take you to where you are now or beyond.

In this chapter the emphasis is on the past. In many cultures, the 'before birth' past and the spirit realm are very important. It may be appropriate to start the time-line further back, and not just before birth.

Think about your physical, mental, spiritual and emotional ups and downs. How has your family life, that is, your extended family or family of origin, changed?

- What about other kinds of personal and professional relationships?
- When you draw the highs and lows, peaks and troughs as well as the plateaux, try to let your hand go freely without thinking too much.
- Indicate what caused you most pain and most joy. Add dates and details using words, pictures, photos, colours and anything else that will help you get under your censors.
- As you look at your lifeline, what are some of the most significant events?
- Write down any insights.
- What are the things you would like to avoid repeating in future?
- What are some of the events, experiences and activities you would like to focus on and possibly recreate?

You may choose to discuss some of your insights with a group or another person. You are in control of what you choose to show that person or group of people, and how much you choose to say about your experiences.

(Continued)

(Continued)

7.8 Sexual expression in your culture

Some visitors from outer space land in your country. They want to understand the sexual culture where you live. Prepare a short presentation for them on sex in your culture(s) e.g. what is sex for? What is thought of as good or bad sex, who is allowed to have sex, who is discouraged or prevented from having sex, how do people learn about sex etc. The visitors are encouraged to ask questions.

(Butler et al., 2010: 177)

This exercise is most enjoyable if carried out in small groups, so that some group members can visit other groups, playing the role of the visitors from outer space.

7.9 Rescued speech poetry

Many therapists, especially narrative therapists, use 'rescued' or 'recovered' speech in poetry, capturing their clients' words and writing them down in stanza form (Crocket, 2010; Speedy, 2008). Such rescued speech poems emerge out of therapy dialogue itself. The therapist usually writes down the words and phrases they have witnessed, spontaneously, highlighting particular phrases or images.

Write from your notes, or immediately after the next therapy session, where you pay attention and notice the richness of language in your client's words.

7.10 What is your psychopathology?

As in other written exercises, it is useful to reflect on our own vulnerabilities and struggles in writing and in private before deciding how to share this material with others.

(McLeod, 2010: 42)

- What is your own core issue or area of psychopathology?
- Can you describe an example from the recent or more distant past?
- What is the pattern of thinking, feeling and action that consistently gets you into trouble or undermines your life goals?
- In terms of well-known models of psychopathology, would you describe yourself as schizoid, obsessional or personality disordered (or as having a tendency in any of these directions)?
- Where does this pattern come from? How did this area of difficulty arise in your life?
- What do you do to cope with this issue, or to manage it? Have you used different strategies at different points in your life? What strategies have been most and least effective?
- Who knows about your 'basic fault'? How open or secretive are you around this issue?

8

Here and Now: Writing the Present

Focuses on current experiences and relationships, both personal and professional

Philip: I'm sitting in the counselling room on the first floor. Although the steep stairs (and no lift) mean that I can't work with some clients in this room, it's my favourite space at this agency. The view is over the back garden and of the trees which are beginning to change colour. I think they are Mountain Ash. The berries are startling orange. Summer is almost over.

I'm waiting for my next client with a heavy sense of loss. I notice it in my stomach, like stone. He was made redundant almost a year ago now and wants to find a way to get over that and start working again. We don't seem to have got very far in three sessions. I wonder if my approach is going to be the best way for him. Time to ask him. Also I need to tell him, 'Sometimes I feel overwhelmed by the amount of detail in what you tell me.'

Anita: This shared office is getting me down but at least I've got the laptop now. I tried to catch my negative thoughts just now with my last client. I have 10 minutes before the next appointment arrives and I'm going to write down what I noticed so that I can take it to supervision. I'm going to use the present tense because it seemed to work last time.

He arrives late. I notice my irritation. I ask him how he got on with the activity scheduling we agreed he would work on over the weekend. He shrugs his shoulders. I remind him that we have only six sessions and that this is the third session. He looks down and I feel I've failed.

In our first session he talked about going to meditation classes. I'm think-ing we could move into some mindfulness practice. I don't know whether this will be useful to him. I ask, 'how is this going today for you, this ses-sion? I'm noticing that we're not connecting somehow.'

He suddenly looks straight at me for the first time.

Jo: I'm going to talk about this situation in supervision next week. I wanted to check that what we're doing is working for my client, Jane, but it seemed to go horribly wrong. I'll try and remember how it went by writing the dia-logue now before my next client arrives.

Me: So how is this going for you?

Jane: OK (she looks a bit startled when I ask her). I filled in that questionnaire at reception and circled all the fives – that's good isn't it?

Me: (feeling embarrassed) No, sorry I didn't mean that. I meant do you want me to carry on listening to what happened at work without interrupting you or shall I ask some questions? What would be most useful for you? We have six sessions and this is the third. I'm not sure that I'm clear what it is you want to change.

This chapter focuses on current experiences and relationships, both personal and professional. It will be informed by three major theoretical frameworks: humanis-tic, narrative and cognitive behavioural. The message is: Stay in the moment!

Several exercises in this book involve mindfulness, which is about paying atten-tion in a particular way, on purpose in the present moment and non-judgementally (Kabat–Zinn, 2005: 4). The work of Eugene Gendlin in experiential focusing is also introduced in this chapter. You might want to borrow or make your own audio recording of mindfulness, experiential focusing or any guided meditation exercises you know and like, so that you can play them before writing.

Activity: Our senses

Eating a raisin mindfully

If you don't like raisins it might be better to use some other fresh or dried fruit that you do like! This exercise is used in mindfulness-based cognitive behavioural prac-tice to prevent depression and relapse.

- Take a raisin between your finger and thumb and feel the texture of it.
- Now look at it very carefully as if you had never seen a raisin before.
- Notice the colour, the ridges on its surface, maybe the way the light shines on it. Then smell it and notice anything about the way the raisin smells.

- Now put it on your tongue without chewing and notice what it feels and tastes like.
- Next bite into it very slowly, savouring its taste.

(Segal, Williams & Teasdale, 2002: 103)

Writing using all of your senses

- List some words about the experience of eating like this and how it compares to your usual way of eating.
- What other experiences might you be missing out on by not being fully aware of the present moment?
- Try to make the list as full as possible.

THEORETICAL FOUNDATIONS

Cognitive behavoural therapy and mindfulness

The point of this introductory mindfulness exercise, now part of contemporary cognitive behavioural practice, is to bring to our attention how much of life we live on automatic pilot. The present moment is lost in thinking about other things, memories from the past, or daydreams projecting into the future. If you are fully aware of thoughts, feelings and sensations in the body (as glimpsed in the 'Eating a raisin' exercise above), even if they are painful experiences, you can choose to accept or change those feelings. Traditionally, CBT aimed to reduce distress or change behaviour by changing thinking, and therefore attitudes, towards life situations and experience. Third-wave cognitive behavioural theorists and researchers harness the power of mindful meditation, in addition to cognitive change, to help people with depression move away from 'automatic pilot' and rumination towards more choices (Mace, 2008; Segal et al., 2002).

CBT, an action-oriented, integrated approach, draws on many aspects of learning theory and cognitive psychology. Philosophically, CBT is aligned with the Stoics. Epictetus, an ancient Greek Stoic philosopher, is often quoted to illustrate some of the key principles of cognitive therapeutic thinking: human unhappiness is often caused by dwelling on the past or worrying about the future. Human beings perceive events in different ways: it is not the situation itself that causes distress, but the meaning and perception of the situation to that person. It may not be possible to change the event, but it is possible to change how we interpret it. For example, a friend who is often affectionately described as negative or a 'glass half empty' kind of person, phoned to say that a tree had blown down in his garden. He wanted to borrow a chain-saw and spent several conversations both on the phone and in person bemoaning his bad luck. His daughter suggested he could use the wood for firewood or give it away. The same event or situation can have different emotional consequences for different people.

Behavioural therapy originated in the first half of the 20th century and is still used in aversion therapy using graded exposure, parenting programmes on TV and dog training. CBT was developed as a short-term, structured, present-oriented psychotherapy by Aaron T. Beck, who had originally trained as a psychoanalyst.

EXAMPLE
Aversion therapy

Overcoming a fear of rats

I (Jeannie Wright) am afraid of mice, rats and anything furry with a long tail. There have been times when I've been able to overcome this fear using a form of graded exposure. The example I wrote using this exercise might help you to see how this worked:

I remember seeing a rat in the street when I was walking home from school. I think that was the first time I'd ever seen a rat. It looked repulsive, its fur all matted, with red bald patches. The long, flesh coloured tail dragged behind it. I stopped and stared at it and I remember my heart was racing. A man who was waiting at a bus stop stepped towards where the rat was darting along a wall and kicked out at it. Some of the women at the bus stop screamed. Later on, when I was a student, we had an infestation of mice in the kitchen of the house I was sharing. The mice would jump out in the dark if I got back late startling me. I'd run out trying to stifle my screams, much to the amusement of my flatmates. It got so bad that I avoided going into the kitchen unless someone else was there. My flatmates would tease me with a soft toy of a mouse, knowing that I would start to move away from wherever it was, probably looking frightened and embarrassed at the same time. I knew I was going travelling and would have to overcome this fear because of the kind of places we would be staying in. I started by looking at pictures of mice and rats in books and taking deep, slow breaths while I looked to control my anxiety. I created a kind of 'safety', telling myself all the time that these pictures could not hurt me. Then I moved on to the soft toy, until I could sit next to it without my heart rate leaping up and my palms getting sweaty. Again, I used intentional slow, deep breathing to counteract my anxiety response. By the time we were travelling, I could eat porridge in the morning in street markets with rats running along the beams above my head.

The difference between 'feel' and 'think'

For the purposes of journal writing, we've highlighted the emphasis on correcting maladaptive thinking in CBT. Identifying the difference between feeling and thinking is vital in CBT practice. In the English language we frequently use 'I feel' (emotion) to mean 'I think' (judgement). One way to clarify this confusion is to check if 'think' can be substituted for 'feel' in a statement, for example:

'I feel that you should take a holiday.'

or:

'I think that you should take a holiday.'

The meaning of this advice is not changed by substituting 'think' instead of 'feel', whereas in:
'I feel he/she is attractive', is clearly wrong and in:

'I think he/she is attractive.'

the meaning is perfectly clear.

Often, with clients, I ask about the physical sensations associated with a particular feeling in order to make clear the difference.

Monitoring the inner critic

Beck (1978) referred to the cognitive triad in depression. He pointed out the inner critic or negative internal dialogue that most of us would recognise as an undermining voice, leading to self-doubt, a negative view of the world and a pessimistic view of the future. For example, when the pressure is on to perform well at work or on the sports field, the inner critic would be muttering, 'That's a hard call, this is not really your strength either'.

FIGURE 8.1 Anxiety

© Liam Wright-Higgins. Reproduced with kind permission.

Being at the front and in the spotlight has never been my idea of a good time. I'm OK working with groups of people I know, but find old patterns of anxiety emerge when all the attention is focused on me. My heart thumps loudly enough so that I'm sure the person next to me can hear it, my palms start prickling and I keep dropping things. The last time I was a keynote speaker, I noticed some of these bodily sensations early on. The lectern had moist handprints on it from where I'd leant against it. I moved into anxiety first-aid. Positive self-talk helped, and I started breathing more slowly and more deeply, deliberately moving my breath from my upper chest right into my stomach. (Jeannie Wright)

Activity: Identifying negative automatic thoughts

For a set period of time, a day or two at most, keep a thought record and monitor where and how your own inner critic emerges. It is important to take specific situations or events as examples.

- Catch the negative feelings, perhaps by noticing changes in your body.
- Write down the self-talk.
- What are you doing and what was going through your mind just before or at the time you catch this negative voice in action?
- Can you spot any potential or persistent triggers?
- If the situation involves other people, what does this mean about how the other person thinks/feels about you? Self-doubt can lead to negative predictions about other people's perceptions of you.
- How easy was it for you to get into the habit of writing down self-critical thinking or negative automatic thoughts?
- How do you experience it?
- How do you respond to it?

Returning to the keynote speech scenario, once I had calmed my breathing and started speaking I could have looked around at the audience and noticed someone looking at their watch and standing up to leave the hall. Instantly deserted by my positive self-talk, I could easily move into assuming that this person was bored. Predicting that whatever I had to say would not hold their attention would only lead to more negative self-talk and anxiety. According to CBT theories, catching these negative thoughts in time might allow me to look for alternatives explanations for their clock-watching and leaving. For example, I don't have any evidence to support my assumption that this person is bored. Some alternative views are that they might be expecting an important telephone call, or have an unavoidable appointment. Self-critical thinking is replaced, and I avoid the trap of assuming that my view of things is the only one possible.

Melanie Fennell, a clinical psychologist and researcher in the UK, talks about mapping your own vicious circle of low self-esteem. For clear examples of how this works, read any of her self-help books, or watch any of the recordings produced by the American cognitive therapist Christine Padesky. If you consult a self-help book based on CBT principles, or a clinician's guide such as the classic *Clinician's Guide to Mind over Mood* (Padesky & Greenberger, 1995), you could work through the exercises systematically and notice what comes up for you. Self-practice and self-reflection is one way of stepping into your clients' shoes, increasing the likelihood of a sound therapeutic alliance.

Thinking muddles – do you notice this when you monitor your thoughts?

Albert Ellis (1962) is often credited with work on thinking muddles (which he called 'errors'), such as:

* *All or nothing thinking*, for example, 'He always keeps me waiting and never apologises.'
* *Catastrophising*, for example, 'You'll never make that deadline and then you'll be on the redundancy list.'
* *'Mustabatory' thinking*, featuring 'must', 'should' or 'ought', for example, 'I must clean and tidy the kitchen every evening before I go to bed.'

Tapping into the power of our own thinking in this way has not only been successful in counselling and psychotherapy but has also been taken up by professional coaching, in sports and in business (Cox, Bachkirova & Clutterbuck, 2010). Glance through the shelves of self-improvement books commonly on sale in railway stations and airports and you'll notice the underlying principles of many of them lie in CBT, often combined with positive psychology.

From this brief outline of some of the foundational forces in CBT, you can see why it is in demand for stress management and coaching.

Humanistic and person centred counselling and psychotherapy

Humanistic approaches to counselling and psychotherapy share commonalities but are also very different from each other. They share a common belief in the potential of the actualising tendency, and that if the untapped abilities of the individual can be reached through therapy, actualisation or personal fulfilment is possible. The individual is able to grow and resolve problems through their own agency, if provided with a nurturing and facilitative environment. A phenomenological stance is another commonality. The way to valid knowledge and understanding is by closely exploring and describing people's experience of things. Phenomenology as a method of philosophical enquiry aims to depict the nature and quality of personal experience (McLeod, 2009).

Person centred approaches, drawing on phenomenology, were developed as a revolutionary alternative to psychoanalysis and behaviourism by Carl Rogers, starting in the 1940s in the USA. Rogers famously described personal experience as 'the touchstone of validity'. The focus on the central role of the therapeutic alliance and the importance of emotions are emphasised in the person centred approach. The foundational principles underlying the suggested writing activities in the next part of this chapter emphasise staying in the present in journal entries, and identifying and following feelings.

Try this: Recognising your feelings

- How are you right now?
- What's between you and feeling fine?

Focusing

Eugene Gendlin used experiential focusing to unlock the body's wisdom. A contemporary of Carl Rogers, and working in the USA, Eugene Gendlin's work on the 'felt sense,' focuses on the heart of what's happening beyond feelings. Writing and drawing provide ways in which that felt sense can be symbolised and expressed.

- Clearing a space is the first step.
- Relax and slowly use your 'felt sense', not your mind or your feelings, to identify concerns.

Gendlin maintained we are inherently interrelation as human beings. He suggested that working with a focusing partner on the phone is preferable to working alone. YouTube offers video clips of Gendlin at work, as well as exercises in focusing.

Like any form of meditation, focusing takes practice.

Empathy

Empathy is a vast and contested subject in counselling and therapy. Carl Rogers, from a person centred view, suggested that it is one of the core conditions of a therapeutic relationship. In order for therapists to understand clients' subjective experience, and accurately convey that understanding, there must be a strong and secure sense of the therapist's own self:

To be with another person in this way means that for the time being you lay aside the views and values you hold for yourself in order to enter another's world without prejudice. In some sense it means that you lay aside your own self and this can only be done by a person who is secure enough in himself that he knows he will not get lost in what may turn out to be the strange or bizarre world of the other, and can comfortably return to his own world when he wishes.

(Rogers, 1975: 7)

An outline of the vast literature on the philosophical thinking influencing Rogers' conceptions of the self might be useful but is outside of the scope of this book. One relevant fact is that Carl Rogers' daughter, Natalie Rogers, has extended person centred theory and practice by introducing creative and expressive ways of working in therapy (N. Rogers, 1993). She writes:

Psychological safety and psychological freedom are the soil and nutrients for creativity, but seeds must be planted. What I found lacking as I worked with my father were stimulating experiences that would motivate and allow people time and space to engage in the creative process. We can sit and talk about being creative but never involve ourselves in the process. (p. 17)

Promoting psychological change using art, dance, pottery, music and creative writing is at the very heart of Natalie Rogers' work.

Activity: Time out

Give yourself the gift of writing for 10 minutes – whatever comes to the end of your pen, pencil or onto your screen. You might want to start by describing:

- What's on top?
- How do you feel at this very moment? (How you feel might, of course, be affected by where you are, and who you are with.)
- When and where do you tend to feel most relaxed?

Congruence

One of the facilitative conditions for positive outcomes in person centred counselling and psychotherapy is congruence, or the therapist's ability to be authentic in the therapeutic relationship. A first step in recognising an emotional state, and therefore being able to work congruently in therapy, is being able to identify exactly how you are feeling and why. Some feelings are more acceptable than others. For each of us there may be some particular emotional states which are not easy to 'own'.

Activity: Drawing and writing feelings – Anger

- What triggers anger in you?
- How often do you notice anger in your voice or behaviour?
- Draw or write what anger looks like to you.
- If you were an animal, what kind of animal would you be when you're angry?
- What kind of weather would you be?

FIGURE 8.2   Anger

© Liam Wright-Higgins. Reproduced with kind permission.

Try this: Emotional vocabulary

Extend your emotional vocabulary.

- How many words or expressions for anger can you list (including slang and local dialect, even 'bad language')? 'Spitting tacks', for example, is local to parts of the UK.
- How do you put anger into words?

Unconditional positive regard

In person centred practice, another of the 'core conditions' is unconditional positive regard or a non-judgemental attitude towards clients. In counselling and psychotherapy education, an exercise asking you to consider what kinds of potential clients you might find difficult to work with usually throws up some interesting and sometimes surprising insights. Again, you are in control of writing about your feelings about your clients. You can either destroy this writing or decide to talk about it in therapy or in supervision.

Activity: Unsent letter

How do you feel about your clients?

Using the 'unsent letter' way of writing (see Chapters 4 and 6), write exactly how you feel about your clients.

   The aim is to be creative and free in your explorations. The non-judgemental paper or screen will not be shocked, or in any way impacted by your feelings, so there is no need to censor.

- Start the letter with 'Dear' and the name of a client.
- Read back over what you have written.
- What is it that you enjoy or find difficult about working with this particular client?

If you repeat this exercise periodically, you may be able to see themes and patterns which might be usefully explored in supervision.

- Now read the example letter below, then write a reply to the client:

Dear Chris

We've had three counselling sessions together now. I like your humour, that irreverence that bubbles up even when you're under a lot of pressure at work. At those times, you are definitely not into pleasing other people. When you start talking about violence, and the harm you've done to yourself, I feel my stomach tightening into a knot. My mouth goes dry – is this fear? I notice I often reach for some water when we're talking about the person you've decided to call 'Mr Knife' who seems to arrive in your life and take over.

Uncomfortable subjects

Which are the subjects you tend to find easy to listen to, and which do you shy away from? For example, monitor your inner response when clients start talking about their religious, spiritual or political beliefs, sexual practices or experience of domestic violence.

   Think about clients you have worked with where either you think it might have been useful to raise the issue of sex or spirituality but you did not. Perhaps you did talk about sex, racist politics or religion but it was difficult and embarrassing. What caused the difficulty or embarrassment? What went well in the conversation?

In some cultures it might be more acceptable than in others to talk openly about spirituality, or about sex and sexuality, for example (Butler et al., 2010: 37).

For various reasons, it may be that your experience is of nervousness and discomfort when certain subjects are spoken about, especially with people of certain ages, gender or religion.

Reflective journal writing is a very private place to begin thinking about unhelpful beliefs and prejudices in the area of spirituality, sexuality and other sensitive subjects.

Two-chair work and writing a dialogue

Many therapeutic modalities now claim empty and two-chair work to be effective, probably because they are very powerful and effective strategies for working with conflict, intra-personal 'splits' and decision making. Usually associated with gestalt therapy (McLeod, 2009: 280), two-chair techniques work well in two main ways, which can be adapted for writing dialogues.

First, an activity if you or your client is stuck (at a point of impasse). Each chair represents a different and conflicted part of the client, as in this example:

EXAMPLE
Two-chair dialogue

Mark, a client of Jeannie Wright's, is unsure about leaving a long-term relationship which has been difficult and unsatisfactory for some time. He agrees that it would be useful to use two chairs to represent his lack of decision and feeling of being stuck. In one chair Mark decides to use a 'voice of reason', not a dominant voice to him and one associated more with his friends. They all think he should get out of the relationship with Lucy as soon as possible. In the other chair Mark uses a voice he calls 'the stuck one', which has become the dominant voice. It is clear how this exercise could be translated into writing a dialogue:

Voice of reason: Come on Mark, this has been dragging on for far too long now – it's not doing you or Lucy any good.

The stuck one: I know that, but if I went, I'd feel so bad – we've been together a long time. We know each other so well and until these last few years, it was the best relationship of my life. If Lucy would go to counselling with me I'd feel more hopeful, but we just keep on bickering, undermining each other, hardly doing anything together any more. We don't laugh at the same things any more.

Voice of reason: So what keeps you there? What do you mean you'd feel bad if you left?

The stuck one: I'm not sure. I think I feel guilty to be the one wanting to move on. I'm also a bit scared – what if I don't meet anybody else and live alone for ever?

Mark is surprised by these strong feelings, which he hadn't 'named' before. He hadn't admitted to the fear of being on his own, nor to the guilt of being the prospective instigator of a break up – 'the baddie'. He can recognise how sad and frustrated he sounds as 'the stuck one', and when he has moved from chair to chair a few more times, agrees he has to do something soon. To write a letter to Lucy, even if it's not sent, describing how he feels, is the starting point.

Second, and in contrast to two–chair dialogue, using 'empty chair dialogue' can be practised as a writing activity for dealing with conflict with another person, or as a way of resolving unfinished emotional business in a person's life. The empty chair can represent a person the client is in conflict with or cannot communicate with for some reason. The therapist directs the client to move from chair to chair, speaking from the point of view represented by the part of themselves or the person they are imagining in that chair.

Some studies have used a metaphor of dominant and suppressed 'voices' rather than the original Gestalt 'top dog' and 'bottom dog' image (Honos–Webb & Stiles, 1998). We choose to use the metaphor of voices here.

Activity: Write a dialogue

- Choose a scenario.
- Think of a part of yourself that is usually marginalised, its voice turned down or drowned out. It may be a party-loving, outgoing voice that rarely gets to be heard because the quiet, conscientious, shy self dominates; it may be the angry voice against the 'not allowed to get angry' voice.
- Create a dialogue between these two parts of yourself in the here-and-now. (See Chapter 3 for how to write dialogues if you are unsure.)

And/or:

- Think of a conflict that's going on at the moment with another person. It may be that it would be impossible to deal with the conflict face-to-face.
- Write a dialogue between yourself and that person.

Putting yourself in the other person's shoes in order to write their side of the conversation might stimulate some new insights from their point of view. Dialogue writing can be particularly useful if there is unfinished and strong emotional response to a relationship with someone who has died, or who is no longer available to have the conversation.

Narrative therapy and externalising

Narrative therapy originated in family and systemic therapy practice. From the point of view of self-writing, narrative therapy is a rich and diverse source (White & Epston, 1990). This approach takes the view that people are competent, can find their own solutions to problems and are experts on their own lives. In this way there are commonalities with the person centred approach. Important differences emerge, and for the purposes of keeping a reflective journal, the narrative emphasis on language and its power in constructing identity will be central.

The narrative approach also takes a different view of mental health to CBT or psychodynamic counselling and psychotherapy, for example, based on contesting 'the language of deficit' (Gergen, 2001). A client might describe themselves as 'narcissistic', 'anorexic' or 'having a sexual dysfunction' according to more traditional therapeutic language. Rejecting the 'problem-saturated' stories that may have been internalised into a person's life and relationships, narrative therapists work to discover new, more positive stories that are co-authored with their clients. Narrative practices provide a radical alternative to the medical model or traditional culture of counselling and psychotherapy,

> One of the key contributions of narrative therapy is the determination not to locate problems as internal to people, but instead to externalise problems and to understand that the ways in which problems are constructed and experienced are related to matters of culture and identity.

> (Russell & Carey, 2003: 7)

Mandy Pentecost, a counsellor and teacher working in Aotearoa New Zealand, asks some questions about perfectionism to externalise and better understand her client Robyn's struggles:

- How does Perfectionism stop you from resting?
- What tricks does Perfectionism use to keep you in its thrall?
- When you get a glimmer of a way of doing things that is not ruled by Perfectionism, what appeals to you about it?

(Pentecost, 2008)

CONCLUSION

In this chapter we discussed writing in the here-and-now, using mindfulness-based exercises and experiential focusing to stay in the present.

Theoretical approaches to writing the present include CBT, humanistic therapies and narrative therapy. The aim of the next chapter is to carry writing into imagining the future.

Write!

8.1 Reflection: Classical conditioning

Choose a situation in which you feel moderately afraid, but which you feel OK about exploring in a written exercise.

- When was the first time you remember feeling like this?
- What were the original unconditioned stimuli and responses from which this pattern originated? It may be hard to remember such an incident if you have had this fear for some time. You may need to imagine a hypothetical situation in which you first experienced this fear.
- What was the process of generalisation that resulted in the present pattern of fearfulness?
- In what ways has this fear led to an avoidance of certain situations or stimuli?
- To what extent has this avoidance resulted in the perpetuation or maintenance of the pattern?
- Applying a behavioural approach, what could you do to extinguish the connection between certain situations, and the fear response that you have identified in this analysis?

(McLeod, 2010: 88)

8.2 First-aid breathing and writing

You have reflected on a situation where you feel afraid. It is likely that remembering that situation has brought back some of the emotional and physical sensations.

- Use mindfulness breathing to come back into the present, slowly taking a breath in to a count of 3, and consciously breathing out to a count of 4.
- Take an inventory of what's going on in your body.
- In this way you become more aware of what's going on for you physically at this moment, whether you are sitting or standing.
- You may also become more in contact with your mind in the here-and-now.
- Make some notes that show the links between the avoidance of certain situations or stimuli.
- How could you set about extinguishing the connection between these situations and the fear response?
- Write a list of those ways.

(Continued)

(Continued)

8.3 Drawing and writing anxiety

- When was the last time you felt anxious?
- What caused it?
- Choose a very specific instance and draw any images you associate with that experience.
- Using the present tense, describe how you felt as if it is happening to you now.
- Write in as much detail as possible.
- Identifying some of the symptoms of that feeling of anxiety might mean noticing shortness of breath, a rapid heartbeat, a dry mouth and other physiological sensations.
- Draw or use words to describe what anxiety feels like in your body.

8.4 Stress and goal-setting

- What are some of the situations where you find yourself feeling stressed?
- Describe, in words or images, one specific problem or issue you have difficulty with.
- What does that stress feel like in your body?
- Starting from your feet and moving right up to the top of your head, can you identify the physical sensations of stress?
- What's happening to your breathing, for example, or your heart rate?
- Breathing more rapidly or in a shallow way is often associated with the triggers of anxiety and stress.
- Now take three long, slow, deep breaths.
- Close your eyes and imagine what would have to happen for the sources of these feelings of stress to reduce.
- Write down these ideas now.
- List your immediate thoughts about what would need to change as quickly as you can, without thinking too hard. It is important you don't censor your thoughts – let your imagination loose with these ideas. Let them be as off-the-wall as you like.
- Now write them as achievable goals.

You might have come across the use of SMART goals in therapy, coaching and future planning. The acronym SMART stands for: **s**pecific, **m**easurable, **a**chievable, **r**ealistic and **t**ime-bounded (or variants of this). It is a way of setting goals that are not too loose, vague and unattainable.

Now look back at your earlier writing about what you need to change about a stressful situation to reduce the anxiety it causes you.

- What is it specifically that you want to achieve or attain?
- How will you know when you've attained this goal?
- How realistic is your goal, for example is it within your control?
- When might you achieve it by?

8.5 Writing a feeling

If, for example, as you clear a space you notice a headache or tension in your body, draw where you locate that in your body.

Feelings may surface first and if, for example, you're feeling irritated, list on paper or the screen all the problems or situations that are making you feel irritated.

What's the trigger for the most powerful sense of irritation?

> I feel irritated every time I'm walking across the park in autumn and one of the maintenance staff is blowing leaves with a loud, diesel powered machine. What's the point? All that is achieved is engine noise and the smell of petro-chemicals. I also feel irritated by electrical hand dryers in public toilets. They are almost completely useless for drying hands and just make lots of noise. (Jane)

8.6 Writing: Talking about sex

The following questions could be responded to individually, in writing, or as part of a group or pairs exercise in a training setting.

- What are your personal fears or anxieties about talking about sex with clients?
- What do you fear may happen if you raise the issue?
- What have been your experiences to date when the issue of sex has been raised in therapy?
- What therapeutic models do you work with and what place does sexuality hold within them?

(Butler et al., 2010: 17)

8.7 Externalise

- Think of a problem that you have struggled with for some time. It could be smoking, over-eating, not exercising, depression.
- Give the problem a name, as Mandy and her client Robyn did in the perfectionism example.
- Using the kind of questions Mandy used, externalise the problem.

8.8 Changing the ending

- Write a story about something you have experienced in your own life.
- Change the tense from the past to the present.
- Now change the ending of that story.

Suggested topics:

- A time when I was frightened
- A time when I was lonely
- A time when I felt abandoned
- I will never forgive ...

(Continued)

(Continued)

- The thing that makes me saddest
- If I could go back and change ...

You could set a time for yourself so that you know, for example, in 20 minutes you will go and do something else. This kind of time boundary is often useful when writing about potentially negative and emotional subjects.

Now answer some questions about the story you've written:

- What would have to be changed in order for the story you've written to have a more positive ending?
- What should have happened?
- You can change history, your own and other people's behaviour, you can even introduce a rescuer or use magic in order to make the story come out right.
- Now re-write the story in the present tense, incorporating the necessary changes for the story to come out right. Remember to stay in the present tense.

9

Looking Back to Look Forward: Writing the Future

Focuses on using imagination to envisage the future

Philip: It is spring. Now the crocuses are out, great banks of them bending in the wind. Yesterday I was sat for a while at lunchtime under a tree, still leafless, the first time I've done that this year. Purple and deep gold crocuses all around me when the trees are still grey and lifeless. We'd been asked to write about ourselves as counsellors in the future. I had my notebook with me and started to make some lists, but it felt very constrained. I haven't really got any idea where I'm going to get a job and I need one. We were asked to write as if there were no rules, wild ideas, anything at all. Here's where I got to: enough income to pay the rent, working with people who don't have to pay but who want to come to counselling, maybe a community agency?

Reading it back now I can see the contradictions, and the tameness of it – hardly wild! Hmmmm. As I come out of the underpass I walked along with some of our group to one of our last seminars as our course comes to an end. I'll have another go at that writing when I'm feeling a bit less anxious.

Anita: It's really difficult to imagine where I'll be in 10 years' time. The job at the GP surgery is permanent and will give me varied experience, so I feel very lucky. I know I don't want to stay here forever. At some point I want to go home. That was the whole point of studying and training for so many years. I just don't know where my training will fit with some of the traditional ways at home. I know if I've got a plan I can create some goals and usually I can be determined and just keep going until things start to happen. I just don't know what I'm aiming for in future and that's what I have to work out. I had a dream where I was dancing with some people I recognised from the course, but I felt I was at home. There was that humidity, just before a storm, when you feel you could wipe the air with a cloth and wring it out. I felt light when I woke up, and somehow energised as if I'd drunk water on a hot, dry day.

The first thing I'll do is write a list. There's a negative voice keeps nagging at me: 'You won't be able to get where you want to be – who do you think you are?' It's not a new voice and I'm conscious of its old self-doubt messages. The important thing will be to stop the downward spiral into loss of self-confidence. The course has gone well, I've had some good results and feedback from tutors, so I will make sure I write down positives and not just the negative and critical.

Jo: I can't believe we're coming to that part of the course where we have to start saying goodbye to people. I know I'll stay in touch with some, but it does feel very strange to have got to know people so well. I saw my friend when I was walking to the shops, in a hurry with my head down. He's so much part of the gay culture here. I used to feel so dowdy and grey and didn't dare speak to him for ages at the beginning of the course. Now he crossed the road and flung his arms around me, shouting 'Hello gorgeous'. He always smells of something delicious, maybe coconut or mango? I felt so much better for seeing him and having a chat.

I've been looking for jobs and there's not much going on. When I imagine where I'd like to work I get really carried away. I can see the wooden and glass floating building. It is surrounded by, almost part of, the gardens full of giant ferns, green creepers and jasmine. The computer's on the table near the window. There are other people around but we each have a room and my view is over to the West, with a low sun behind the trees. Dreams.

I don't want to lose touch with the networks I've built up doing the online work. Also, it's easier to keep clocking up practice hours towards professional membership via the odd face-to-face hours that come my way at the community agency. So I'll stay volunteering until I can get some paid work.

Chapter 8 focused on the magical qualities of imagination and fantasy to envisage the future. Working in counselling and psychotherapy brings us into contact with people's past and present experiences; anxiety about the future is also a common reason to consult therapists. This chapter will introduce three ways of writing the future:

- knowing your ancestry and what that might mean for your future ambitions
- knowing what you want and where you want to be and creating goals to get there, and
- using fantasy to explore future options.

LOOKING BACK TO WRITE THE FUTURE

Proverbs reflecting age-old wisdom in many cultures suggest that knowing the future means searching the past. In your family, do you have photographs of your grandparents and great grandparents? Perhaps there is somebody in your extended family who has done some work on genealogy and produced a family tree. How strong is that sense of family connection to the past? Maybe at weddings, funerals or other family get-togethers, some of the aunties and older generation start telling stories about how one of your cousins reminds them of their grandfather. He has the same smile, got into a lot of trouble at school for being cheeky, ended up leaving school early and finding a job on a building site. The cousin, just like his grandfather, loves this physical work and loves being outside. It's a shame, the aunties say, that he hasn't followed his father into a professional job as a teacher, but it's no good trying to make him something he is not. In the same way, some family members, perhaps the first to go into higher education, cause discomfort at family gatherings. They no longer fit.

To what extent do you believe that what happens to us is predetermined in some way through ancestry? Depending on your political view, you could argue that gender or socio-economic class has far more to do with where we end up than ancestry, in any genetic or predetermined sense. By analysing statistical information from around the globe, recent research by epidemiologists Wilkinson and Pickett (2009) examine social problems in the world's developed countries in terms of the gap between rich and poor:

> The solution to problems caused by inequality is not mass psychotherapy aimed at making everyone less vulnerable. The best way of responding to the harm done by high levels of inequality would be to reduce inequality itself. (p. 31)

Social class and income differences are not the only factors studied. Gender also plays an enormous role in inequality in all but a few so-called developed countries. For most women living in developed economies during the past 50 years, professional and educational opportunities have widened beyond the imagining of their grandmothers. Until relatively recently in most developed economies, even if a woman worked outside the home, she would not earn the same as a man for doing the same job.

THEORETICAL FOUNDATIONS

Socio-economic class, gender and life/career planning

It is also certainly true that in Britain, until relatively recently, social class and gender would determine your future life and career to a significant extent. The

Granada TV documentary series *Seven Up* interviewed children at expensive private schools and at schools in the then predominantly white, working-class East End of London. Watching the series now with the early episodes, starting in 1964, in black-and-white highlights how the children's social and economic 'place' predicted their future. The 7-year-olds at the private school talked about their plans to go to a particular college at Oxford or Cambridge universities, join a particular legal firm, and then become a judge. The documentary series continued to interview the same children in 7-year intervals. When interviewed 28 years later, this is exactly what had happened to one boy. He had progressed through a particular Oxford college and had been called to the bar, working at a particularly prestigious law firm where his family had had connections for generations. And then, when interviewed for the next series, his ambitions had been fulfilled: he had become a judge. Rather than using a crystal ball, he knew his ancestry and his class position in Britain in the last half of the 20th century and so could predict the future.

By contrast, the pupils who attended the relatively deprived state school in the East End of London in those years had few ambitions. Most of the girls knew they wanted to get married and have children. One boy wanted to be a jockey. Most knew their place and talked about jobs befitting their social, economic and class background. One or two, however, managed to bend the rules. One of the boys made a lot of money in taxi-driving in London, and retired to Spain with his wife who had helped him build up a thriving business. The documentary film, made when he was 49, showed him sitting by his swimming pool, tanned and relaxed, surrounded by his children and grandchildren. Would it have been possible for a fortune-teller to have predicted this outcome?

Try this: How do you limit your aspirations?

- I have to ... or else.
- I can't ... because ... .

Fortune-telling

Fortune-telling is an ancient practice. There are almost as many psychics, clairvoyants and palm-readers advertised on the Internet or in the telephone directory *Yellow Pages* in most industrialised cities as there are psychotherapists and counsellors. Years ago I can remember feeling deeply insulted when a client told me they had tried seeing a palm reader and decided to try counselling as well. What this shows me about my changing awareness is:

- how fortune-telling was related to marginalised cultures, travellers and Romanies who came round with the annual 'Goose Fair' where I was brought up;
- how Eurocentric and 20th century my views about such mysterious practices were, as well as about my lack of cultural flex at the time. (Ramirez, 1991)

Now looking to astrology and fortune-telling seem to make more sense, especially in situations where human agency seems limited. In some cultures, where consulting with The Great Mystery is part of everyday life, it would be unthinkable to choose a future course without ritual or consultation. I look at the advertisements for those claiming special powers. Here at the seaside in the UK, for example: 'Tarot card readings in confidence; Love, career, luck, happiness – corporate clients can provide testimonials; clairvoyant to the stars.' I can also see why, even in this diluted form, it might be an attractive proposition to know our fate, especially for people anxious about the future, for whatever reason.

A modern Western view might say that it is necessary to take charge; it may be all too tempting to ascribe power to a higher being, to another person or to 'fate' and hand over personal responsibility. Sitting passively to hear what lies ahead is not the way. Shakespeare's plays, on the other hand, are full of references to rituals used in foretelling the future. Witches and other seers arrive with unwelcome prophecy as well as predictions of victory on the battlefield.

In some cultures of course, human agency is thought to be very limited. In parts of the East, for example, geomancy or seeking cosmic harmony and future foretelling are a way of life and no decision would be thinkable without consultation (see McLeod, 2009: 306 for examples from Taiwan and Japan). With the writing activities suggested in this chapter, you are the person with agency, in control. But there are examples of the way in which writing can become as magical as any palm or psychic reading: giving hope, benefiting self-confidence, increasing assertiveness and reducing anxiety.

SOLUTION FOCUSED THERAPY AND POSITIVE PSYCHOLOGY

This chapter will refer to some of the traditional theories of the power of planning and goal setting, familiar to Western approaches to career counselling (Okun & Ziady, 2005). The key concepts of humanistic and CBT are more present and future focused than psychodynamic practices tend to be. All three traditional 'forces' however, are more problem focused than the newer, possibly less well-known solution focused therapy which, as its name suggests, pays much more attention to the solution than to the problem. Take, for example, the miracle question which asks you to imagine a time in the future when your problem has been resolved. Read through the paraphrased miracle question below:

Imagine when you go to sleep one night a miracle happens and the problems we've been talking about disappear. As you were asleep, you did not know that a miracle had happened. When you woke up, what would be the first signs for you that a miracle had happened? (De Jong & Berg, 2008)

USING IMAGINATION AND FANTASY TO WRITE THE FUTURE

Activity: Miracle question

- Choose a situation which you have been trying to change for some time.
- Write down the miracle that would need to happen for this situation to change.
- What would be the first signs to the people you live with, or know you well, that this miracle had happened?
- Write a letter to the people who know you well, celebrating this change in your life.

Here's an example of how imagining an ideal future and scanning for strengths helped a woman who had been suspended from her nursing job because of an unjust accusation. A subsequent tribunal dismissed the case against her, but she left her job in the hospital anyway. She was searching for purposeful activity, not necessarily paid work, and wrote in answer to the miracle question:

> I am lying in a hammock on a wooden terrace built on stilts over the water. All I can hear is the wind in the bamboo and the sounds of children playing in the street. When I open my eyes, the sea and sky are joined in a blue line. The water is so smooth it looks ironed. It is four o'clock in the afternoon and time for me to go for a swim after checking the evening appointments. The holistic health centre is part of a project I helped to set up with local people. Since I came here my blood pressure problems have disappeared, the irritable bowel syndrome too, and I've stopped smoking. I sleep well both at night and most afternoons after lunch. We offer massage at the health centre, groups for creative therapies and counselling, have links with the local market gardeners for fresh food as well as providing prescriptions for antibiotics for infections. When I finish work, I can be home in just a few minutes, walking up the hill through avocado groves. Sometimes the division between home and work seems to blur. I like the people I work with very much and we meet in each other's houses, sometimes after work and sometimes at weekends. We eat together, play guitar and sing. (Susan)

When Susan showed me this piece of writing we both laughed and cried. The place she had created, the ideal life/work, was so radically different from the concrete, grey, windowless, bureaucratic workplace and life of commuting for over an hour a day she had just left.

She decided it was too soon to retire and she wanted to use her skills and experience, but in a very different kind of health setting from the one she had just resigned from. A few months after she had written about this ideal environment, Susan applied to Voluntary Service Overseas (VSO). Her application was successful, and she was offered a post in Indonesia. She specified certain geographical areas in her interview, knowing that going to work in the tropics was part of her ideal.

This is why it is important to know what you want and how your past might have influenced your wishes. See Exercise 9.3 at the end of the chapter.

DRAWING AND WRITING: IDEAL THERAPIST

New developments in technology mean that we can work online with therapists, either real or imagined. What would your ideal therapist look like, sound like?

EXAMPLE
Imagining the ideal therapist

The beginning of this story is inside a room, like any other therapy room. I designed it, inside my head. Today it has two long windows, sun pouring in, some rich-coloured rugs – dark red and indigo. A simple room but the details are luxurious – a smooth soapstone carving, deep upholstery. The person facing me, the avatar therapist, was also created inside my head. Sometimes I change her to a him, change race, age or height. She doesn't say much. I do most of the talking during our meetings. I know she loves me. She's welcoming, warm, hugs me when I first sit down and when I leave. I let her do this. Let them alter the programme to do this. It took time. I had never let anyone else put their arms around me. At the beginning, she mostly nodded, smiled, made encouraging sounds, 'Hmmm, yes'. She'd also pick up some of my words and put them together with my body movements, facial expressions and tone of voice. I knew she had no axe to grind. I felt understood.

The scans were accurate. The brain images had shown a deficit in my early bonding – an attachment disorder, they said. The mapping produced a series of statistically meticulous representations of those areas of the limbic brain which needed balancing. The instructions suggested attention might be directed to this medication (with side-effects in bold) or to this or that form of psychotherapy. I'd opted for relational sessions and self-designed avatar – more expensive than drugs in time and money, but I was wary of trusting anything, swallowing anything and having so little control of the consequences. So far, we had met six times. I'd opted for a 10-session package and could view the recordings of our meetings freely, at will. When I watched myself in the room with her, it seemed I was beginning to soften. Gradually, I could see a relaxation of some of the muscles around my mouth. The shoulders dropping a little, hands and arms looser, fingers relaxed.

(Continued)

(Continued)

I also followed a series of 'writing in therapy' exercises. I've never been easy about talking to other people about my thoughts and feelings. I could write in private, whatever I liked and when I liked. I could also see, when I re-read the writing, that I was beginning to switch perspective. Less about the past and what had become, in my mind, 'the pit' and more about the present.

After six sessions, the scan showed progress. As I left the room after the eighth meeting, I was handed the recording as usual and a disk. That evening before eating with some friends, I played it: 'Attention might usefully be paid to movement,' it said. 'Choose from the following: movement with music, drumming, dancing water and waves, five rhythms.' I would find out more about what was on offer.

(Based on Wright, 2003a)

KNOWING WHAT YOU WANT: GOAL-SETTING

Using your imagination is a good place to begin goal-setting exercises. If your goal is to set up your own website as a practitioner, there will be practical steps to take to reach that goal. However, first comes the exciting part where you envisage how the website might look and how you would want the messages you convey to come across.

Activity: Designing a website

This exercise is about envisaging your professional future. It asks you to create a website advertising yourself, but this is the design stage so you don't need technical skills. You will need colours, images, photos and a large sheet of paper or a screen if you prefer.

- What kind of counsellor or psychotherapist are you?
- What is the service that you're offering?
- Who needs this service?
- Who would pay for it?
- What kind of sounds or music might your website play?
- Imagine the first impression you want to create – colours, shapes, images.

Now write some words inviting people to access the site, pointing out what you're offering for the 'Home Page'.

EXAMPLE
Imagining the future

The room was in the basement of a community meeting house in the centre of the city. It looked out on a garden of lavender-edged lawns in the summer, and cherry blossom now in spring. The group sat on the floor mostly, drawing on white paper with wax crayons. She drew in response to the question 'Where would you see yourself in five years time? Don't hold back, let your imagination free.'

She drew a yellow wash with palm trees around the edges. An orange-red sun hung in the centre of the sky, so hot she could feel it on her back. There was no blue crayon blue enough to match the picture in her mind. Two children played near a house on the beach. She recognised them as her son and younger daughter.

A year later she left her job, permanent and well paid, that had changed around her and become draining. She applied for something paying less than half her current salary, at an organisation in the West Indies. The form-filling was done in January at a computer wearing fingerless gloves and a woollen scarf – and this was necessary against the cold indoors. By July they were on the plane and emerged to 34 °C heat.

Once you have a clear goal, and it must be SMART, set the steps in place that you will need to reach that destination. SMART is an acronym for goals that are **S**pecific, **M**easurable, **A**chievable, **R**ealistic, **T**ime-related.

'What I need to do first is ... .'

POSITIVE PSYCHOLOGY

Therapy is about change, and we wouldn't do this work if we didn't believe people are able to change their thoughts, feelings and behaviour. All approaches to counselling and psychotherapy are positive in this sense. However, in the last decade, strengths-based and positive psychology have come to the fore, mostly associated with the American psychologist Martin Seligman. Widely known for his work on the theory of 'learned helplessness', Seligman and his associates have worked on mental *wellness* rather than illness. The cliché about 'a glass half full or a glass half empty' thinking illustrates how positive psychology works.

EXAMPLE
Positive thinking

In a community choir there are five times as many women as men, resulting in some women choosing to sing with the tenors, usually a male part. For a long time there was no bass section, also usually

(Continued)

(Continued)

sung by men, making some harmonies thinner. One particular evening only one member of the bass section turns up. 'I feel sorry for him', said the choir leader pulling a sad face, 'Oh dear, only one bass.' A choir member joined in, 'No, hurrah – he came, we have one bass!'

How does this way of thinking fit with your particular approach to life/career planning? Too often we are limited by negative thinking.

CONCLUSION

Thinking about the future means confronting some of your basic values and assumptions. This chapter discusses three ways of writing the future in terms of your life/career choices: knowing your ancestry and where you come from, not just in terms of geography but in terms of gender, social and economic class; setting goals for yourself and working out how to achieve them; using fantasy to explore possibilities. Once you have some less constrained options and have overcome any 'identity crises', setting SMART goals is easy.

The aim of the next chapter is to explore blocks and obstacles and how to overcome them.

Write!

9.1 Telling the future

Write some lists about what you would like to know about your future, starting with, What, How or Why.

- What is it you'd like to be able to foretell?
- To what extent do you read your stars or consult higher powers to know your fate?
- What are the attractions of looking to astrological charts, the I Ching (or Yi Jing) and other mysterious forces for guidance?

9.2 Social class

Write some notes about where you fit economically and socially in the culture you now live in.

- Where do you belong in terms of social class, that is, were you born into a particular class group?
- How important has social class been in your life?

- Have you been socially mobile in your lifetime? For example, were you the first in your family to go to university or aspire to a professional occupation?
- Could you have predicted the kind of work you now do, or want to do, by looking at your class background?

9.3 Extending your lifeline – the choices we make and the chances we take

You were asked to draw your lifeline in Chapter 7. This is an invitation to explore that lifeline again, looking for patterns in choices and taking chances. You could also extend that series of memories to project into the future. You might even want to continue on the same large sheet of paper, or the same file on your computer.

Whether as part of a group or working on your own, this can be fun. Look in particular at the chances you took – how did they pan out?

If you can, identify where there were choices to be made and reflect on why you took one particular track and not another. For example, education usually offers different points where choices are necessary. How did you make those decisions? Did you get any help with those choices from a career counsellor or a teacher? How central was your family in the decision making?

If you think this activity might bring up painful memories, make sure you have some support in place before you start.

9.4 Photographs – looking back to look forward

Find a photograph of your grandparents, and ideally photographs of your great-grandparents.

- Greet them. How much do you know about them?
- Where would they have been at your age and what would they have been doing?
- Where were they born?
- How much do you know about their work, their religion, the kind of community they live(d) in?
- Now imagine you can ask for some information or advice from one of your grandparents or great grandparents.
- What are the questions you'd like to ask them?

9.5 Imagining your ideal work/life environment

- Imagine your ideal work/life environment.
- Draw it.
- What are the colours like?
- What are you wearing?
- Where would this life/work be?
- What kind of people are you working with?
- Write a wish list of this new environment.

(Continued)

(Continued)

- Imagine what it will feel like to be a therapist 5 or 10 years from now.
- Write a letter to and from this 'experienced therapist' to your present self.

9.6 Scanning for strengths

You might have noticed when you apply for jobs, courses, funding or anything else that requires a curriculum vitae how difficult it might be to stay with positive thinking outlined here. You might also have experienced how emotionally draining such personal and professional audits can be.

This writing exercise, which might take no more than 20 minutes, helps you focus entirely on the positive.

- Make a list of all the work you have done, paid and unpaid.
- To see if you can find the positives in each role, concentrate on the strengths you brought to this work.
- Focus on some of the people you worked with and how much you learned from them.

There will possibly be some tangible benefits in each job (paid or unpaid) you've done; for example, qualifications you completed, or a friend you met and still love seeing.

9.7 Writing down the positives

Just before you go to sleep, scan through the day searching for positives. Even if they seem very trivial, don't dismiss them.

- Write down three things that went well today.

This may sound ridiculously simple, but research suggests this kind of writing can have powerful effects. It has certainly been taken up by those talking therapists who work as coaches (Cox et al., 2010).

PART THREE

SIGNPOSTS

10

Getting Stuck: How to Deal with Blocks, Overcoming Obstacles and General Difficulties

How to develop hope and resilience

He toi whakairo he mana tangata. Where there is artistic expression, there is human dignity.

(Māori proverb)

Philip: I'm feeling very stuck. Most of the people on the course seem to have their lives sorted out. They have jobs to go to, homes, partners. As usual the old patterns emerge when I'm feeling like this. I isolate myself. It is as if I don't want anybody to know because it's shameful in some way. So, when friends or colleagues ask how things are going I smile, nod, say inane things like 'fine thank you'. Polite, hiding the vulnerability I feel. It's about not daring to trust anybody with what is underneath the mask.

Anita: Dear Lee

I wish you could have come up this weekend. You've got a lot of work to do and good grief I understand that – so have I with all these deadlines for the course! Tell you the truth, I could do with going home. Do you ever feel like that? If I could get on a bus at the end of the road and be there, it wouldn't matter how many hours the journey would take: aeroplanes aren't like that are they. I'm tired and I'm beginning to notice how some of the stories I hear at work are staying with me. I've been reading about burnout and I wonder if I should take a break from the clinic. It's beginning to feel mechanical the work that I'm doing.

Jo: There's been a suicide, a boy in the school nearby. It's left me wondering about online therapy. What can we do if someone is in such despair? Logically, I realise that face-to-face work may not have helped him either. His death has caused a real sense of shock in the office. He used the phone line and then texting. We're all coping with it in different ways. For me, I prefer being together with other people and I really need the meeting on Friday when we're going to spend the afternoon together talking about what happened.

Isabel Allende, Chilean novelist and activist, lost her adult daughter Paula to a rare disease. In the introduction to *Paula*, which started as a letter to her daughter as she lay in a coma, Allende writes, 'Of all the reasons to write, survival is the most powerful' (Allende, 1996).

From the beginning of this book, we emphasised that working in counselling and psychotherapy takes its toll. This chapter looks at how writing and other expressive ways of working can strengthen your resilience, both in work and in life. Resilience is about being able to work with traumatic stories without being overwhelmed. As in previous chapters, we are assuming that no one way is best and will refer to a range of theoretical and research sources.

Three different ways of looking at resilience will come into focus:

- Witnessing trauma, reasonable hope and narrative practices.
- Compassion and working with shame using mindfulness.
- Overcoming obstacles by using creative activities, including writing.

WITNESSING, REASONABLE HOPE AND NARRATIVE PRACTICES

In Chapter 2, we looked at various theoretical paradigms in working with trauma. In particular James Pennebaker's 'writing paradigm' was outlined, which is predominantly associated with cognitive behavioural psychology. This section of the book will refer to the work of Kim Etherington, Mandy Pentecost and Kaethe Weingarten (Etherington, 2003; Pentecost, 2003; Weingarten, 2003), therapists and researchers who are committed to narrative theories and ways of working.

Mandy Pentecost teaches and works as a counsellor in Hawkes Bay, Aotearoa New Zealand. Mandy uses different kinds of writing in counselling, including therapeutic letters, 'rescued speech' poems based on clients' words spoken in counselling sessions and short stories. In this letter written to Robyn, who is grieving and feeling down, Mandy uses Robyn's own words about ways of coping, keeping a spark of interest going against the pain and sadness:

It has to be something that has enough interest to grab your attention. Most of you will still be where it was, but if you find something that grabs enough of you, it eases the pain the slightest bit, and gives you a bit of a rest from it …

It's like a new horse, when it stands up and it's all shaky; when it falls down it keeps getting up again till finally it stands securely on its own legs. The secret is in being able to keep getting up again, not letting yourself get so far down you can't get up again.

Then back in her own words, Mandy continues in the letter to Robyn:

I was not surprised to hear when I phoned that you had been taking this advice you gave yourself, and writing – as you said, creative activities like writing and playing the guitar take your concentration and won't let you think of not going on. As you said on the phone, it helps you feel more in control.

(Pentecost, 2008: 23)

Activity: Therapeutic letter

Think of a time when you have been facing great difficulty, struggling with obstacles and feeling overwhelmed. Write a letter to yourself, using words in the way that Mandy Pentecost's writing demonstrates, highlighting your strengths.

The conventions of therapeutic letters in narrative therapy told me to capture words that held the possibility of accounts counter to the dominant, problem-saturated story; they told me I didn't need to comment or evaluate, just present what you had said and ask questions that further thickened that alternative account.

(Pentecost, 2008: 23)

COMPASSION AND WORKING WITH SHAME USING MINDFULNESS

Resilience and hope

There is increasing agreement about the need to prepare those in therapy training to be resilient in listening to, witnessing and re-authoring, sometimes extremely traumatic stories. Some of the qualities that make up that resiliency include: optimism, creativity, motivation, flexibility, resourcefulness, imagination, persistence, determination (Bernard, 2004).

Activity: List ways of coping

Write a list of those ways you use in your counselling work to compose yourself when the pain of what you're witnessing becomes too much. Do you: make a hot drink? Play a game on the computer? Look out of the window? Take a break and go for a walk?

What are your particular ways of coping?

Overcoming obstacles using mindfulness

The first step in noticing the danger of a block or an obstacle is to notice. Thought monitoring, drawn from cognitive therapy, is a tested way to notice – in writing (Greenberger & Padesky, 1995).

This sounds paradoxical but is crucially important. When stressed, it is likely that the usual ways of caring for ourselves and ensuring that we stay competent to practise are diminished. Clinical supervisors, professional peers and friends play a significant role in providing feedback, honest and possibly hard to hear, about how we seem to them. The practice of mindfulness, referred to in several other chapters, encourages us to pay attention, non-judgementally, in the moment and on purpose (Kabat-Zinn, 2005).

Activity: Mindful breathing

- Take a moment now to review how you are.
- Close your eyes if it helps you to focus on your inner state and reduce external distraction.
- Take a long, slow in-breath, feel the air filling your lungs so that they expand sideways.
- Count to three.
- Breathe out, slowly. Notice any pain or discomfort in your body.
- Notice any urgent thoughts, worries, plans. Let them drift by like clouds in the summer sky.

Mindfulness is a process. We do not *achieve* a perfect state of mindfulness, rather it comes and goes. Mindfulness will become a regular habit if you let it. It's almost like a rescue remedy, or first aid. Combined with finding a compassionate voice, a non-judgemental presence you can talk to and listen to in writing, you have a powerful package that will enable you to overcome obstacles.

New developments in cognitive behavioural psychotherapy are harnessing neurophysiology, mindfulness and new conceptualisations of compassion to overcome severe depression (Gilbert, 2005). Paul Gilbert, well known for his therapeutic work on depression, knew about the feeling of being depressed from his own experience (Wright, 2007). Realising the central part shame plays in mental health and that the antidote to shame is love and care, Gilbert looks to Eastern philosophy, Jung, Bowlby and Buddhist practices – an unusually pluralistic view – in his work. Experiencing self-compassion is a vital part of this change process.

Activity: Self-compassion

Imagine: You have woken up one morning feeling very low. You're crying without knowing why. There doesn't seem to be anything worth getting up for. Sit up in bed and find something to write on. You're going to write a letter to a person, perhaps a part of yourself, who will not judge or criticise. When you think about this person, or this part of yourself, the qualities shown to you would be warmth, acceptance, caring, openness and support.

Start the letter with the name of that person, or create a compassionate image for yourself.

- How would you like your ideal compassionate image to look?
- What would their voice sound like?
- What other sensory qualities can you give to this image?

An example of how self-compassion can be beneficial is given below:

Jane is a natural journal writer and successful professional woman. She has tried counselling and found it helpful but was worried about the dependency it seemed to encourage. Combining some reading of self-help books and her instinct to write down and reflect on her thoughts and feelings, she has developed a way of writing dialogues. Every morning she writes as if in conversation with a compassionate presence. She describes it as 'a nurturing, mothering, very caring loving presence.'

These qualities could also be seen as some of those conditions for therapeutic change Carl Rogers exemplified (C. R. Rogers, 1957, 1974). The person centred approach in its original and earlier forms has been critiqued by those who would argue that it is focused too much on the individual and too little on the social and cultural pressures around them. I asked Jane why she thought women tended to be subject to these 'contradictory expectations' (Greer, 1999) of work, home and family in spite of feminist successes. She said:

And I think women worry about these sorts of things too, how do you deal with relationships and communities and obligations? … It seems to me that as a woman one of the things we do try to do is to hold things together. Somebody has to be there, sending birthday cards, you know talking with the children when you really just want to go to bed, you know somebody has to be there for those key relationships even if they're not always all that positive. Somebody has to have a view on the long-term network and that tends to be what women do a lot.

In common with many women who hold down stressful full-time jobs as well as meeting the needs of elderly parents and children, Jane has found that making time for the dialogue writing improves her mood and enables her to be more assertive (Wright, 2009b):

I actually feel my energy go up, I feel better … and I'm not reassuring myself or anything like that – you are although all of that is part of it, affirming myself, reassuring myself but actually it's as if there is someone inside myself that I'm still finding that knows more about, that can help me more get through this world in a good way and enjoy it.

So I think I mean why would I write down, I think I write it down because it really does focus me. And sometimes I'm writing and I'm writing really quickly and it's all just kind of coming out and you know I'm obviously then in a really rich seam with feelings and, I think, so I think it's what writing is often it is very focused and you can reflect and it makes you stay with that.

Jane's writing could be said to be a form of mindfulness. The writing helps her slow down and stay focused.

Try this: Mindfulness writing

Give yourself 6 minutes to breathe and write.
   Address your writing to a part of yourself, or another person, who nurtures you, offers you that complete acceptance, without judging.
   Whatever comes to the end of your pen or onto your screen is right.
   Gag the inner critic!

OVERCOMING OBSTACLES USING CREATIVE ACTIVITIES

In the literature on creative therapies, the traditional forces in psychology, counselling and psychotherapy still take their different views, based on their fundamental understanding of how human beings flourish and cope with distress. The person centred approach for example, represented by Carl Rogers' daughter, Natalie Rogers, looks to the actualising tendency as the source of human imagination and creativity (N. Rogers, 1993). The psychodynamic approach, in all of its rich variations, has traditionally been at the heart of creative therapies in Europe at least, drawing on theories of archetypes, conflict and the unconscious (Meekums, 1999, 2000). Recently, psychotherapists such as Margaret Wilkinson, drawing on attachment theory, Jungian psychoanalytical psychology and neuroscience, provide clinical examples of how trauma and neglect can be overcome. The plasticity of the brain, and creative therapies, aid therapeutic change (M. Wilkinson, 2010).

Even with the theoretical knowledge and years of experience of a therapist like Susie Orbach, listening to sadism, or systematic abuse, the hurt that has happened to people can sometimes be hard to hear, 'I felt as though I had been punched in the heart and that my mouth might be hanging open' (Orbach, 1999: 129).

Sand-play therapies and drawing, dance, music and other creative activities can be used as antidotes to the stresses of therapeutic work, as well as therapeutic modalities in their own right.

Activity: Being creative in therapy

Creative work is play. How do you like to play?

- Write or draw a list of 10 things you enjoy doing.
- When was the last time you allowed yourself to do these things?
- List the ways you managed to find time to play this week (e.g. dancing, painting, talking with friends, driving, walking etc.).
- Who are the people you like to play with?
- Who do you like talking to about the things you like to do?
- Finish the sentence:

  o When I was little, I used to like to ... .
  o I don't do it much but I enjoy ... .
  o If I had time, I would ... .

EXAMPLE
Using word play to create a poem

Steve Lang, a counsellor and counsellor educator in Aotearoa New Zealand, uses word play to create a poem.

(Continued)

(Continued)

Reflections on reflections

Its the last day of our training workshop and my concern begins to build about what to say at the close. We usually go onto the Māori meeting house to say our farewells and in such a spiritual space we invite the students and staff to say whatever they wish which reflects their spiritual beliefs. This is in line with our collaborative and pluralist approach, and yet my anxiety is 'what to say myself?' as an atheist who believes in other people's rights to their religious beliefs.

As I walk across the car park I try to relax the tension in my shoulders and allow ideas to flow. The tension release feels like gliding as opposed to pushing against the issue, and the words of a poem 'come into view' – 'you can glide if you want to …'. The teaching day is a busy one and yet at odd moments other lines appear, and the poem begins to appear as if out of a mist. I am surprised as it does so at the rhyming which is not a frequent characteristic of my poetry. However, I begin to warm to the neatness of it, as if in some way it reflects the tidied up ends of a counsellor education workshop; all the papers that have been signed and returned; the hasty meetings in corridors and lunchtimes that have taken place to resolve concerns; all concluded; all rounded off. And so it seems to fit somehow that there is a rhyme and an attempt at rhythm though I do not have time during the busy last day to revisit the words, rather they were spoken as they appeared.

Not until a few days later, when at four in the morning I am awake in bed counting off syllables under the sheets. I had awakened with a strange dream about being awkward in a church, and then my thoughts turned to my own debrief on the workshop, and then to my reflections on the poem and how it rhymes but does not yet have a rhythm. It feels important to make the poem just right!

I resolve to give it rhythm … so I count on my fingers. 'You can glide if you want to = 7, Ride thermals to great height = 6, Do battle with tornadoes = 7, And push boundaries of flight = 7, Take whichever way with grace = 7, For hope will see you through = 6, May you be true to what you believe = 9! And may what you believe be true = 8. Just as we try to refine the workshops to meet our learning outcomes so I appeared to reflect this vigour in my pursuit of rhythm and meter. Ideas began tumbling around in my head and I struggled with the idea that I might not get back to sleep till this was done! So I persevered.

I liked 'great new height' it sounded like 'brave new world' and so a total of 7 syllables per line evolved. I then approached the word 'For' as in 'For hope' and I remembered Kaethe Weingarten's (2000) work on *reasonable hope* but that has too many syllables and I thought of 'honest hope' and liked that too. There are too many words in the next line and I reflected on my verbosity in workshops and cut out the 'May you' as not necessary. And similarly the last line manages just fine without the 'And' at the beginning. And so a revised poem was shaped and I went back to sleep!

You can glide if you want to
Ride thermals to great new height

Do battle with tornadoes
And push boundaries of flight
Take whichever way with grace
Honest hope will see you through
Be true to what you believe
May what you believe be true

(Lang, personal correspondence)

Here's a story:

> Mere, one of Jeannie Wright's clients, had made several suicide attempts. She had been in a strong relationship and was devastated when her partner left, after 16 years. He seemed not only disinterested in Mere, but also in their children, which enraged her. A turning point in the counselling happened when I asked about Mere's clothes, which were always spectacularly colourful, in unusual materials. This resulted in Mere bringing in a bag full of fabric, fun fur, Lurex, cotton prints and velvet. We used those fabrics to look at her current situation and hopes for the future.

STUCK WITH WRITING: WRITER'S BLOCK

Finding there's no words there to write happens to all of us. The pen poised over the page with no arterial blood coursing down to it. It can feel as if no thought or reflection or memories or feelings are possible, particularly to be written.

The first strategy to try is just to leave it for the time being. Go away, do something entirely different and return to it at a different time of day or night in a different place, perhaps even with different writing materials.

Then find a peer to do a writing session with. One of you lead, setting you off on the *6-minute writing exercise* (see Chapter 4), and then suggesting a further exercise, then re-reading your writing silently to yourselves, then sharing and discussing it with each other. If that doesn't work try one of the activities below.

Activities: Combatting writer's block

1 Re-read Chapter 4 'Starting out'; try the exercises you didn't do previously, or re-do one you found constructive then.

(Continued)

(Continued)

2 Write a letter to your *writer self*. Pour out all your feelings of frustration at not being able to write.

   o Write the reply.

3 Write a list like this:

   o If my writer's block were a weather or time of year it would be a ... .
   o If my writer's block were an animal it would be a ... .
   o Continue with different categories such as type of landscape (e.g. huge mountain), article of clothing, piece of furniture, mode of transport, then invent your own.
   o Think widely in response to each one (armour or locked filing cabinet for example), and write a line or two in response to each rather than a single word.
   o Write a letter to one of them, and then write the reply. For example 'Dear Black Dog on my shoulder, you are NOT dear at all, I would strangle you if I could ... .'

4 Write a detective or quest story about searching for facility in writing.
5 If none of these work, give writing a break for a while, and try drawing, painting, dancing or singing.

CONCLUSION

> Yet there is, I believe, a much more important reason for my writing. It seems to me that I am still – inside – the shy boy who found communication very difficult in interpersonal situations: who wrote love letters which were more eloquent than his direct expressions of love ... That boy is still very much a part of me. Writing is my way of communicating with a world to which, in a very real sense, I feel I do not quite belong. I wish very much to be understood, but I don't expect to be.
>
> (C. R. Rogers, 1978: 80)

Carl Rogers knew how writing could overcome obstacles. This chapter has suggested three ways to work when the going gets rough:

- Building resilience and hope using narrative ideas.
- Mindfulness and building a compassionate image.
- Creative therapies and activities.

When life's rough, the tough write – or draw, sing, dance, paint, play, find a way.

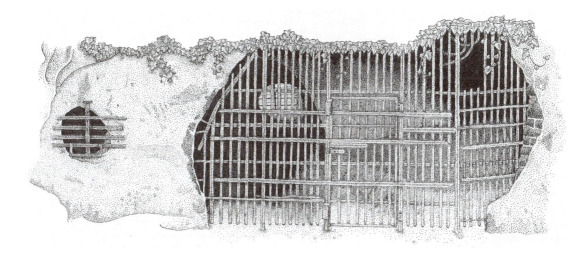

FIGURE 10.1 Trapped

© Liam Wright-Higgins. Reproduced with kind permission.

Write!

10.1 Written applications

The selection process for accreditation and membership of professional bodies in counselling and psychotherapy often involves autobiographical writing. Application for initial training courses also tends to include a written application form. Some of these written applications ask you to write autobiographical statements, such as:

'Briefly describe a time of difficulty in your life and how you overcame it.'

It may be, therefore, that you have already had some experience of writing about your past. The purpose of this autobiographical writing, if you are ready to start or continue it, is to make links between your life history or life experience and your way of being as a counsellor or therapist (McLeod, 2010).

10.2 Writing about reactions

Write about some work with a client that has caused you some distress. What is it that is not going well?

(Continued)

(Continued)

Questions, such as why you react as you do to particular client stories, may be the focus of some work in clinical supervision. You could also write about those reactions.

10.3 Writing a song lyric

This could be a light-hearted activity. It could also be sad or angry, depending on what you decide to write about.

- Choose your favourite song. What is it about the words that you particularly like?
- Start with free writing – let the words pour out.
- Rhythm – rewrite and see how the writing becomes more like speech by using a stanza form to write it down.
- Try rhyming.

11

Supervision, Reflexive and Reflective Writing

Reflective practice is one of the cornerstones of professional therapeutic relationships

Philip, letter to supervisor:

Dear Claire

Supervision has been really helpful these last few weeks, and I feel much less uncomfortable having my work scrutinised as time has gone on. When I take a counselling session recording now and we listen to me stumbling, trying to stay within the client's frame of reference, I don't squirm with embarrassment like I used to. After each supervision session where we've talked about growing edges and what I would have done differently, I write a letter to myself. The voice I use is not the fierce, critical one at all. I try to offer myself genuineness, empathy and acceptance.

Thank you for agreeing to fit me in at short notice for tomorrow. I saw a client for the first time last Tuesday and wanted to talk over with you some of the ethical dilemmas I foresee. Leroy is 65 and has just lost his wife to cancer. They had been married for over 40 years and the rest of his family is now back in the West Indies. He says he's not sleeping, not eating and that, 'it doesn't matter what I do'. The focus would seem to be self-care and some obsessive behaviour the GP mentioned in the referral letter. He visits his wife's grave several times a day. It is very likely that I will be leaving this agency within the next couple of months and I'm unsure the time is right to start working with Leroy. Also, his story brought back acute memories of my recent losses. I'm in need of perspective. Leroy told me he did not want to come to counselling but his GP persuaded him. Are we a good cultural fit? The right person is possibly from his church which seems to be his main support at the moment.

Anita, e-mail to supervisor:

Hi Martin

As you know, one of the most useful things about keeping the personal journal this year has been deciding to set myself some goals at the end of each entry. Recently I worked with a child (K) for the first time. It was a surprise to me that I enjoyed the session so much, as I have always thought that I would work with adults. After writing up my notes about the session and some more personal observations about what seemed to go well in my journal, I had a look at the outcome rating scales, and the working alliance inventory which had been adapted for use with young people. K seemed to get the hang of these questionnaires and tick-boxes. Her use of the sliding scales mostly seemed to fit my sense of how we had got on – she was mostly positive: she had felt understood and respected; she felt heard and that the session had been right for her. She had circled the other end of the scale in the goals and topics domain, i.e. we did not work on or talk about what she wanted to work on and talk about. I felt a bit baffled.

In our next supervision session I'd like to reflect on this and have set myself some goals. I've been asking myself some questions, such as what I would like to change in my practice and how I would know that it had changed.

Goal/task: Write up the notes for the session as if I were the girl?

Jo, e-mail to supervisor:

How are you Mere?

I'm glad we decided to use e-mail while you're working away. I miss our face-to-face sessions but this writing gives me an opportunity to connect with you in a different way. I'm also wanting to start writing case studies as part of a course assessment and this introduction to a client I'm currently working with might help me. It means I have to sit down and begin! Do you remember I mentioned Sam? He started texting soon after I began work at the agency and was one of my first clients. He's now decided he'd like to meet face-to-face and has made three appointments, cancelling them all. Finally, last Friday, he arrived and stood in the waiting room with his headphones on. It was an edgy meeting but we both agreed we would like to continue. It's not my job to diagnose, and you know I hate labels, but I'd agree with his own description of being somewhere on the 'Aspergers' continuum. It's as if he is engaged in the conversation some of the time and then disappears.

All of my old self-doubt flooded back in.

In this chapter we consider how, together with supervision, reflective journal writing is a vital component of professional development and self-care, helping ensure practitioners work safely and effectively with clients. Counselling and psychotherapy are complex and emotionally demanding professional activities. Along with the need for personal resilience, therapists must continue examining and improving their practice in order to develop professional skills. These practices also offer support when therapists are under particular personal or professional stress.

Freud advised therapists to return to personal analysis every five years because of frequent exposure to primitive repressed material which he likened to dangerous exposure to X-rays. Cognitive behavioural therapists, at the other extreme, have not tended to expect to be in personal therapy either during training or after. All counselling and psychotherapy orientations share, at least in most parts of the world, a commitment to ongoing, professional or clinical supervision; it is essential for professional accreditation in the UK and many other parts of the world, although this is not the case in the USA.

'Supervision' is a problematic term, with implications of surveillance rather than a professional relationship between peers. Its purposes and impact on therapists and their work with clients has been considerably debated in recent years (Wheeler & Richards, 2007). Regulation and the culture of professionalisation are causing disquiet in the UK, Aotearoa New Zealand and other parts of the world. New and critical views of supervision draw very effectively on ideas underpinning the narrative approach (Crocket, 2007; Crocket et al., 2007).

We use the term 'supervision' here to mean a working alliance between a supervisor and a therapist, where there is an opportunity for therapists to reflect on their work in relationship with a trusted colleague or colleagues. One of the objectives is to enable the therapist to work ethically, confidently and creatively, ideally offering quality assurance to clients and the wider community in which counselling and psychotherapy sit (Bolton, 2010; Wright, 2003b).

Reflective journal writing can be a vital element of supervision. Most codes of ethics provide a definition of professional supervision or a statement of purpose, such as:

> professional supervision is for counsellors to reflect on and develop effective and ethical practice. It also has a monitoring purpose with regard to counsellors' work. Supervision includes personal support, mentoring professional identity development and reflection upon the relationships between persons, theories, practices, work contexts and cultural perspectives.
>
> (NZAC Code of Ethics, 2009: 33)

REFLECTION AND REFLEXIVITY

Reflection is about learning from experience; uncovering new meanings from the ground up. This might be as simple as reviewing a particular therapy session or part of the session, working out what went well, what made a difference or seemed to trigger a breakthrough for a client, and what you might have done differently.

Researchers in cognitive behavioural practice have recently developed and studied ways for students and practitioners to self-practice and self-reflect: 'In essence, reflective practice is what distinguishes the expert therapist from the average therapist, and SP/SR (self-practice/self-reflection) directly facilitate this' (Bennett-Levy et al., 2003: 153).

Reflection is like looking in a mirror and seeing an image of practice. Reflective practice has to go deeper than a mere inverted image. The writing exercises in this chapter enable this process. Focusing upon and making developmental use of your case notes (not process notes) involves reflection. (For an explanation of reflexivity, which is a slightly different process from reflection, see Chapter 3 and Bolton, 2010.) Kim Etherington (2004) points out that reflexivity is a way of being we develop in therapeutic practice:

> Reflexivity is a skill that we develop as counsellors: an ability to notice our responses to the world around us, other people and events, and to use that knowledge to inform our actions, communications and understandings. To be reflexive we need to be aware of our personal responses and to be able to make choices about how to use them. We also need to be aware of the personal, social and cultural contexts in which we live and work and to understand how these impact on the ways we interpret our world. (p. 19)

Celia Hunt (2000) examines the difference between reflection and reflexivity:

> Where reflection could be said to involve taking something into oneself – a topic, an event, a relationship – for the purpose of contemplation or examination, reflexivity involves putting something out in order that something new might come into being. It involves creating an internal space, distancing oneself from oneself, as it were, so that one is both inside and outside of oneself simultaneously and able to switch back and forth fluidly and playfully from one position to the other, giving oneself up to the experience of 'self as other'. (p. 156)

Activity: For tutors and students – writing to a future you

For many years, at the end of the first year of counsellor training, we take envelopes along to the last day of the block course. We ask students to write themselves a letter to be opened in 6 months' time. On the board is written the instruction:

- Write your name on an envelope.
- Write a letter to yourself and seal it in the envelope. You've got about 20 minutes.

- Use your first language – nobody else is going to see this writing. For example, if Samoan is your first language, please write in Samoan/English or any combination you choose (or you could use visual images – crayons and pastels are always available in our teaching rooms).
- We'll return the sealed letters to you when we next meet in 6 months' time.

Students then discuss the process in small groups, responding to questions like:

- What was it like to write this letter?
- What kind of audience are you imagining might read it?
- How do you think you'll feel when you read it?

When we return the letters, the instruction is:

- Read as if this is unknown writing from an unknown person.
- Who wrote it?
- How do you feel reading it?
- What does this writing have to say to you?
- What will you do with it?

Here's a diary entry, in the form of writing to herself, and then an example of reflexive writing from Kitt, a practitioner whose first language is Danish:

Dear Kitt
my emotions
it's like squeezing into clothes
I don't like
too small and is
too big and
too hot for summer and
too light for winter
I-am-hot-cold-small-big
all at the same time
nothing fits
me
it's like I can never fully fit into myself
as if I am no longer who I was and who I was no longer part of who I am now
I can't find a fit with my new language
English
the English version of me doesn't fit the Danish version of me

it really hurts
and nothing fits anymore
will my Danish self ever fit my English clothes?

The above writing is an excerpt from a diary I kept when training as a psychotherapist. I had lived in Aotearoa New Zealand for five years and English was very much still a struggle for me. Not so much the act of stringing together sentences for everyday conversation. It was the self-reflective writing exercises we were asked to do as part of our training that became a painful struggle for me. They really hurt.

I often felt split and ungrounded when writing and reflecting in English. Rather than finding and making sense of myself, as others in my group so often reported was their experience, I had the experience of creating a self, my English-speaking self. For many years I had the experience of not fitting into myself, as expressed in the above poem.

Today, 10 years later, I still don't fit − but I feel less disturbed by the emotions not fitting brings up inside me. Those feelings have become treasured teachers. In particular, when working therapeutically with other immigrants for whom English is a second language and finding a sense of themselves here in Aotearoa New Zealand is a struggle. Knowing how reflective writing has helped me come to terms with my Danish and English identities, I have at times suggested to clients the possibility of it being a useful tool for them to explore and reflect on their struggles. One woman began exchanging letters between her native self and her immigrant self, writing in both English and her native language. Through her letter writing and reading she told me she began to feel more 'peaceful' inside. I felt so inspired by her experiences I began writing letters to myself in Danish. It was like receiving letters from an old friend telling me I was okay and that not fitting is okay, I needn't be so scared. It really helped ground me. Today I write to myself in Danish and to others in English. It creates a space where my Danish and English selves are able to meet and exchange experiences.

SUPERVISION

Sharing client work through journal writing

Yalom, in his inspirational open letter to a new generation of therapists and their patients, *The Gift of Therapy* (2002), passes on gems gained from years of therapeutic experience. Acknowledging the challenges of working with human problems, Yalom encourages therapists to cherish their occupational privileges:

> Not only does our work provide us the opportunity to transcend ourselves, to evolve and grow and to be blessed by a clarity of vision into the true and tragic knowledge of the human condition, but we are offered even more. We are intellectually challenged. We become explorers. (p. 258)

The following writing illustrates how reflective practice can help us in this personal as well as professional exploration. Jenny O'Connell (not her real name) is a counsellor in a school in Aotearoa New Zealand. She responded to questions and instructions to help analyse a specific incident which happened in school. She was asked to describe this particular situation and its impact on her, not only as a counsellor but also as a person. The opening instruction was:

> Briefly describe a piece of work with a counselling client that has triggered a personal issue of your own.

EXAMPLE
Jenny's need for supervision

A personal issue of mine that I have become aware of is that my own parents were so busy getting on with what was happening in their own lives when I was a teenager that they did not nurture/parent me enough.

I have a very well developed 'nurturing parent' and in my counselling work I have to be careful that I am not mothering to the students. This week a traumatic incident happened at the school where I work. A 13-year-old boy was with four others in the corridor of one of our school buildings. In this building there has been some construction work happening and an electrical wire from a smoke alarm was left hanging down, someone had knotted and looped it so that it was like a noose.

The boy was showing off and put his head in the noose – but he slipped and the wire went tight around his neck. A teacher arrived on the scene and found the boy not breathing and had to lift him to release him from the noose. When the teacher managed to release him the boy fell and hit his head and cut his chin.

At the hospital I had to go in with him while he was attended to by the doctor and nurses. At one stage he cried and I could feel myself getting emotional, so I held his hand while he was being treated. I felt overcome with sadness and anger that this boy, who is in foster care, was here in hospital after such a traumatic event and his caregivers and social welfare had still not arrived after two hours of being contacted. I kept thinking where this boy's own mother/father are at this time and why are they not caring for this young boy who so needs nurturing. I had to work very hard to repress my emotions so that I had the appearance of not being affected by all this.

Another issue that was noticed was the boy was wearing school shorts that had been ripped down the side and he had stapled them up. The teacher told me his pants had been like that for over two weeks. I told the teacher that I would organise to get him a new pair of school shorts.

When the male caregiver arrived, his attitude was that this was not too serious and that the boy was still alive and his only wound is a cut chin so he will be alright and that we were not to make too much fuss about it. This added to my sadness about how this boy needed to be nurtured and cared for more.

I am now in a position of needing to work with the boy as a client. I had a discussion with two psychologists around the work that I would need to do with this boy. I am aware that I must maintain personal boundaries around my approach with working with this student.

(Continued)

(Continued)

At this school I deal with a large number of clients involved in being placed in foster families. Often in foster families there are not the same emotional ties or nurturing. Occasionally there are also some families who use this as a means of income and may not spend the money on specifically providing for the needs of the young person. Statutory services are responsible for monitoring how placements are working to support the young person. I need to remember that as a school counsellor I can challenge them about whether the practical needs of the child are being met, but it is not my role to step in and provide the nurturing needed.

I realised that I was trying to nurture and rescue him by saying I would buy him some new school shorts. I made the decision that if I was going to work successfully with this boy I could not take on a rescuer role, therefore it was not my responsibility to get the shorts.

After a traumatic incident such as this I needed to attend supervision. I plan to talk about my reaction and my need to keep checking my response to working with this client.

For Jenny, supervision after this incident might have focused on the complex mixture of feelings about her relationship with this client, her sense of pressure to work professionally and within ethical boundaries, and her role as a school counsellor. She might also decide to talk about personal issues the incident has raised for her.

Try this: Clients triggering personal issues

Briefly describe a piece of work with a client that has sparked a personal issue of your own.

What has this reflective writing revealed?

WRITING REPORTS

Activity: Waiting for your client

Let's imagine you're waiting for your counselling client. Close your eyes and think back to when that last happened.

If you've not yet been in that situation, in either chair, let your imagination find the space, the time of day, the thoughts and feelings about how you can prepare for the person who is about to arrive.

During a radio interview, the novelist Pat Barker said that only creative writers think and feel at the same time in their work. I'd disagree. When I'm working with a person who's telling me about why they've come for counselling, there is a very real emotional, cognitive and sometimes spiritual dimension in that work. I use all of myself in the therapy room. The effects of working in this way, using all of yourself, can be stressful. So can writing reports about that work.

In a study about sexual abuse counselling based in Aotearoa New Zealand, therapists were asked about the effects of listening to details of traumatic events. Angela describes writing reports:

> When I have to write without being in relationship to them [clients], that's the worst for me. Sometimes, I've just got to walk away or I'd sit there and yell at them [the reports] [laughs]. A lot of what is in the reports, content wise, is, of course, quite cruel and violent as well as sexual. I find that traumatic. [Voice trails off. Pause to self reflect] It can't help but affect your spirit, your whole being, working with someone who tells you these things. It's like your heart just punctures, really.

> (Pack, 2009: 47)

It may be that report writing, unlike expressive writing where you 'really let yourself go', re-stimulates traumatic experiences. Perhaps that's why for some, writing becomes a burden, associated with that dread. When Angela uses the metaphor of her heart just puncturing, the need to take some of this anguish to supervision, to move out of isolation and to work with another individual or a group of colleagues, becomes apparent.

USING WRITING IN SUPERVISION

Reflective and reflexive writing can be used before, during or after a group or one-to-one supervision session. Technology also provides choices for clinical supervision and can sometimes involve text-based practice, such as e-mail (Lago & Wright, 2007; Wright & Griffiths, 2010).

Traditionally, clinical supervision has taken place face-to-face. It has mirrored traditional therapeutic practice, with chairs, a low table, a clock and usually some tissues. Telephone supervision is, however, now commonplace and, increasingly, the use of the Internet (Skype, e-mail) is reducing distance and improving limited choices for practitioners who work in remote areas. You may want to work with a clinical supervisor who lives or works at a distance. Working in Fiji and later in Aotearoa New Zealand, I have used e-mail as a vehicle for clinical supervision. E-mailing my supervisor, who lives an hour's drive away, I explained why I don't like the extra time writing takes, but prefer it to the phone.

I prefer writing because essentially it gives me time to reflect (and backspace). When I was practising online in the UK (Wright, 2002), I developed useful habits which have transferred well to telephone and e-mail supervision, for example preparing for our phone supervisions by writing a list to clear the chatter in my mind and writing or drawing some key points after the phone call. I like writing rather than the 'real time' of the phone because I feel less pressured and more in control. I can express whatever I like on paper or on the screen and then re-read and edit before anyone else sees the writing.

(Wright & Griffiths, 2010: 695–6)

ONLINE OR E-MAIL SUPERVISION

There is now some research and published writing into the use of technology in clinical supervision. Most useful perhaps are the case examples with ethical guidelines (Anthony & Goss, 2009). See the website of the International Society for Mental Health Online (www.ismho.org) if you're interested in finding out more. Examples you will find there include case practice from the USA and Europe.

My experience of online counselling began at Sheffield University in 1999. I experimented with e-mail supervision but found it too time-consuming: my typing speed simply couldn't match talking. On the other hand, there was no choice but to use e-mail when I worked as a counsellor in Fiji. Since then using e-mail to communicate with a supervisor has, at times, been both frustrating and illuminating. I'm talking to my supervisor here in Aotearoa New Zealand about our occasional e-mail supervision sessions:

In the e-mail dialogues, we're both likely to feel more 'exposed'. Yet, I'm well aware of being in control of the 'raw material' and of 'editing' before sending you the message. The writing enables me to explore new professional identities, values, new cultural learning. Reflective practice is at the core of this process, whether or not I work with the 'internal supervisor' or with you. (Jeannie)

See Exercises 11.1, 11.2 and 11.3 at the end of this chapter for ways to explore using writing before, during and after supervision.

What is your relationship with technology? In spite of all these years of campaigning and advocating for the use of the Internet in therapy and supervision, I have a very ambivalent relationship with the technological hardware. I find myself writing notes to data projectors, such as this one written on the back of a green flyer and found years later. I had asked participants to do some writing in a workshop on supervision in London, during a heatwave: 'Dear data projector, why did you stop? Are you too hot? In this small room, all 16 supervisors (oops! no, 17) are writing now, mostly women, all over 40, elders.' Or even more heartfelt:

Dear Computer,

I need to finish this writing. You are very old now and beginning to behave erratically. Sometimes fonts change without me doing anything. Sometimes underlining appears, sometimes not. Installing that database that was supposed to make referencing easier was the most desperate mistake. I can't work it. I panic about losing all that I've already done. Sweat breaks out on my scalp. It seems to make you crash. Now I don't know how to uninstall it.

The feeling of not being able to fix it, to be in control of how the finished writing looks, upsets me out of all proportion to the problem. Is this to do with age? Having to use you and other newer computers has contributed to the stress of this writing in untold ways. So, I'm telling those ways now. It has taken all the joy of writing out of it. Yes, you have made Tipp-Ex and other whiting-out tools obsolete but ... I prefer paper and pen/pencil. Maybe newer technology – voice activated? – will help, maybe, maybe not.

Yours truly,

Jeannie

Activity: What is your relationship with technology like?

- Write a letter to your computer, your phone or whatever form of technology you choose. What do you like about it?
- What do you wish were different?

BLOGGING

The Internet provides alternative ways to make professional connections. Blogs, or online public journals, could be useful for practitioners to record their thoughts and receive messages from others in a similar situation. One advantage of blogging is that you can choose to remain anonymous (see www.blogspot.com). Blogs are usually free to set up. Web logging, or blogging, is similar to the process of journal writing, and can be a lot more flexible and accessible.

CONCLUSION

Reflective practice is one of the cornerstones of professional therapeutic relationships. Witnessing pain, working with people who are in despair, or at times expressing rage or the deepest anguish, takes its toll. Writing reflectively and reflexively, whether in supervision or not, can offer insight and inspiration and can restore calm.

Practitioners need to find their own way to be themselves in practice in counselling and psychotherapy. In the early stages of professional relationships, it can be tempting to revere and mimic the supervisors' ways of being and professional identities. Reflective and reflexive writing enables practitioners, whether novice or more experienced, to be themselves, in private on the page, and then to choose what to share in supervision.

In this chapter and the next we look at ways of continuing to develop reflective and reflexive journal writing as lifelong habits.

Write!

11.1 Reflecting on practice

This exercise in reflective practice would work best if you have recorded some of your counselling or psychotherapy sessions, audio or video recording, whichever is acceptable to your clients. You could then select a particular passage which you think is critical in the work you're doing with an individual client.

- Choose an incident from your counselling or psychotherapy practice.
- Describe the incident or situation in some detail.
- Consider what the personal impact was for you, for example how did you feel during this incident? How did you feel after the situation or incident had finished?
- List what your professional learning from this incident might be – what went well?
- What might you have done differently?

11.2 Before supervision

Take three long, slow breaths, close your eyes and focus on your current clients for a few minutes. When you open your eyes, you might be aware of some gaps in your recollection of your current clients. Write notes in response to these questions:

- Does one client come immediately to mind?
- Of your current clients, who is persistently not present?
- Whose face/voice/presence seems to be hard to conjure up?

Your pattern in supervision might be to follow your impulse. You might want to experiment to see what you actually tend to focus on using this kind of writing. Alternatively, your supervision might be highly structured, working through each client in turn with your case formulations and plan. Writing some notes before supervision about what is 'on top' for you will save time and help focus the session.

11.3 During supervision: writing/drawing

I tend to doodle and scribble notes during supervision so I can remember key points. I might also use other expressive and creative methods, like drawing or a sand tray. Negotiate with your supervisor or supervision group how you might use writing.

- Make a decision to notice the kinds of metaphors you use to describe clients or colleagues in supervision.
- Write them down.
- What can you learn about your relationships with clients and supervisor by focusing on the metaphorical language you use in supervision?

11.4 After supervision

You might decide immediately what the focus was, what you've learned from that supervision session, and spend five minutes free writing before you get back into your day's work or routine.

Try a free writing exercise immediately after your next supervision. List what you have learned. See below for an example.

After a recent phone supervision, where I was working on the need for greater clarity with a colleague, I wrote the following notes in the car before leaving for my next appointment:

When we worked through the particulars of that difficult piece of communication I wanted to rehearse, there was a light-bulb moment. I realised it is the last step in the assertiveness model we were using that I habitually forget. So, I described the problem specifically enough; I expressed how I felt without getting too angry or upset; I explained how I would like the problem to be solved, but then I 'forgot' to name the consequences, either positive or negative, the rewards or the negative consequences that will result if we don't resolve the situation. I didn't lay my cards on the table! I tend to cave in too easily, and if I can break the habit of forgetting the final stage, it would help me hold my own, and lead to clearer communication with this person.

11.5 Advice to yourself

Imagine you could go back in time and meet yourself at the very beginning of working in counselling and psychotherapy. It might be your first day of training, or your first session with a client.

- What advice would you offer?
- Don't just think it or speak it: write it down.

(Continued)

(Continued)

11.6 Blogging

You need an Internet connection for this exercise, because a blog is a web page, an online journal which you can access wherever you are. A user-friendly provider can be found at www.blogger.com. Video instructions are provided. It should take you no more than five minutes to set up; it's easy to register and the page will then have its own URL.

If there is nothing that comes to mind that you want to write about immediately on your new blog, you might want to write about the present, using some of the forms of writing we suggested in Chapter 8, 'Here and now: Writing the present'. The first step in this kind of writing is to observe how you are right now.

As before, pausing and reflecting, using the technique of first-aid breathing – three long, slow, deep breaths – provides a springboard to start writing.

12

Assessment

Signposts for assessing personal development writing

Philip: Exhausted – we just spent a whole afternoon on assessing the personal journals. We had to write one page, a distillation they called it, about our learning during the course, based on our personal journal writing. I stayed up most of the night just re-reading my journals. In groups of three, we then gave feedback to each other, pointing out any obvious omissions or blind spots in the one-pager. Finally, when we all got back together as a group, we each read out our one-page, summarising our personal development. There was then an opportunity for staff and other students to comment. So nervous – I don't know which I was thinking would be worse, having to comment on the others in the group or hearing what they and the tutors had to say about me. It felt good when it was over.

Anita: So, it seems a few years ago, students had to hand in their personal development journals to tutors for assessment. I'm glad they put a stop to that. Now we look at the self-practice/self-reflection we've worked on, some of the material anyway, in small groups. It seems the assessment is based on how we had engaged with those exercises, as much as anything. The criteria for pass/fail seem pretty fuzzy to me, observing our 'thoughts, beliefs and feelings' – how? I can see how we can observe if someone's used Socratic questions and other technical skills. At the end of all this we have to write a blog, a summary of the experience of self-practice and self-reflection. We'll see.

Jo: It was pretty obvious which of us in the group had taken the personal development journal writing seriously. There were some embarrassed looks when we had to discuss where we were up to in the writing. I think some people just don't get it and see it as a chore. I think if you write the whole lot at the end of the course, pretending to reflect on the experience, it's just a waste of time. I really object to tutors having the right to read our journals. Self and peer assessment is probably the best way to assess personal writing like this.

I (Jeannie Wright) asked a group of counselling students if they would keep a personal journal as part of their therapeutic training if it weren't assessed. There were some sheepish looks. One smiled and said, 'Sometimes I'm feeling fine and have nothing to say. Then I worry and feel guilty because I'm not writing in my journal.' Another said, 'I write anyway, it's for me.' Several admitted that they would probably not keep it going if they knew the journal would not be assessed at all, and 'It feels as if you value it more if it's assessed.'

Some counselling and psychotherapy students feel strongly about their subjective experiences and personal reflections being assessed, and especially graded:

If anyone sits down to mark it in an academic framework, it would be nonsense anyway, because I might have written one entry, erm, 'daughter's birthday today – got drunk' as a splurge on to a piece of paper, against one and a half pieces where I might bring in, for example, authors or research into that bit, so there are things all over the place anyway. It seems impossible to score.

(Sutton et al., 2007: 395–6)

The very idea of assessing something so subjective seems nonsensical:

It's such an individual thing. How do you mark it whether it is passed or not? If it's your own reflections it could mean something to you but be absolutely meaningless to somebody else, 'cause it is purely personal. So how do you say if that's good or bad? (p. 396)

This chapter considers how expressive and reflective writing can be evaluated as part of counselling and psychotherapy education and CPD. It may be that this chapter is more interesting to tutors/assessors than to students; however, that assumes a tutor-assessed model. Many counselling and psychotherapy programmes use self and peer assessment of personal journal writing, as Jo advises above.

How a personal journal is used and assessed will depend on the theoretical orientation of the programme. All assessment, however, depends on students knowing how and why they are being assessed and on what, whichever therapeutic orientation is offered. Most teaching and learning now involves providing clear assessment criteria so that students can judge for themselves how they measure up.

ASSESSMENT CRITERIA AND GOALS FOR PERSONAL DEVELOPMENT

Here's an example of a goal for personal development journal writing from a psychodynamic perspective:

> Identify ways in which past history, family of origin and life experiences have impacted on the current way of relating to others and demonstrate an ability to process the negative impact as it may manifest itself in a counselling relationship.
>
> (Wheeler, 2002)

From a cognitive behavioural point of view, 'self-as-therapist' is the term used to enable practitioners to manage the limits of their therapeutic relationships and their personal reactions to clients. Therapists and need to be aware of their own thoughts, feelings and beliefs, and the following is an example of how that might be assessed from a CBT perspective:

> Choosing a specific issue of your own, apply Socratic dialogue and write down the results. When you apply the conceptualisations to yourself, how easy or difficult is it to see your assumptions and core beliefs? Reflect in writing on this experience.

Another example, from a reflective writing course, provided the following list, which could be applied to therapeutic practice. It asked students for:

- Writing with careful, detailed observation of events and situations.
- Writing showing examples of empathising with other people.
- Writing that notices the various emotional dimensions of events and situations.
- Writing addressing the complexities of issues, events and situations.
- Writing that makes connections between different events and situations, and between specific details and general principles derived from a range of professional knowledge.
- Writing that demonstrates learning, in response to both professional experience and the process of reflecting upon/writing about it.

(Winter & Sobiechowska, 1999: 108)

Competence in particular areas of counselling and psychotherapy practice and training will probably increasingly be guided by nationally recognised standards, drawn from core curricula. This list is a good starting point, however, which can be adapted to meet the particular theoretical orientation and needs of CPD and therapy training.

If your counselling and psychotherapy course provides clear criteria for your personal development writing, such as those listed above, you might be able to see how you can ensure success in assessment. Here's an example:

EXAMPLE
Ensuring success in assessment

Criterion 1: writing careful, detailed observation of events and situations

This morning a boy came to see me – he'd been 'sent' for counselling by his teacher. He made no eye contact at all, from me opening the door to him leaving five minutes later. He texted throughout our meeting, chewed some sort of fruit-smelling gum, and every now and then blew bubbles from it.

Criterion 2: writing with examples of empathising

I knew something about this boy and that he was often in trouble. Kids have so little power in schools. Counselling, when mandated, becomes part of social control. He looked closed down, pale, angry.

Criterion 3: writing that notices emotional dimensions of events and situations

He somehow pressed all my buttons. I suppose we all want to be, famously, the one highly skilled professional who can get through to disaffected adolescents like this. I just felt a complete failure.

Criterion 4: writing that addresses the complexities of context

I knew that if he was suspended from school again, he would be at risk of permanent exclusion. So, from meetings with the head of year, and from the exasperation some of his other teachers expressed in the staff room, I suspected that this boy had run out of chances.

Criterion 5: writing that makes connections

The boy's father had phoned me after his last suspension. He wanted me to know that the boy's mother had recently left home, taking two of their children with her. They would all be going to a new school, but the boy had begged his father not to make him start a new school, again. I needed to weigh up the ethical dimensions of some of this information.

Criterion 6: writing that demonstrates learning in response to both professional experience and process of reflecting upon/writing about it

With my supervisor, I looked at the options for how I could intervene in any way in this situation. We also discussed the strong feelings that came up and what that might be about. For me, when faced with apparently intractable school systems, and the kind of rage I used to feel at school, I want students to know where I stand. I might look like part of the system, but ...

Had I been a tutor or peer assessing this work I would have passed this piece of writing, which is concise, insightful and meets all six criteria very effectively.

SELF, PEER AND TUTOR ASSESSMENT

Research into the assessment of writing for personal development in counselling and psychotherapy is very limited. Reflective writing and reflective practice in other disciplines have a much more extensive research base (Bolton, 2010). If you are a student, learning outcomes and assessment criteria will flow from the orientation of your particular counselling or psychotherapy course.

A person centred programme would manage the process of assessing reflective writing according to the values of the person centred approach (see example below). Person centred practitioners may see personal development writing as part of experiential group work.

CBT training, on the other hand, is unlikely to require personal experiential group work as a means of personal development. However, as a training tool to enhance CBT practice, self-practice and self-reflection are increasingly encouraged (Bennett-Levy et al., 2001).

We take the view that if students know that their personal journals will have to be submitted for assessment, even if only on a pass/fail basis, the writing will be inhibited and/or results will be skewed (see Bolton, 2010). For example, students might write for the tutor, 'I wanted my tutor to know ....', or would censor the writing in various ways:

> I've certainly withheld mine. There's a lot of information that I could have used but withheld because I don't want anyone else reading it. It's very personal stuff.
>
> (Sutton et al., 2007: 396)

Clear criteria and protocols need to be agreed at the outset, however assessment of personal journals is managed. Some students use journals for therapeutic purposes and need to know where to go for support if distressing patterns emerge, for example. If students are required to submit their personal writing, they need to understand how feedback will be offered:

> It can be quite scary, especially when there is no comeback, you know, it's like, if you had a client who phoned and told you something and you just totally ignored it.
>
> (Wright, 2005: 514)

Practitioners and students need to be in control of their own personal writing. It therefore follows that they are given the right to assess that writing against whatever criteria are appropriate if they are in a training programme.

The example below would be consistent with a person centred counsellor education programme. Criteria for assessing personal development journals are:

- The personal journal will contain examples of how a person has developed a sense of and sensitivity to the cultural contexts that individuals exist in, and how this might affect the helping relationship that they can offer to others in counselling.
- The writing in the personal journal shows how the person reflects on their own experiences, at an emotional and cognitive level, in relation to their understanding of person centred theory. Reference to Carl Rogers' six conditions for therapeutic growth are useful but not exclusive (Rogers, 1957).
- The writing indicates how the person has related effectively with others in the training group, reflecting on their responses and behaviour and how it affects others.
- The writing examinees prejudices and provides evidence of ways in which interpersonal difficulties and prejudices have been faced and overcome.
- The journal writing shows how the person is able to trace changes in their thoughts, feelings and behaviour as the course has progressed. These changes may be directly related to learning or personal goals they have set themselves.

Using these criteria, we will use a brief example of Philip's writing to consider self and peer assessment.

Self assessment

Drawing on what we've called 'the raw material' of the writing takes time. Re-reading that raw material is very much part of the reflective process, as is condensing what might amount to hundreds of pages into a reflective statement. Reflective practice models, well-known in nursing, social work, teaching and other human services, are perhaps less well known and less researched in counselling and psychotherapy (Bolton, 2010).

Philip's experience of an intensive small-group activity is one example of how this 'reflecting on the reflections' might be managed. It is usually an intense session and needs careful facilitation (Bleakley, 2000). Producing his one-page personal learning statement might have taken several hours. Here's an extract:

Philip: I notice when I read the notes I write after working with clients how often I pick up on feelings, theirs and mine, and that my perceptions are usually accurate. The feedback forms at work are also rated high on 'feeling understood'. Empathy and unconditional positive regard are some strengths that others have noticed.

Growing edges: I find it much easier to stay with the client and not challenge them. Work in supervision with one particular ethical dilemma helped me sort out how to challenge and when, but I don't think it will ever be very comfortable for me to challenge others in group work. For example, I have often disagreed with one particular student in our group but stayed silent. I would have liked to have intervened and have written down some ways I might have said something earlier.

In supervision I've worked on my lack of assertiveness and think I am improving in building stronger and clearer communication skills. For example, I have written a lot in my journal about one particular client and how hard it was not to judge, and yet challenge his prejudices. I did challenge him, however, and the result, on the recording of the session, was useful for him.

Peer assessment: giving and receiving constructive feedback

Giving and receiving feedback is a skill which can be developed. It may well be part of the counselling or psychotherapy initial therapeutic education you are currently involved in or have undertaken. Particularly in skills training exercises in triads, you have probably experienced working as client, counsellor and observer. Taking the role of the observer during therapeutic practice means that you are already familiar with giving feedback to one of your peer group who is taking part in the triad as the counsellor.

Constructive feedback, given skilfully, increases self-awareness and offers alternatives to current ways of behaving. Feedback needs to start with the positive. Most people need encouragement, to be told when they're doing something well. In formal education, the focus has often been on mistakes, rather than on strengths. When looking at what could be improved, be specific. For example, if you say, 'at that point in the session, you seemed to be imposing your values on the client', you are providing more opportunities for learning if you pinpoint the exact sentence or moment in the counselling session.

Similar guidelines might apply in giving feedback to one of your peers on their personal and reflective writing. We suggest that support and challenge are key. Mutual congratulation and back-patting can become nauseating; however, destructive and unfocused criticism is even more unproductive. Therefore, following the principles of the positive/negative (or 'growing edge') sandwich, here's an example in response to Philip's one pager:

Positive feedback: One of your great strengths, Philip, as this writing indicates, is your ability to stand in other people's shoes. You seem to tune in to other people's feelings very readily. You also seem to be able to communicate that empathic response and during this course you have demonstrated that many times in the group.

Growing edge: A suggestion would be for you to be more assertive in your challenging. You seem to hold back, particularly when you're working with people in the group who are louder than you are. There is an example in your reflective writing when you talk about … .

Positive: I celebrate the way you have taken risks in challenging stereotypes and prejudice in your work with clients.

Tutor assessment

Gadamer (2004: 393) quotes Plato as having said that the specific weakness of writing was that no one could come to the aid of the written word if it fell victim to misunderstanding, intentional or otherwise. When I write an assessment on a student's personal writing, I can sometimes become totally paralysed by the fear of being misunderstood.

As in clinical supervision, a climate of trust is crucial for critical reflection to flourish. So, in practice, a gentle approach, often asking questions rather than making statements, can be useful (Morley, 2007). Positioning my assessment so that the student does not feel personally criticised by the process, yet gains something from my written comments, takes time. Here's an example of a response to a student who wrote about feeling burned-out after having taken on an additional placement:

> You have gone out of your way to seek ways of increasing your practice hours. I can understand your dilemma, and applaud your honesty and insight in this writing; however, self-care is another ethical principle that seems to need some attention. How are you going to look after yourself if you take on this additional work? I would ask you to consider talking about this extra placement in supervision, if you haven't already. (Jeannie Wright)

Assessing the personal journal is fraught. A student on a CBT programme says:

> It's threatening to complete it rather than motivating to complete it because you've got to pass it or fail it. It's not a good feeling.

> (Sutton et al., 2007: 397)

Across the occupational areas where reflective practice is part of the initial training curriculum, and increasingly part of CPD, triadic assessment – by self, peers and tutors – seems to be most acceptable (Bolton, 2010).

SOME RECOMMENDATIONS TO ASSESSORS

Ensure that criteria for assessment are made clear to candidates, and linked to learning or professional objectives. If possible, allow time and space for assessment criteria to be negotiated with candidates. Professional bodies seeking to assess CPD may find this process difficult. Counselling and psychotherapy education lends itself to class discussions where criteria for the assessment of personal development journals can be debated. Self-assessment is usually acceptable to students, and although giving feedback to peers is uncomfortable at first, its value is quickly grasped.

Other forms and opportunities for reflective practice, for example clinical supervision, could and should be linked to personal journal writing. Some professional bodies require a written letter to support a candidate's application for membership or accreditation. Again, this process takes time and the supervisor would be wise to ask for the candidate's written application well ahead of writing a letter of support.

Communicate clearly during training situations – and not just at the beginning of the session – how sensitive material in personal journal writing will be managed.

Recommendations to practitioners and students

Ensure that you know what the criteria for assessment of your personal development writing are. If they are not made clear to you, keep asking. Assessing the journal against criteria such as those given as examples in this chapter takes a significant amount of time, so it is unwise to leave this process to the last minute. For example, you might be asked for peer and self assessment of your personal development writing against the following criteria:

- Identifying personal strengths.
- Identifying growing edges and blind spots and suggesting ways in which these may be overcome.

Decide who you are going to share some of your personal journal writing with and from whom you will seek feedback. Then consider which of the feedback you want to keep and which you want to let go of. Check how and where you are going to carry out this peer and self assessment. It is always valuable to be specific and to reflect on particular incidents, rather than to make vague claims. The implications of this learning for your work with clients, in whatever setting, acts as an important backdrop to what might appear to be a mechanistic exercise.

CONCLUSION

Assessing personal and professional development writing is complex. The purpose of the writing and the criteria for evaluation must be clear and explicit, whether in initial training or CPD.

To assessors: If your programme requires students to submit their personal development journals to staff for assessment, clarify what this means. For example, does this mean you are expecting students to edit the raw material of their journal writing in some way? A self/peer/tutor assessment model is recommended.

Write!

12.1 Significant events

List the significant activities you have undertaken over the past year, for example conferences, courses, seminars and workshops attended or offered/delivered. Assess how these activities have improved your practice.

12.2 What have you read?

List any professional reading, books, articles, reports or reviews that have made a significant impact on you recently. Describe how this reading has contributed to your practice, giving at least one detailed example.

12.3 Future plans

What are your plans for future professional development? Explain how you anticipate the value of these activities and how you expect to make use of this CPD in practice.

12.4 Application for accreditation

Reflective responses in writing are often at the heart of applications for membership of professional bodies or for accreditation. What is your experience of applying for professional membership? How did you assess your achievements? What would your most brutal critic say about your application? Write a response to their criticism.

12.5 Write a reference for yourself

Write a reference for yourself as if you were writing it for someone else. Use the third person, for example: 'Jo often goes the extra mile, especially to ensure ethical practice. She has become a valued colleague and someone to whom we all tend to turn when we are facing ethical dilemmas.'

There are often strong cultural and social values that cause us to feel discomforted by being 'a tall poppy' or 'blowing our own trumpets'. If you find this exercise uncomfortable, team up with someone who can help you with 'professional boasting'.

13

Arrivals and Continuing the Journey

Reflective writing for CPD; essential questions

I'm making connections now between professional knowledge, theory and the emotional dimensions of work with clients. Taking the time to write in my journal, and re-reading my own words, still helps me to gain a more balanced perspective.

(Therapist at a CPD workshop)

Philip: Where I work now, it suits me – for a start, it's important to me that people who can't afford private therapy get a good deal. And they do at this agency. I always enjoyed client work, and that's got better if anything. Some of my colleagues get on my nerves. I have written letters to some of them about things that have happened, and, by the time I've finished, I've thought: 'I'm not sending that' because I feel better and I don't need to do anything else, other than just get rid of all this crap.

Anita: I never thought I'd carry on writing this journal but I have. What I've written recently is more like having a moan – a catalogue of the moans and groans that go with everyday irritations. Since I moved back home, I've got used to some things – like intermittent power cuts when you're in the middle of writing a report, or trying to use e-mail for supervision. Sometimes the entries get smaller, especially when work is hectic, but I still use a lot of what I write before supervision in my e-mails to my supervisor back in the UK. There have been some particular ethical knots where the writing has been really useful. I never imagined I'd end up working with children, but I love it.

Jo: After I qualified and got a job, and worked my way through professional accreditation, I went downhill a bit with my journal as well, just too busy. I suppose that's how it is – sometimes you need to write more than others, and sometimes you make a space to write. I loved the personal development writing more than others in my group, but over the last few years it's become much more a part of my practice and not something I do separately on my own. This workshop about using client's words 'rescuing speech', in fact only using words that clients have spoken in therapy was fantastic. I started writing 'rescued speech poems'.

CONTINUING PERSONAL AND PROFESSIONAL DEVELOPMENT WRITING

Personal and professional development writing can be a lifelong, profession-long practice. The methods explained in this book can help develop clarity in ethical thinking and decision making. Writing creates a closer focus, a reflective, attentive slowing-down similar to meditation, which can also be crucial for self-care. This concluding chapter addresses both these issues.

To end the book, Philip, Anita and Jo are still asking developmental questions, some of which they address directly to us, Jeannie and Gillie. Our answers offer a range of reasons to continue personal development writing, with examples based on our experience and theoretical understandings. Here, as throughout the book, we offer maps, navigational aids and signposts without claiming prescriptive knowledge about the impact of reflective and autobiographical writing on professional practice.

AUTOBIOGRAPHICAL MEMORY AND WRITING

The ancient Greeks and Romans viewed regular introspective writing as part of moral self-discovery, and ultimately an aid in living a better life. As mentioned in Chapter 5, autobiographical writing is a classical Western tradition. Do you come from a culture where self-writing is a longstanding way of training yourself to live a good life? There are many spiritual traditions in which 'confessional' writing has a long history (Abbs, 1998). For example, in the Christian tradition, the image of the 'recording angel' is strong. Saint Ignatius, before every period of prayer, asked himself: 'What do I truly want?' (Johns, 1996). Is this kind of self-discovery more associated for you with talking, or possibly meditating?

Theories change, and are illuminated by developments in research. Relatively recent studies in neuroscience cast additional light on autobiographical memory and consciousness:

We are not conscious of which memories we store and which memories we do not; of how we store memories; of how we classify and organise them; of how we inter-relate memories of varied sensory types, different topics and different emotional significance. We have usually little direct control over the 'strength' of memories or over the ease or difficulty with which they will be retrieved in recall. We have all sorts of interesting intuitions, of course, about the emotional value, robustness, and the depth of memories. We have a solid corpus of research on factors governing learning and retrieval of memory, as well as on the neural systems required to support and retrieve memories. But direct, conscious knowledge, we do not have.

(Damasio, 2000: 226)

Some kinds of writing suggested in this book aim to reach into unconscious knowing, just as other creative therapeutic activities do. Other kinds of writing aim for logic and clarity, and especially where the goal is to think more clearly about an ethical dilemma, for example.

ETHICS AND PROFESSIONAL PRACTICE

After a group of counsellors and psychotherapists had just finished a 6-minute free write, I ask for their comments:

'Writing enables me to see what I think.'
'It's easier to write it than to say it face-to-face.'
'I was struggling with that particular ethical issue, and now I've written it down, it's clear what I need to do.'

Ethical decision making in the talking therapies is increasingly complex; there is no simple, prescribed ethical code to follow and therapists must use ethical reasoning to reflect on options (Bond, 2010). Ethical dilemmas and possible solutions emerge in the moment: writing can productively assist the process. The very act of writing down a dilemma can help resolve it. Sharing the process with a colleague or clinical supervisor can also be useful, for example:

> A therapist in supervision said, 'Yes, now I've written the e-mail I don't need an extra appointment. Seeing my thoughts on the screen – it's just like hearing myself talk out loud.'

Activity: Ethical anxiety

Think of a recent client who created ethical anxiety for you. Perhaps you regarded them as at risk of self-harm or suspected of illegal activities. Briefly write down the key points of your concerns (see Exercise 13.2 for a useful framework for analysing a situation before discussion with colleagues or supervisor).

SELF-CARE

Some details of clients' stories stay with you. Counselling conversations can stay in the mind, becoming 'intrusive thoughts', even causing sleeplessness and symptoms of stress. One practitioner compared writing out a particularly 'hard to hear' story as a kind of exorcism: 'I just had to get that stuff out'.

Most professional ethical guidelines apply to practitioners as well as to clients: everything relevant to clients' well-being is also relevant to practitioners. Yet it is very easy to forget this ethical responsibility to ourselves. Counselling and psychotherapy are rewarding activities – practitioners often comment upon the privilege. Therapeutic work can also be demanding and draining, however.

EXAMPLE
Self-care at work

David works in a hospital paediatric setting:

People ask me 'How do you work with critically sick children and their families?' I sit in the chapel when I arrive at the hospital and go through my major personal concerns, carefully laying them aside there, to be picked up later. I use the chapel, despite not being religious, as I can be certain of being undisturbed. Then, before I leave, I return and reflect upon the patients and parents I've seen, leaving my care for them in the chapel – so I don't take them home with me; well of course I do, but as less of a burden and with more hope. And I pick up my own concerns again. And do you know? My own bag of cares feels so much lighter after reflecting upon the horrors faced by those brave kids and their families. (David)

Self-care in counselling and psychotherapy is not optional. It is embedded within a number of professional codes of ethics, and links with competence to practice.

> Attending to the practitioner's well-being is essential to sustaining good practice ... practitioners have a responsibility to themselves to ensure that their work does not become detrimental to their health or well-being by ensuring that the way that they undertake their work is as safe as possible and that they seek appropriate professional support and services as the need arises.
>
> (BACP, 2010: 10)

Practitioners have sometimes noticed how negative some of their 'self talk' can be through writing dialogues or letters to themselves. Writing can help turn down or submerge such critical voices, allowing kinder words to be heard. Self-doubt can be turned into self-counselling. One therapist, Chris, wrote to herself:

> Dear Chris
>
> I like your humour, that irreverence that bubbles up even when you're under a lot of stress – it's not ingratiating. You're not into pleasing other people much. I also noticed how self-critical you can become, particularly when you're tired and stressed. As your internal wise adviser, I would suggest you keep some of that laughter in your life. You need to take care to self-care.
>
> Best Wishes
>
> Chris

Supervision is an important part of self-care. Sharing problems in an empathic, collegial relationship allows space for healthier perspectives. Making notes to take to supervision can help express feelings, create priorities, and help clarify thinking. Here's Chris again with some notes to take to supervision. She got up and wrote in the middle of the night:

> This big move coming up is already keeping me awake, and then waking me up far too early. The new job itself isn't the problem; I've noticed my old patterns of displacing my anxiety into very minor things. Some trivial things that are worrying me at four o'clock in the morning will make you laugh: for example, will I be able to use the electric stapler in the new office (I still can't use that one in my old office and I've been trying to for 5 years – it's become an office joke).

Chris came away from supervision with a checklist of old stress patterns to notice, and reminders about how she coped before in similar transitions: 'Walk to work instead of driving; book to go swimming with a friend at least once a week; take extra magnesium and other supplements; listen to the mindfulness relaxation recording at least twice a week.' It's not that we don't know how to manage self-care, it's more about reminding ourselves and connecting with that knowledge. With these commitments written in her diary, and discussed in supervision, Chris moved into more constructive ways of dealing with the normal stress associated with moving jobs.

MINDFULNESS

Mindfulness is a way of including spiritual dimensions in writing in counselling and psychotherapy. Some of the benefits of mindfulness include:

* being fully engaged in the moment, whatever the activity
* developing an alert yet calm focus on the current situation

- fostering links between body and mind
- being with the breath, which is grounding and can make contact with emotional states
- preventing ruminative, uselessly circular thinking
- paying attention to the simple – often more effective than analysis of the complex
- building an ability to focus and direct attention.

Jack used mindfulness to enable him to intuit the needs of his counselling clients:

> Sally bounced in, so different from last time. 'I wrote what you said; I did my homework!' I smiled and nodded, not even trying to remember what I'd suggested. She read me her deliciously bright account of a first birthday party. 'You can't believe the difference it's made to remember happy times. I've read this to both our parents, and others; and we've got the old photos out too.'
>
> I smile at her more broadly. I know I won't remember what I'd said to encourage her to focus upon good times with her baby before he died. Because I never know what I'm going to suggest people write: I listen to them, and then open my mouth knowing that whatever I say will flow from the clarity of my focus upon them during the session. It wouldn't work if I planned it, or consciously thought about what would be best for them. My suggestions to them come from my awareness of them, my mindfulness in the moment with them. (Jack)

You may have found other ways to create space for reflection as part of your professional development. You may also still have queries about how to use reflective writing. Below, Philip, Anita and Jo raise some questions to which Jeannie and Gillie respond.

SOME QUESTIONS AND RESPONSES

Anita: They say I can just write anything. This whole thing makes me nervous, it is too swampy. How can I feel less overwhelmed by journal writing? It sometimes seems too chaotic.

Jeannie and Gillie: Yes, like swimming in the sea, whether the English Channel or the Pacific Ocean, you might want to swim within the flags at first, and limit the time you spend in the water. It might also feel safer to swim with a companion.

Your important question concerns boundaries. Reflective writing is most useful when you create your own boundaries to give sufficient structure and safety. These boundaries might change and develop, just like you might swim within your depth and with lifeguards on hand until you feel more confident. You might decide upon a time duration, a specific time and place to write, and whether or when to write with company or alone, and when, how and with whom to share your writing. You can also make decisions about content before you start; for example, one day you might only write about client issues and on another day allow yourself to focus upon tricky personal material. You can decide to use certain forms which you know will take you in deep, such as some of the letter writing exercises described in *Reflective Writing in Counselling and Psychotherapy*; or you might feel like playing safe sometimes by describing a situation minutely, promising to re-read critically to develop it reflexively at a later date when you feel stronger.

Boundary is a metaphorical term indicating how counsellors and psychotherapists put up fences as if a session were a field. For example, sessions are given with specific appointment times within quiet, private spaces – ethical frameworks and therapeutic contracts are created promising confidentiality and professional conduct.

Writing will hopefully take you out of the shallows where you've practiced swimming. The exercises within the book, whether at chapter end or within the chapters, have encouraged you to practice personal and professional development writing. Even if it sometimes feels risky, you can write anything because, although you aim to get underneath your censors, you set the boundaries. As in counselling and psychotherapy practice, you can decide which boundaries you need in place and how to change them, depending on the context and situation.

Philip:	How can I allow myself to write about clients and other people? It feels really dangerous.
Jeannie and Gillie:	Writing about other people, especially clients, needs great care. The ethical framework you work within applies here and you need to ensure that ethical principles are respected. For example, it makes sense not to write real names, or too many recognisable details which might breach confidentiality contracts. You are the first and only reader of your writing unless you decide otherwise, so you keep this material private, changing details or using code if you decide to share it. You must take responsibility for either ensuring the writing is encrypted (if it's digital), destroying the writing if it's on paper, and/or safeguarding clients' rights within the writing.

Experimenting with the exercises which suggest writing in the third person and about fictional characters might help you feel more comfortable with expressing honestly your thoughts and feelings about other people (see Chapter 8, 'Here and now: Writing the present'). Reflective and expressive writing about other people must follow clear guidelines. Here are some starting points: ideally, write in such a way that the people themselves would be able to read and collaborate; if you need to, conceal the identity of the person you are writing about to the point where they would not recognise themselves, by using a composite of people, changing gender, identifying details and so on. If you have to use writing to vent some very negative feelings, as Philip did at the beginning of this chapter, make sure you destroy the writing immediately.

Anita:	I still struggle with this subjectivity of it all. Certainly at the beginning of keeping a journal I was constantly worrying about using 'I'. One of my early journal entries reads: 'Surely for this course I'm not allowed to use "I" – it feels more like writing stories. We did this in primary school.'
Jeannie and Gillie:	In personal development writing, using 'I' means you 'own' what you're saying. It says clearly how you position yourself to the feelings and thoughts being expressed.

Writing in the first person, using 'I', is personal and expresses thoughts and feelings with immediacy. For example: 'I suddenly felt anxious, even my stomach started churning'. Formal, scientific and conventional academic writing aims for objectivity, and distances the reader by using the third person, 'the author', 'he' or 'it', banishing subjectivity. For example: 'The counsellor felt anxious and said the anxiety was located in her stomach.' Traditional academic disciplines do not forbid the use of the first person; the highest rating journals over the world contain many papers freely using that little but expressively vital word 'I'. Counselling and psychotherapy encourage writing subjectively to claim your voice, just as you use 'I' with clients in practice.

Most exercises in *Reflective Writing* encourage your own voice to come through strongly, to enable effective writing about life and work experiences. The exceptions are where distancing is useful, and when writing from the point of view of a third person narrator can feel safer (see Kim Etherington's examples in Chapter 7).

Jo:	Writing pins me down too much. How can I shake off that feeling of being exposed in writing?
Jeannie and Gillie:	Perhaps this comment is about feeling uncomfortable when you start writing in visible places. Even if what you are writing seems boring or mundane, the chance that your writing might attract readers causes anxiety. Your writing is for your eyes only until you choose otherwise. Seeing what you're thinking or feeling in writing is magical, because you can change it. Rather than feeling pinned down, perhaps you could try writing on a children's magic pad, where when you lift the page the writing disappears. The reflective or expressive writing is then only visible to you or anyone else for an instant.

On the other hand, as bloggers and tweeters know, there is a collective value in taking the time to reflect and write about challenging things. You make a connection with others who might think as you do; on the other hand, they might disagree. You know about this, Jo, the Internet as both a curse and a blessing, because you've been blogging for years. I wonder if you feel as exposed in your blogging?

Philip:	I am beginning to wonder what I'm going to do with all my journal and other writing. I can see the benefits of expressing how I'm feeling and what I'm thinking, but by storing some of the writing and being asked to re-read it, I sometimes go back to places I don't find particularly positive or useful. Why do I have to re-read?
Gillie and Jeannie:	Because this writing is a dialogue with yourself. It's only on re-reading that you discover certain elements in the writing. It's also very easy to forget what you've written, even if it seemed incredibly exciting at the time. The process of writing is itself a learning process. The initial dash of writing can be deeply inspirational or even cathartic. Then re-reading to the self can be a surprisingly educative: *yes I did write this, I do remember/feel/think this!* And then sharing it with another is the third stage; reading your writing aloud can be important, as this gives it voice, really brings it into the world of consciousness. Another's response can be vitally useful; they might point out elements or connections we'd missed and would never have noticed or intuited ourselves.

Writing reflectively, following re-reading or discussion with another, can be very useful too. There are many suggestions in *Reflective Writing in Counselling and Psychotherapy* for ways of rewriting stories of experience (such as from the point of view of someone else who was present).

Some writing is best destroyed unread, however; follow your instinct as to what's best for you at the time. Otherwise, as far as possible, write, re-read, share significant pieces with another or a group.

Jo:	Sometimes when I'm writing to vent irritation or contempt, I really don't like myself very much. It gets it out of my system and often stops me from getting into all kinds of tensions with people. But I really don't know that I want to express some of this bile. What do you mean, I can't write the wrong thing?
Gillie and Jeannie:	You will write about your own experience. You are the world authority on your own experience and so can't get it wrong.

You were probably taught there are right and wrong ways to write, as I was. But that was writing for a public audience, the youthful equivalent of the final manuscript of a book, essay or article. A journal is a different type of writing. The personal content is the only thing that matters, the story you are able to tell about events with their attendant thoughts, feelings and memories. If you can put on one side anxiety about the *form* of the writing, and allow yourself to write what's there to be written within you, you will do it well. And it will communicate to the tiny readership for which it's intended. Even it you follow none of the suggestions and activities in this book, as long as you write openly, expressively and exploratively, then the content of that writing will always be right *for you*, even if the grammar is sometimes wrong.

Anita:	How can I be sure writing it down won't make me feel worse? There's something about seeing my thoughts and feelings on the screen – when I see things in writing, they become more real.
Gillie and Jeannie:	Well, it depends what you mean by *worse*. It might make you feel initially more vulnerable. It will almost certainly make you more uncertain of yourself for a while because you will be questioning assumptions and taken-for-granteds which have hitherto been seemingly safe boundaries for your life. One of the functions of this journal writing is to question our status quo. Journal writing's job is to shake our certainties, facing us, for example, with those occasions when our actions are *not* consonant with the values we tell ourselves and others we hold.

Our practice and habitual ways of being are questioned in the writing process. I suppose this can be expressed as 'feeling worse as a result of writing'. The old adage 'no pain, no gain' has some resonance here (though I don't think we always have to suffer pain to gain the goodies of life). Like anything worth doing, personal and professional development is neither comfortable nor easy, though it certainly does have its joys. If it seems to be straightforward and personally undemanding, then it's probably not doing very much for you.

If you do ever feel really shaky, then find the right person to talk to and be with about it – a peer, counsellor, therapist or tutor. Remember your life partner might not be the best person initially.

All these negatives are about immediate response to journal writing. Once the stage of uncertainty and tackling the difficulties of change is over, then the benefits of that development can really be reaped.

Write!

13.1 Where will you be in 5 years' time?

Fantasy is a great way to allow you to be aware of possibilities, alternate lifestyles and career choices.

Start by closing your eyes and gaining a sense of quiet. Write as soon as you're ready, in any way that frees you up, on paper or on screen.

Discussing your writing with a trusted colleague or friend could open up even more resources and possibilities.

13.2 Ethical dilemmas and professional practice

Briefly describe the ethical issues involved in the problem you were asked to think about earlier in this chapter. If you didn't come up with one then, take a few moments to think of an ethical dilemma that is current for you.

- Whose problem is it?
- Consult the appropriate ethical framework you work with and select relevant principles, including particular clauses you need to consider.
- Identify any potential organisational difficulties involved in relation to this dilemma.
- Consider the options open to you and write them down.
- Describe any actions you have already taken to resolve the dilemma or ethical issues facing you.
- Who else might be involved? Have you consulted anyone else so far?

13.3 Letter writing: what do you truly want?

- Write a letter to yourself for 5 minutes without stopping, on 'What do I truly want?'
- It doesn't matter if you repeat the same sentence or the same words, and remember that none of the usual rules of correct spelling and grammar count.
- Start with, 'Dear' and your name.
- Don't let yourself stop to answer the phone or to pay attention to any other distraction.

13.4 Learning from fictional characters

- Think of a character you identified with in a film, TV or radio drama/soap, book or play.
- What was it about them that held your attention?
- Write down what you learned about your own behaviours from connecting with them. For example:

There was a film on television about a woman who was grieving. I can't remember the name of the actor but she was able to show her feelings on her face and in her body with real subtlety. At one point she said 'No, don't hold me, I don't want to be held,' and ran out of a room full of people who wanted to help her. I could actually see myself in the stiff way she held her body. She avoided people when she was most upset, and so do I.

13.5 Reviewing

At the end of the day/week/month/year you might find it useful to review your writing and ask yourself some questions:

- What was most playful – which pieces of writing make you smile?
- Which pieces of writing came up with most insights or surprises?
- What exercises involved the most risk?
- What would you like to do less of?
- What would you like to do more of?
- Where do you need to reflect further to work out what you'd do differently?
- Where can you see achievement and learning in the writing?

References

Abbs, P. (1998). The creative word and the created life: the cultural context for deep auto-biography. In C. Hunt and F. Sampson (Eds.), *The self on the page: theory and practice of creative writing in personal development*. London: Jessica Kingsley.

Adler, J. M., & McAdams, D. P. (2007). Time, culture, and stories of the self. *Psychological Inquiry*, **18**(2), 97–128.

Allende, I. (1996). *Paula*. London: Flamingo.

American Psychiatric Association (1994). *Diagnostic and Statistical Manual of Mental Disorders* (4th ed.). Arlington, VA: American Psychiatric Association.

Anthony, K., & Goss, S. (2009). *Guidelines for online counselling and psychotherapy with guidelines for online supervision* (3rd ed.). Rugby: British Association for Counselling and Psychotherapy.

Bakewell, S. (2010). *How to live: a life of Montaigne in one question and twenty attempts at an answer*. London: Chatto and Windus.

BACP (2010). *Ethical Framework*. Lutterworth: British Association for Counselling & Psychotherapy. Available at www.bacp.co.uk/ethical_framework.

Ballinger, E., & Wright, J. K. (2007). Does class count? Social class and counselling. *Counselling and Psychotherapy Research*, **7**(3), 157–163.

Beck, A. (1978). *Cognitive therapy and the emotional disorders*. Harmondsworth: Penguin.

Bennett-Levy, J. (2006). Therapist skills: a cognitive model of their acquisition and refinement. *Behavioural and Cognitive Psychotherapy*, **34**, 57–78.

Bennett-Levy, J., Turner, F., Beaty, T., Smith, M., Paterson, B., & Farmer, S. (2001). The value of self-practice of cognitive therapy techniques and self-reflection in the training of cognitive therapists. *Behavioural and Cognitive Psychotherapy*, **29**, 203–220.

Bennett-Levy, J., Lee, N., Travers, K., Pohlman, S., & Hamernik, E. (2003). Cognitive therapy from the inside: enhancing therapist skills through practising what we preach. *Behavioural and Cognitive Psychotherapy*, **31**, 143–158.

Bernard, B. (2004). *Resiliency: What we have learned*. Oakland, CA: West Ed.

Bleakley, A. (2000). Writing with invisible ink: Narrative, confessionalism and reflective practice. *Reflective Practice*, **1**(1), 11–24.

Bolton, G. (1999). *The therapeutic potential of creative writing: writing myself*. London: Jessica Kingsley.

Bolton, G. (2001). Open the box: writing a therapeutic space. In P. Milner (Ed.), *BAC counselling reader, Vol. 2* (pp. 106–112). London: Sage.

Bolton, G. (Ed.) (2003). Opening the word hoard. *Journal of Medical Ethics: Medical Humanities*, **29,** 97–102.

Bolton, G. (2008). Boundaries of humanity: writing medical humanities (full keynote paper First ANZ Association of Medical Humanities conference (2006)). *Arts and Humanities in Higher Education*, **7**(2), 147–165.

Bolton, G. (2009). Writing values: reflective practice writing, *The Lancet*, **374,** 20–21.

Bolton, G. (2010). *Reflective practice: writing and professional development* (3rd ed.). London: Sage.

Bolton, G. (2011). *Write yourself: creative writing and personal development*. London: Jessica Kingsley.

Bolton, G., & Wright, J. K. (2004). Conclusions and looking forward. In G. Bolton, S. Howlett, C. Lago, and J. K. Wright (Eds.), *Writing cures: an introductory handbook of writing in counselling and psychotherapy* (pp. 228–231). London: Routledge.

Bolton, G., Field, V., & Thompson, K. (2010). *Writing routes: a resource handbook of therapeutic writing*. London: Jessica Kingsley.

Bond, T. (2010). *Standards and ethics for counselling in action* (3rd ed.). London: Sage.

Bowlby, J. (1988). *A secure base: clinical applications of attachment theory*. London: Routledge.

Bruner, J. (2004). The narrative creation of self. In L. E. Angus and J. McLeod (Eds.), *The handbook of narrative and psychotherapy: practice, theory and research* (pp. 3–14). Thousand Oaks, CA: Sage.

Burkeman, O. (2010). Can worries really be sealed in an envelope? *The Guardian Weekend*, 9 October.

Burr, V. (2003). *Social constructionism* (2nd ed.). Hove: Routledge.

Butler, C., O'Donovan, A., & Shaw, E. (Eds.) (2010). *Sex, sexuality and therapeutic practice: a manual for therapists and trainers*. London and New York: Routledge.

Castenada, C. (1993). *The art of dreaming*. London: HarperCollins.

Chantler, K. (2005). From disconnection to connection: 'race', gender and the politics of therapy. *British Journal of Guidance and Counselling*, **33**(2), 239–256.

Chen, J.-Q., Moran, S., & Gardner, H. (2009). *Multiple intelligences around the world*. San Francisco, CA: Jossey-Bass.

Clarke, H. (2000). Journal writing. *The Adlerian Yearbook*. London: Adlerian Society.

Cooper, M. (2008). *Essential research findings in counselling and psychotherapy: the facts are friendly*. London: Sage.

Cox, E., Bachkirova, T., & Clutterbuck, D. (Eds.) (2010). *The complete handbook of coaching*. London: Sage.

Crocket, K. (2007). Counselling supervision and the production of professional selves. *Counselling and Psychotherapy Research*, **7**(1), 19–25.

Crocket, K. (2010). Rescuing speech: teaching and writing aesthetic for counseling practice. *Journal of Poetry Therapy*, **23**(2), 73–86.

Crocket, K., Gaddis, S., Day, C., Flintoff, V., Lammers, M., Malcolm, P., & Schoffelmeer, E. (2007). Shaping supervision practice through research: effects of supervision for counselling practice. *New Zealand Journal of Counselling*, **27**(1), 55–69.

Damasio, A. (2000). *The feeling of what happens: body, emotion and the making of consciousness*. London: Vintage.

Damasio, A. (2010). *Self comes to mind: constructing the conscious brain*. New York: Pantheon Books.

Daniels, J., & Feltham, C. (2004). Reflective and therapeutic writing in counsellor training. In G. Bolton, S. Howlett, C. Lago, and J. K. Wright (Eds.), *Writing cures: an introductory handbook of writing in counselling and therapy* (pp. 181–188). London: Routledge.

De Jong, P., & Berg, I. K. (2008). *Interviewing for solutions.* Belmont, CA: Thomson Higher Education.

Diaghilev, S. (2010). Quoted in A. O'Hagan, Diaghilev: Lord of the Dance. *Guardian Review* (pp. 16–17). Saturday, 9 October.

Diamond, S. L., & Gillis, J. R. (2006). Approaching multiple diversity: addressing the intersections of class, gender, sexual orientation and different abilities. In C. Lago (Ed.), *Race, culture and counselling: the ongoing challenge* (2nd ed.). Maidenhead: Open University Press.

Duncan, B. L., Miller, S. D., & Sparks, J. A. (2004). *The heroic client.* San Francisco, CA: Jossey-Bass/Wiley.

Durie, M. (2010). *Whaiora: Maori health development.* Auckland: Oxford University Press.

Ellis, A. (1962). *Reason and emotion in psychotherapy.* New York: Lyle Stuart.

Enns, C. Z. (2004). *Feminist theories and feminist psychotherapies: origins, themes and diversity* (2nd ed.). New York: Haworth Press.

Ernst, S., & Goodison, L. (1981). *In our own hands: a book of self-help therapy.* London: Women's Press.

Etherington, K. (2000). *Narrative approaches to working with adult male survivors of child sexual abuse: the clients', the counsellor's and the researcher's story.* London: Jessica Kingsley.

Etherington, K. (2003). *Trauma, the body and transformation.* London: Jessica Kingsley Publishers.

Etherington, K. (2004). *Becoming a reflexive researcher: using ourselves in research.* London: Jessica Kingsley Publishers.

Fairhurst, I. (Ed.) (1999). *Women writing in the person-centred approach.* Wiltshire: Redwood.

Fanthorpe, U. A. (1996). In G. Bolton, and D. Padfield (Eds.), *Reflections in writing* (poetry/prose anthology). Kelso: Curlew Press.

Figiel, S. (1999). *They who do not grieve.* Auckland: Random House.

Foucault, M. (1997). Technologies of the self. In P. Rabinow (Ed.), *Ethics: subjectivity and truth.* Essential works of Foucault 1954–1984. (Vol. 1, pp. 223–252). London: Penguin.

Freud, S. ([1933]1973). *New introductory lectures on psychoanalysis.* Harmondsworth: Penguin.

Freud, S. ([1915]1991). *The essentials of psycho-analysis.* Harmondsworth, Penguin.

Gardner, H. (2006). *Five minds for the future.* Boston, MA: Harvard Business School Press.

Gergen, M. M. (2001). *Feminist reconstructions in psychology: narrative, gender, and performance.* Thousand Oaks, CA: Sage.

Gilbert, P. (2005). *Compassion: conceptualisation, research and use in psychotherapy.* London: Routledge.

Grace, P. (2004). *Tu.* Auckland: Penguin.

Greenberger, D., & Padesky, C. A. (1995). *Mind over mood: change how you feel by changing the way you think.* New York: GuilfoGreer, G. (1999). *The whole woman.* New York: A.A. Knopf.

Helman, C. (2006). *Surburban shaman: tales from medicine's front line.* London: Hammersmith.

Holmes, J. (2001). *The search for the secure base: attachment theory and psychotherapy.* London: Brunner Routledge.

Honos-Webb, L., & Stiles, W. B. (1998). Reformulation of assimilation analysis in terms of voices. *Psychotherapy*, **35**, 22–33.

hooks, b. (1993). *Sisters of the yam – black women and self-recovery.* London: Turnaround.

hooks, b. (1999). *Remembered rapture: the writer at work.* London: Women's Press.

Horney, K. (1942). *Self analysis.* New York: Norton.

Hughes, T. (1982). Foreword. In S. Brownjohn (Ed.), *What rhymes with secret?* London: Hodder and Stoughton.

Ivey, A. E., & Ivey, B. M. (2002). *Theories of counseling and psychotherapy: a multicultural perspective* (5th ed.). Boston, MA: Allyn and Bacon.

Jacobs, M. (2006). *The presenting past: the core of psychodynamic counselling and therapy* (3rd ed.). Maidenhead: Open University Press.

Johns, H. (1996). *Personal development in counsellor training.* London: Cassell.

Jung, C. G. (1998). *The essential Jung: selected writings.* London: Fontana Press.

Kabat-Zinn, J. (2005). *Coming to our senses: healing ourselves and the world through mindfulness.* New York: Hyperion.

Kelley, A. (2007). *The bower bird.* Edinburgh: Luath Press.

Kipling, R. (1902). *Just so stories.* London: Macmillan.

Lago, C. O. (Ed.) (2006). *Race, culture and counselling: the ongoing challenge* (2nd ed.). Maidenhead: Open University Press.

Lago, C. O., & Smith, B. (Eds.) (2010). *Anti-discriminatory counselling practice* (2nd ed.). London: Sage.

Lago, C. O., & Wright, J. K. (2007). Email supervision. In K. Tudor & M. Worrall (Eds.), *Freedom to practise: developing person-centred approaches to supervision* (Vol. 2, pp. 102–118). Ross-on-Wye: PCCS Books.

Lapworth, P. (2011). *Tales from the therapy room.* London: Sage.

Levinson, M. (2010). Working with diversity. In A. Grant, M. Townend, R. Mulhern, and N. Short (Eds.), *Cognitive behavioural therapy in mental health care* (pp. 181–191). London: Sage.

Mace, C. (2008). *Mindfulness and mental health: therapy, theory and science.* London and New York: Routledge.

Macran, S., Stiles, W. B., & Smith, J. A. (1999). How does personal therapy affect therapists' practice? *Journal of Counseling Psychology*, **46**, 419–431.

Malcolm, J. (2003). The kernel of truth, *The Guardian Review* (p. 4), Saturday, 25 January.

Matthews, G. B. (1980). *Philosophy and the young child.* Cambridge, MA: Harvard University Press.

McLeod, J. (2009). *An introduction to counselling* (4th ed.). Maidenhead: Open University Press.

McLeod, J. (2010). *The counsellor's workbook: developing a personal approach* (2nd ed.). Maidenhead: Open University Press.

Meekums, B. (1999). A creative model for recovery from child sexual abuse. *The arts in psychotherapy*, **26**(4), 247–259.

Meekums, B. (2000). *Creative group therapy for women survivors of child sexual abuse.* London: Jessica Kingsley Publishers.

Milne, A. A. ([1928]1958). *The world of Pooh (the house at Pooh Corner).* London: Methuen.

Mitchell, J. (1974). *Psychoanalysis and feminism: a radical reassessment of Freudian psychoanalysis.* London: Allen Lane.

Moodley, R. (2007). (Re)placing multiculturalism in counselling and psychotherapy. *British Journal of Guidance and Counselling*, **35**(1), 1–22.

Moodley, R., & West, W. (Eds.) (2005). *Integrating traditional healing practices into counselling and psychotherapy*. Thousand Oaks, CA: Sage.

Morley, C. (2007). Engaging practitioners with critical reflection: issues and dilemmas. *Reflective Practice*, **8**(1), 61–74.

Munno, A. (2006). A complaint which changed my practice. *British Medical Journal*, **332**: 1092.

Norcross, J. C. (2005). The psychotherapist's own psychotherapy: educating and developing psychologists. *American Psychologist*, **60**(8), 840–850.

NZAC (2009) *Code of ethics*. Hamilton: New Zealand Association of Counsellors. Available at www.nzac.org.nz/ethicscode.html.

Okun, B. F., & Ziady, L. G. (2005). Redefining the career ladder: new visions of women at work. In M. P. Mirkin, K. L. Suyemoto, & B. F. Okun (Eds.), *Psychotherapy with women: exploring diverse contexts and identities* (pp. 215–236). New York: Guilford Press.

Oliver, M. (1992). The summer day. In M. Oliver, *New and Selected Poems*. Boston, MA: Beacon Press.

Orbach, S. (1999). *The impossibility of sex: stories of the intimate relationship between therapist and patient*. London: Penguin.

Orbach, S. (2009). *Bodies*. New York: Picador.

Pack, M. (2009). The body as a site of knowing: sexual abuse counsellors' responses to traumatic disclosures. *Women's Studies Journal*, **23**(2), 46–57.

Padesky, C. A., & Greenberger, D. (1995). *Clinician's guide to mind over mood*. New York: Guilford Press.

Paterson, D. (2010). 'Lust in action': Shakespeare's sonnets. *The Guardian Review* (pp. 2–4). Saturday, 16 October.

Payne, M. (2000). *Narrative therapy: an introduction for counsellors*. London: Sage.

Pedersen, P. (1997). *Culture-centred counseling interventions: striving for accuracy*. Thousand Oaks, CA: Sage.

Pennebaker, J. W., & Beall, S. K. (1986). Confronting a traumatic event: toward an understanding of inhibition and disease. *Journal of Abnormal Psychology*, **93**(3), 274–281.

Pennebaker, J. W., & Chung, C. K. (2007). Expressive writing: emotional upheavals and health. In H. Friedman and R. Silver (Eds.), *Handbook of health psychology* (pp. 263–284). New York: Oxford University Press.

Pentecost, M. (2008). A letter to Robyn: explorations of the written word in therapeutic practice. *The International Journal of Narrative Therapy and Community Work*, ('Normality' the written word and teaching narrative practice), **1**, 17–27.

Ponterotto, J., & Pedersen, P. (1993). *Preventing prejudice: a guide for counselors and educators*. London: Sage.

Proctor, G., Cooper, M., Sanders, P., & Malcolm, B. (Eds.) (2006). *Politicizing the person-centred approach: an agenda for social change*. Ross-on-Wye: PCCS Books.

Rainer, T. (1978). *The new diary: how to use a journal for self-guidance and expanded creativity*. London: Angus and Robertson.

Ramirez, M. (1991). *Psychotherapy and counseling with minorities: a cognitive approach to individual and cultural differences*. Oxford: Pergamon.

Rich, A. (2006). Legislators of the world. *The Guardian Review* (pp. 2–4). Saturday, 18 November.

Riessman, C. K., & Speedy, J. (2007). Narrative inquiry in the psychotherapy professions: a critical review. In D. J. Clandinin (Ed.), *Handbook of narrative inquiry: mapping the methodology* (pp. 426–456). Thousand Oaks, CA: Sage.

Rogers, C. R. (1957). The necessary and sufficient conditions of therapeutic personality change. *Journal of Consulting Psychology*, **21**, 95–103.

Rogers, C. R. (1974). *On becoming a person: a therapist's view of psychotherapy.* London: Constable.

Rogers, C. R. (1975). Empathic: an unappreciated way of being. *The Counseling Psychologist*, **5**, 2–10.

Rogers, C. R. (1978). *Carl Rogers on personal power: inner strength and its revolutionary impact.* London: Constable.

Rogers, N. (1993). *The creative connection – expressive arts as healing.* Palo Alto, CA: Science and Behaviour Books.

Rowan, J. (1990). *Subpersonalities: the people inside us.* London: Routledge.

Rowan, J. (2005). *The transpersonal: spirituality in psychotherapy and counselling* (2nd ed.). London: Routledge.

Russell, S., & Carey, M. (2003). Feminism, therapy and narrative ideas: exploring some not so commonly asked questions. *International Journal of Narrative Therapy and Community Work*, (2), 76–84.

Sartre, J. P. ([1938]1963). *Nausea.* Harmondsworth: Penguin.

Segal, Z. V., Williams, M. G., & Teasdale, J. D. (2002). *Mindfulness-based cognitive therapy for depression: a new approach to preventing relapse.* New York: Guilford Press.

Seneca, L. (1969). *Letters from a stoic.* London: Penguin.

Shields, C., & Howard, B. (2000). *A celibate season.* London: Fourth Estate.

Sloan, D. M., & Marx, B. P. (2004). Taking pen to hand: evaluating theories underlying the written disclosure paradigm. *Clinical Psychology: Science and Practice*, **V11**(2), 121–137.

Smyth, J. M. (1998). Written emotional expression: effect, size, outcome types and moderating variables. *Journal of Consulting and Clinical Psychology*, **66**(1), 174–184.

Speedy, J. (2008). *Narrative inquiry and psychotherapy.* Basingstoke: Palgrave Macmillan.

Sutton, L., Townend, M., & Wright, J. K. (2007). The experience of reflective learning journals by cognitive behavioural psychotherapy students. *Reflective Practice*, **8**(3), 387–404.

Tan, L. (2008). Psychotherapy 2.0: MySpace blogging as self-therapy. *American Journal of Psychotherapy*, **62**(2), 143–163.

Turkle, S. (2011). *Alone together: why we expect more from technology and less from each other.* New York: Basic Books.

Walker, A. (1982). *The color purple.* New York: Pocket Books.

Wampold, B. E. (2001). *The great psychotherapy debate: models, methods and findings.* Mahwah, NJ: Erlbaum.

Weingarten, K. (2000). Witnessing words and hope. *Family Process*, **39**(4), 389–402.

Weingarten, K. (2003). *Common shock: witnessing violence every day: how we are harmed, how we can heal.* New York: New American Library/Penguin.

Wheeler, S. (2002). Assessing personal development. *Counselling and Psychotherapy Journal*, **13**(7), 40–41.

Wheeler, S., & Richards, K. (2007). The impact of clinical supervision on counsellors and therapists, their practice and their clients. A systematic review of the literature. *Counselling and Psychotherapy Research*, 7(1), 54–65.

White, M., & Epston, D. (1990). *Narrative means to therapeutic ends*. New York: Norton.

Wilkins, P. (1997). *Personal and professional development for counsellors*. London:

Wilkinson, M. (2010). *Changing minds in therapy: emotion, attachment, trauma, and neurobiology* (1st ed.). New York: W. W. Norton.

Wilkinson, R., & Pickett, K. (2009). *The spirit level: why more equal societies almost always do better*. London: Allen Lane.

Williams, N. (2008). How I write, *Time Out* (p. 75), 25 September.

Williamson, M. (1996). *A return to love: reflections on the principles of a course in miracles*. London: Thorsons.

Winnicott, D. W. (1971). *Playing and reality*. London: Tavistock.

Winter, R. A. B., & Sobiechowska, P. (1999). *Professional experience and the investigative imagination: the art of reflective writing*. London: Routledge.

Woolf, V. (1985). *Moments of being* (2nd ed.). London: The Hogarth Press.

Woolf, V. (1969). Montaigne. In A. McNeillie (Ed.), *Essays IV* (pp. 71–81). London: Hogarth.

Wright, J. K. (2002). Online counselling: learning from writing therapy. *British Journal of Guidance and Counselling*, **30**(3), 285–298.

Wright, J. K. (2003a). Future therapy stories. *Counselling and Psychotherapy Journal*, **14**(9), 22–25.

Wright, J. K. (2003b). Writing for protection: reflective practice as a counsellor. *Journal of Poetry Therapy*, **16**(4), 191–198.

Wright, J. K. (2005). 'A discussion with myself on paper': counselling and psychotherapy masters students' perceptions of writing a learning log. *Reflective Practice*, **6**(4), 507–521.

Wright, J. K. (2007). The compassionate mind [interview with Paul Gilbert]. *Journal of Counselling Psychology*, **20**(1), 97–103.

Wright, J. K. (2009a). Dialogical journal writing as 'self therapy': 'I matter'. *Counselling and Psychotherapy Research*, **9**(4), 234–241.

Wright, J. K. (2009b). Unfinished business with feminist thinking and counselling and guidance practice. *British Journal of Guidance and Counselling*, **37**(1), 73–82.

Wright, J. K., & Griffiths, F. (2010). Reflective practice at a distance: using technology in counselling supervision. *Reflective Practice*, **11**(5), 693–703.

Wright, J. K., & Ranby, P. (2009). 'Composing myself on paper': Personal journal writing and feminist influences. *Women's Studies Journal*, **23**(2), 57–67.

Xinran, X. (2003). *The good women of China: hidden voices*. London: Chatto and Windus.

Yalom, I. D. (1989). *Love's executioner and other tales of psychotherapy*. New York: Basic Books.

Yalom, I. D. (2002). *The gift of therapy: an open letter to a new generation of therapists and their patients*. New York: Harper Collins.

Yalom, I. D., & Elkins, G. (1974). *Every day gets a bit closer: a twice-told therapy*. New York: Basic Books.

Yeats, W.B. (1962). *Selected poetry*. London: Macmillan.

Index

Page numbers in *italics* refer to figures and boxed material.